OUR SACRED SIGNS

ALSO BY ORI Z. SOLTES

Fixing the World: Jewish American Painters in the Twentieth Century

ORI Z. SOLTES

OUR SACRED SIGNS

How Jewish, Christian, and Muslim Art
Draw from the Same Source

A Member of the Perseus Books Group

Published by Westview Press,
A Member of the Perseus Books Group

Books published by Westview Press are available at special discounts for bulk pur-
chases in the United States by corporations, institutions, and other organizations. For
more information, please contact the Special Markets Department at the Perseus
Books Group, 11 Cambridge Center, Cambridge, MA 02142, or
special.markets@perseusbooks.com.

Library of Congress Cataloging-in-Publication Data

Soltes, Ori Z.
  Our sacred signs : how Jewish, Christian, and Muslim art draw from the same
source / Ori Z. Soltes.
    p. cm.
  Includes bibliographical references and index.
  ISBN-13 978-0-8133-4297-9 (hc : alk. paper)
  ISBN-10: 0-8133-4297-X (hc : alk. paper) 1. Art and religion. 2. Symbolism in
art. I. Title.

N72.R4S65 2005
704.9'48—dc22

                                                                    2005013053

05 06 07 08 / 10 9 8 7 6 5 4 3 2 1

Dedicated to the memory of my father, Avraham Soltes
and my mother, Sarah Rudavsky Soltes,
who first taught me to love the arts,
and of my beloved father-in-law, Martin Shampaine,
whose legacy is the best-formed works of art imaginable

CONTENTS

There is a cave complex on the Nullarbor Plain in Australia that to reach by foot requires a journey of many days from the nearest source of human sustenance. The complex consists of a series of chambers hundreds of feet below the surface of the earth. On the walls and ceilings of the deepest caves are markings that were made by humans perhaps as many as 35,000 years ago. Why would a group of individuals walk so far and then make their way deep into the earth to systematically decorate the surfaces of that underground world? The most likely explanation is that they were responding to an urge—whether from within or from without is a separate question—to be in contact with forces that they believed had created them and therefore had the power to destroy them, to help or harm, bless or curse them. And somehow they had come to believe that this particular spot was conducive to making such contact. Whatever verbal or other means they may have used to generate that contact, they understood that visual means were essential to the process of connecting with those forces.

That urge seems to be universal, and the means of addressing it, though varying from time to time and place to place, connects the art of Upper Paleolithic caves to the architecture of the pyramids to the shaping of Michelangelo's *Pieta* and Leonardo's *Virgin of the Rocks*. While one can trace the visual patterns of seeking access to the realm of "the

Other" across the entirety of human history and geography, the intention of this book is to explore visual self-expression as it has emerged and evolved in the three primary Abrahamic traditions—Judaism, Christianity, and Islam. I do so by focusing only on symbolic language, as opposed to style and subject, except to the extent that these are interwoven with symbolism.

I pursue this goal with three specific ideas in mind. First, there are sources common to all three traditions that predate them all. Thus, the first part of the book explores symbols in the art of the ancient pagan Near East and East Mediterranean, which were subsequently absorbed, adopted, adapted, and altered by the Abrahamic traditions. Second, the three Abrahamic traditions share an enormous range of symbols in common, but each utilizes the identical symbols in accordance with the needs of its particular faith requirements. Third, contrary to an oft-espoused view, the impulses expressed in the pre-Abrahamic and Abrahamic eras have not been eclipsed by the secularizing trend of Western thought during the past three centuries. The impulse to speak in symbolic terms, and even to address particularized spiritual needs, is found not only in obviously "religious" works of art but also in art that is conventionally understood to be secular.

There are at least two things that this book is not. It is not a comprehensive history of any of the three visual traditions that are its primary focus. I have carefully, and perhaps idiosyncratically, chosen the works upon which I focus to articulate my point regarding symbols. Space has limited both the discussion of images and, even more so, their reproduction. And I have spent far less time discussing sculpture than I have painting and even architecture because, from the point of view of symbols, sculpture seems less fruitful and more redundant with respect to symbolism as one moves forward in Christian art beyond its early phases, and in Islamic and Jewish art sculpture is virtually nonexistent until Jewish art in the late nineteenth century. With all this in mind, I have also spent a minimum of time discussing form and other aspects of art endemic to such discussions. Therefore, this is not a conventional book on art history, in which such issues would play a significant role. It is simply an introduction to an aspect of the history of human experience.

———— ❧ ————

My thinking about symbols in the visual self-expression of the Abrahamic faiths began when I was asked to guest-curate an exhibition at the

Spertus Museum of Judaica in Chicago nearly twenty years ago. I would like to acknowledge the splendid cooperation of my colleagues at Spertus who, both in conceiving and installing that exhibition and in inspiring my larger thinking on the matter of symbols, were so important: then Director Arthur Feldman, curator and then registrar Olga Weiss, and designer and installer-without-parallel Mark Agulian. In the aftermath of that exhibition, other individuals and institutions were enormously important in the formation of my thinking, especially Rex Moser, former Curator of Education of the Art Institute of Chicago, who first encouraged me to offer lectures on this subject; David Ariel, President of Siegel College in Cleveland, Ohio, where I first gave courses on aspects of it; and Cliff Chieffo, former Chair of the Department of Art, Music, and Theatre at Georgetown University, who embraced the unconventionality of a university course on this mixed topic. Needless to say, I hold none of these individuals responsible for whatever errors in thinking are manifest in this volume, but thank them sincerely for affording me the opportunity to formulate that thinking—errors and all.

I thank my visionary friend Peter Corsell for facilitating—through the help of Bill Nitze, whom I also thank—contact with Perseus Books. I am also grateful to David Shoemaker, my superb editor, for helping carve too many words into fewer. Lastly, which is to say, firstly, I thank Leslie, Brahm, and Nadav, whose love is more than a mere symbol of faith in humankind and as sacred a sign of hope for the future as has ever existed.

INTRODUCTION:
SYMBOLS OF FAITH

ART AS AN INSTRUMENT OF RELIGION

The Encounter with the Sacer

Religion presupposes a dichotomy between the realm of the here and now and that of the Other. The Romans used the term *profanus* to refer to the first of these: the realm of the known, the everyday, the community, the safely circumscribed of daytime and awareness, of events that happen when and where they should according to the patterns of our expectations. From the Latin word *profanus* we derive our term "profane." Its opposite is the term *sacer,* from which our term "sacred" comes.

The realm of the *sacer* is the unknown in all its aspects. It is what lies beyond the edge of the community: wilderness, forest, desert, outer space. It is the realm beyond the daytime and the everyday: night, sleep, dreams. It is the space beyond reason and awareness: the irrational and subconscious. It is the time beyond the fathomable: before birth and after death. It is the boundless inhabitation of hope and fear, of benevolent and malignant deities and demons and spirits, unpredictable and inaccessible through the five senses or even the intellect—or simply, the realm of God.

The potential of the *sacer* to affect us either negatively or positively—it is intrinsically neutral, but potentially benevolent or malevolent—is obvious as we venture into the realm of sleep: we may not dream at all, or we may experience a horrific nightmare or the sweetest of dreams. That potential is clear when we enter another aspect of the *sacer*, the woods of traditional fairy tales. On the one hand, nothing may happen. On the other, wolves or thieves may tear us apart, or our fairy godmother may tap us on the shoulder, offering wishes that transform our existence.

We don't know whether our death is the true end of our lives or whether some part of us continues. Every belief system that posits a continuation also assumes that the *sacer* realm offers *elysium* or *tartarus*, heaven or hell—or something between that is neither as positive as the one nor as negative as the other. Literature explores these possibilities in works ranging from the ancient Mesopotamian *Epic of Gilgamesh* to Dante's *Divine Comedy*.

Most disturbing of all, when we interface with divinity, we don't know whether it will respond positively or negatively, or simply ignore us. We find this aspect of the *sacer* disturbing because we assume that it has created us and thus has the power to destroy us—to harm or help, hinder or further, bless or curse us.

It is the province and purpose of religion to negotiate on behalf of the *profanus* with the *sacer*—to engage divinity on behalf of humanity—in order to ensure blessing rather than curse, help rather than harm. Thus religion is fundamentally and ultimately about survival—either as an individual or as a community. It may refer to avoiding accidental injury, living healthily and happily to one hundred rather than forty, or going to Paradise rather than to Hell when one dies; or it may mean that there is enough rain for our crops to flourish, but not so much that we drown, or that there is game in the woods when our hunters seek sustenance for us; or it may refer to the women of our community giving birth to healthy babies who will continue us into the next generation.

Religion's engagement of the *sacer* is not simple, for the *sacer*—the Other—speaks its own language, not ours. So how does religion accomplish its task? The answer to this question is shared by every religion known to humanity: revelation. Every faith begins with the belief that the *sacer* reveals itself, at certain times and places, to certain individuals, who are thus able to guide the rest of us in how to think, speak, and act in order to ensure the survival of the community of which we are part.

The one who can guide us—the one to whom the *sacer* reveals itself—is called a *sacerdos* in Latin.[1] Not surprisingly, the term is composed of the word *sacer* and the root of "give,"[2] for the *sacerdos* is the one who can give us access to the *sacer* and vice versa. Whether by birth or by training, the *sacerdos* has special knowledge of the *sacer*. The rest of us lack this knowledge. In fact, if we all possessed it, the *sacer* would become the *profanus*. Instead of operating according to its own logic, it would abide by ours; instead of being unfathomable, it would be conceivable. Only the individual with a foot in each of the two realms—a part of the community even as he or she remains *apart* from the community—has some grasp of how to confront the *sacer* properly, how to cross the border that separates it from us, and how to communicate our hopes and needs to it and its demands and desires to us.

Just as the *sacer* itself has various analogical aspects, so the *sacerdos* may be understood as a border creature of various analogous aspects: a priest(ess), a prophet(ess), a hero(ine), a pharaoh, a shah, an emperor, a king, a poet, an artist. All of these share an inspiriting connection with the *sacer* that the rest of us lack. It is the *sacerdos* who, as prophet, presents us with behavioral guidelines prescribed by God, through which we can achieve God's blessing. It is the *sacerdos* as priest who offers gifts to the gods on behalf of the community, or who instructs an individual offender as to how he or she might assuage an offended divinity.

The instruction will invariably be marked by several features. The *when* will be not only precisely indicated but will invariably be a *border* time: sunrise, sunset, noon, midnight—times when day *(profanus)* meets night *(sacer)* or at the precise midpoint (where the "rise" meets the "fall") of one or the other. The *where* will also be precisely indicated: a spot where there has been some evidence of propitious *sacer-profanus* contact, which has thus been marked as a temple, a sanctuary, an altar.[3]

The propitiousness of such a spot will be clear to the *sacerdos*-priest, as knowledge is inherited from the *sacerdos*-prophet who was part of the founding history of a given community *(profanus)*. When the biblical Jacob, fleeing his brother Esau's anger, sleeps in the wilderness at night (a *sacer* place and time), he has a dream (a *sacer* experience) of a ladder with angels ascending and descending—a connection between heaven *(sacer)* and earth *(profanus)*. When he wakes up in the morning, surprised that "the God of my fathers Isaac and Abraham dwells here," he marks the spot where he slept with a pile of stones (beginning with the one upon which his head rested as he slept and dreamed), thereby creating an altar. He names the spot *Beth-El*—"House of God"—and it becomes the subsequent site of a sanctuary—a *sacer* place—for his Israelite descendants.

The *sacerdos* indicates the precise time and place of addressing or appeasing the *sacer* and utilizes a precise *method*—a ritual. There are those rituals that are part of the daily, weekly, monthly, seasonal, or annual life of the community. There are those that address an offense of the *sacer* by an individual within the community. Indeed, it is likely in such a case that the offending individual will need to leave the community, since as long as he remains within it, there is a danger that the anger of the offended deity will be visited upon the entire community. When Oedipus offends the gods by killing his father and sleeping with this mother—even though he is not aware of having committed either offense—he brings plague onto the community of Thebes, which is lifted only when he goes into exile.

How, then, can someone like Oedipus assuage the anger of the god(s) he's offended? Frequently, a precise method in a precise time and place is prescribed. It usually entails a surrogate of the offender—for example, a goat, a bull, or a lamb—that is offered as a gift to the offended deity. If it is offered to the *sacer* and accepted, then the gift itself becomes *sacer*. In Latin "to make *sacer*" is *sacer facere*; clearly such a process took place often in the Roman world, since the two words eventually coalesced to form one: *sacrificare*.[4] The English-language descendant of that term is clear: "sacrifice." To appease the gods, the offender offers a surrogate of himself. He transfers the guilt, the sin, the curse from his own shoulders to those of the goat or lamb and kills it—since that is an obvious way to enter the *sacer*.[5]

Relieved of being *sacer* (outside the community, the *profanus*, because he endangered it by offending the *sacer*) the offender is now once again *profanus*—part of the community. This return is facilitated by the fact that the *sacer* has revealed to the *sacerdos* the time, place, and method of appeasement, just as the *sacer* also reveals to the *sacerdos* the means by which the *profanus* can maintain an ongoing, positive relationship with the *sacer* through periodic time-specific communal offerings. Such offerings are carved out of conceptual territory analogous to that involving an individual offender. The assumption is that the community as a whole may have offended its gods in the course of a day or a year. The offerings to the gods play the same sort of role as the offerings of an individual offender: they are not merely gifts but surrogates, bearing on their shoulders the guilt of the community.

This principle applied to the community of Israel in the time when the temple stood in Jerusalem. Not only were there daily and seasonal offerings of a prescribed nature, but on the annual Day of Atonement (Yom Kippur)—accompanied by a twenty-four-hour fast and following ten days of intense spiritual introspection—the high priest would take upon himself a year's worth of sins from the entire population. Having confronted God in the holy of holies *(sanctum sanctorum)* within the temple—that ultimate meeting point between *sacer* and *profanus*—he would transfer those sins to a goat (called the '*Azazel,* or scapegoat) by laying his hands upon it. The goat was subsequently released over the precipice of the temple mount—into the *sacer* of the wilderness and the *sacer* of its presumed death over the edge—carrying Israel's sins with it as a surrogate for the people, all of whom might now hope to live another year, or at least not be struck down due to sins of the previous year.

The process of expiation presents a series of paradoxes and contradictions that suggest the ungraspable, problematic nature of the *sacer.* Time and space are infinitely amorphous in the realm of the *sacer.* Past, present, and future are indistinguishable from each other; spatial arrangements follow no pattern coherent to us. Actions fail to conform to our logical expectations. There is no beginning or end to the *sacer* that we can discern. Yet the expiation process requires absolute precision of time and place and method. The *sacer* itself has provided the *sacerdos* with the secret knowledge of the precisely defined conditions of engagement so that there can be interface between *sacer* and *profanus.*[6] It is as though in our need to grasp the *sacer,* we wrestle the borderlands of our would-be encounters with it into a precise framework.

The point to which the precise method of sacrifice pushes—rendering a surrogate *sacer* by killing it (or somehow disposing of it into the wilderness)—is inherently paradoxic. To the extent that to survive means to live, we generally think of death as a negative; the animal that becomes our surrogate seems, from a common *profanus* perspective, to suffer an unhappy fate. But if we assume that the gods are not only bearers of curse but also bearers of blessing, and if death is their analogue and thus both a realm of potential positive and a realm of potential negative, then it is possible that the animal enjoys a happy fate, sent into the bosom of the *sacer*. This paradoxic possibility was further extended by those traditions that focus "survival effort" on what happens after death—that is, the hope that we go to heaven (or its equivalent) rather than to hell (or its equivalent).

The paradox of death, particularly sacrificial death, as both blessing and curse, is at the heart of Christian belief, for in the extended moment in time-out-of-time that carries Jesus up Golgotha to his earthly demise—the ultimate symbol of self-*sacrifice*—and culminates with his resuming his place on the throne of heaven, he who has taken the sins of humankind onto his shoulders is certainly more cursed than any sacrificial animal referred to in other narratives; but returned to the realm of God the Father he is surely more blessed than we can imagine. It is not a coincidence that an image repeatedly used to symbolize Jesus is the *agnus dei*—Lamb of God—for he is pure and innocent and personifies the paradox of being sacrificed to atone for others' sins.[7]

In our need to make the *sacer* more accessible—to establish *entente*—we humans have evolved myriad religious systems with their particular rites and rituals. *Religio*—religion—is the binding that connects us to the *sacer*; different *religiones* are defined by the individuated ways in which they understand and seek to access and bind themselves to the *sacer*.[8] Some are polytheistic, suggesting the existence of many different gods; dualistic systems, such as Zoroastrianism, suppose a pair of opposed forces contending for control of reality; monotheism posits a single God. Judaism, Christianity, and Islam traditionally understand the One God to be all-powerful as well as all-knowing and all-good.[9]

The rites and rituals associated with all forms of religion govern for their constituencies the boundary between themselves and the *sacer*; rites and rituals indicate how and when such borders may be approached or even traversed. Moreover, accounts have evolved—*mythoi* as the early Greeks called them, before that term came to mean "myths"—of how the powers of the *sacer* brought order out of chaos, creating the world we know. Such accounts are recorded by the *sacer-dotes* to whom such information regarding the beginning of time and space as we understand them has been revealed by the *sacer* itself. This is why poets are analogues of the priests and prophets who function as intermediaries between *sacer* and *profanus*.[10]

Such myths, together with prayers directed to the *sacer*, are among the primary verbal instruments of religion. Myths address the power of the *sacer*, and religion molds myth into a verbal means of approaching that realm and of influencing those powers to approach us with benevolence. Thus the *Enuma Elish*—the Mesopotamian account of how Marduk slew Ti'amat at the beginning of time as we understand it and from her body parts created the physical world as we know it—is not merely a story of a long-ago event.[11] Since Ti'amat is an inert, serpent-dragon-like being, contrived of the waters that overflow the banks of the Tigris and Euphrates rivers, bringing flooded destruction, then part of what Marduk accomplishes is the confining of those waters within their properly ordered place not only at the beginning of time but throughout all time.[12]

So the narrative of Marduk's feat will be repeated each year as the flood season nears its hoped-for end to assure that it *does* end in due time—and re-enacted by the Mesopotamian priesthood in order to capture Marduk's attention and encourage him to repeat his accomplishment, lest the uncontrollable waters of the rivers wreak havoc on the community that worships Marduk. The myths are not limited to verbal repetition but are embedded in more complex theatrical intermediations between *sacer* and *profanus*. The gods are encouraged to be there for us, and the community is reminded of how powerful the gods are; awe ties the two parts of the process together.

Symbols in Art

Throughout most of human history and geography—from prehistoric cave paintings to Upper Paleolithic sculptures, from the ziggurats of Sumer to the temples of Rome, from China to Central America, from the medieval through the baroque eras in Europe to contemporary art in the United States—visual art has been a vehicle of focus on the *sacer* and thus intimately intertwined with religion. But just as differences of time, place, and circumstance have engendered a plethora of different religions, each with its own versions of common mythological themes, so each has transformed the details of art into specific forms. Faith reverberates in variant, sibling patterns across human history and geography, each pattern in turn begetting variant, sibling visual symbols.

What are symbols? Entities that stand for and represent something other than themselves. The term—from the Greek *symballein,* meaning literally "to throw together"—referred originally to the exchange of objects between the representatives of two contending forces, as they waged a peace agreement. Each threw into the situation an object—

a *symbolon*—that stood for the good will of the giver in a concrete manner, visible and tangible to all.[13] In art, the term has come to refer to an image (or aspects of an image) that stands for something other than the image itself. The process of symbolizing is usually not arbitrary but has a logic to it that those who understand the language of symbols can readily recognize.

Thus a lamb representing Christ (because of the imputation by us of purity and innocence to lambs and their association with sacrifice, and the association of the same qualities with Christ) is a *symbol* of Christ. Within the Christian context, every time we see a lamb, we think of Christ (see Figure 1). Since in telling the story of Christ's life and earth-bound death, we find the particular narrative associated with Luke most exemplary of Christ's sacrificial nature, the symbol that comes to represent Luke and his Gospel is the ox/bull—another prototypical sacrificial animal. By contrast, Mark is symbolized by a lion, king of beasts, since his Gospel is understood by his constituents to represent most distinctly the royal nature of Jesus as descended from the house of David. Each Gospel text has its distinctive symbol.

There are various types of symbols. Christian art is particularly rich in representational imagery: humans, animals, and plants. In addition to its figurative richness, Christian art also features geometric forms, colors, and particular numbers as symbols. Thus, red often symbolizes blood. Blood is associated with sacrifice—the flowing out of the life blood that is part of death—and so when the infant Jesus is wrapped in a red garment, or his Virgin Mother wears one as he sits on her lap, it reminds us

FIGURE 1 *Apse mosaics, Church of San Clemente, Rome (with* Agnus Dei *below). Thirteenth century*

OUR SACRED SIGNS

of the self-sacrifice he will make in the prime of his adulthood. The number five is associated with the five wounds in Christ's body. In contrast, for Jews the number five suggests the five books of Moses, the Torah or Pentateuch, which is the beginning of the Hebrew Bible. For Muslims the number five is associated with the Five Pillars that represent the fundamental principles of Islam. Thus, one symbol may be interpreted differently among diverse spiritual traditions (see Figure 2).

Several issues naturally arise in the discussion of sacred symbols. One concerns how Jewish art and Islamic art differ from Christian art with regard to figurative representation, since the Jewish and Muslim understandings of the *sacer* are absolutely nonfigurative, whereas Christianity understands God to take human form. Moreover, many of the symbols of the *sacer* and its concomitants used in Jewish, Christian, and Muslim art originated not with any of these three traditions but rather with the visual vocabulary of the various pagan, polytheistic religious traditions of antiquity that formed the historical and conceptual context in which these three faiths were born. Furthermore, the same symbols were interpreted differently by each tradition. Finally, a particular symbol may have undergone a succession of subtle or radical visual transformations over time and across space. Nevertheless, these transformations may only barely disguise the idea suggested by the original symbol's form. For example, a tree of life becomes a column becomes a sacerdotal figure becomes a fountain of water, but in each case that entity centers a composition in which it is flanked by rampant wild animals—variously lions, snakes, deer, winged bulls—for reasons that we shall explore.

———— ⊗∞⊗ ————

Why is it that religion requires all of this instrumentation? We have observed that the foundation of every faith is revelation. But sooner or later, whether after the death of the founding *sacerdos* or after a progression of generations of *sacerdotes* to whom and through whom the *sacer* speaks to the

FIGURE 2 *Moroccan synagogue lamp with* hamseh. *Nineteenth century*

profanus, that process stops. The sacerdotal founder who knows what the proper rites and rituals are, who understands precisely what the *sacer* would have of us and how to interface with it, leaves a legacy of answers that, over time, solidifies into certainties for some and evolves into doubts and questions for others. The community asks what it was that the founder(s) said, or later still, what it was that the founder(s) meant by what was said. Beyond the ground level, the edifice of religion is built of interpretations.

The words are written down—to the best of his followers' recollection, if not by the founder himself—and more words follow to interpret and explain and further explore the meaning of the relationship with the *sacer.* Each generation drinks in with its mother's milk the teachings of the generation that preceded it—or rejects those beliefs for one reason or another. The circle of belief widens and begets variations of itself, similar but not identical to each other. Every religion evolves and undergoes transformation.

Although words are the instruments that make humans unique—that distinguish us from other species, providing a unique means of shaping questions, answers, doubts, and certainties—they are limited and also limiting instruments. If it is difficult to capture with words the exquisite perfection of a sunset or the love of a mother for her child, how much more will words fall short in trying to articulate God? So in our desperation for *entente* with the *sacer,* we have used other instruments—music, dance, the visual arts—whenever words have been insufficient or when the majority of the *profanus* has lacked access to words or understanding of the written word to represent the *sacer* and its relationship with us. Art and its transformative symbols are a means of concretizing the absolute abstraction of divinity and its interface with us, helping religious adherents to grasp the ungraspable.

There is still more to this equation. Throughout history, as the arts have served religion, religion has been a handmaiden of politics. The deification of a pharaoh or a shah or a king—or merely the ascription of a *sacer* connection to such figures—not only transforms these individuals into *sacerdotes* but also reinforces and legitimizes their authority. We are less likely to rebel against a ruler whose source of power is the *sacer* than against one whose power is derived merely from the *profanus.* In turn, then, art, the servant of religion, has served politics, as religion has served politics. The depiction of the pharaoh Chefren (Chafra) with the hawk falcon representing the god

Horus behind him, its wings extended to embrace him around the shoulders, reminds his constituents in strong visual terms—concrete terms, one might say—of the divine basis of his rule (see Figure 3).

This reminder extends to generation after generation, encompassing one ruler after the next, all of whom are understood, within the circle of Egyptian belief, to be a progression of avatars of the same divinely empowered principle. Similarly, the image of a medieval Christian king, enthroned and flanked by acolytes, calls to mind (perhaps unconsciously) the image of Christ enthroned and flanked by angels and encourages viewers to associate that king with Christ and the *sacer* (see Figure 4).

The *mythos* of symbols is a complex of interwoven elements that involve the here and now and the hereafter, the present and the utterly Other. It is an account of a dynamic tension between the elements that are forever the same and those that are in constant flux. It is a story of the relationship between words and images, and between the word as it was revealed and as it is interpreted, and the image as it was originally shaped and its ongoing interpretative recasting. It is about ourselves and that which is outside ourselves, in the myriad conscious and unconscious ways in which we seek to survive—however we interpret that word.

FIGURE 3 *Chephren (Khafra), Fourth Dynasty, diorite, Giza (detail), ca. 2550 BCE.*

Jews, Christians, Muslims, and History

This complicated sensibility is as far-flung as humanity. It carries across geography and history. For the purposes of this narrative, however, I shall examine one particular, if far-reaching, branch of humanity in its threefold siblinghood. Judaism, Christianity, and Islam all find their beginning point in the spiritual revolution that they ascribe to Abraham, who, by their common estimation, lived about 4,000 years ago. The faith founded by Abraham developed for a little more than two millennia before it split into two contending religions, Judaism and Christianity. Islam emerged about half a millennium after its siblings. But each of these progeny of the Abrahamic tradition understood and continues to understand itself to be the true offspring of that tradition and has seen the others as bastard children who have gone off the proper path of relationship with the *sacer.*

Moreover, in the centuries between the time of Abraham and the birth of these three religions, the adherents to the Abrahamic tradition did not exist in isolation. On the contrary, the post-Abrahamic world of the Near East and the East Mediterranean was one of diverse religious systems with which the Hebrews, Israelites, and Judaeans—and subsequently Jews, Christians, and Muslims—contended. In the earlier contact with pagan, polytheistic traditions, none of these aspects of Abrahamic faith could remain absolutely free of influence from them; in the later contact and contention with one another, they could not remain free of influences and counter-influences from each other.

FIGURE 4   Registrum Gregorii: *Otto II receiving the Homage of the Nations. 983* CE

Over the centuries, Christianity and Islam became enormous, far-flung seas, with Judaism an archipelago of islands strung out across both sets of waters. Christians and Muslims confronted each other as infidels for centuries across three fronts in the Mediterranean region. In Spain, the two worlds collided for nearly eight centuries—between 718 and 1492—in what Christian historians refer to as the *reconquista*. In the Holy Land, a series of nine major crusades pitted the two forces against each other between 1096 and the mid-fifteenth century; and with the growing prominence of the Ottoman Turks, that confrontation continued until World War I. In between those geographic endpoints, Sicily spent 200 years in Muslim hands before Christian hands wrested it away.

In all three cases, conflict did not impede commercial and cultural interchange, regardless of how the political picture shifted. In Sicily, for example, the Muslim cultural presence remained for generations after Muslim political control of the island had been eliminated. Similarly, in all three locations, but especially in Spain, the Jews acted as cultural, commercial, and political intermediaries, adding further threads to the warp and woof of the complex tapestries of interaction being shaped through the centuries.

At the same time, each of the three faiths was experiencing its own internal traumas: questions of belief and interpretation, of custom and tradition. Each struggled not only with the truth claims of the other two but with schisms, heresies, and disagreements regarding the *sacer* from within its own theological and historical perspective. As with every belief system, each of these three is overrun with both theological and historical details recognized as self-contradictory by those outside the circle of belief but simply accepted by those within the circle. That should not be surprising, given the paradoxic and problematic nature of the *sacer*.

All of these political and theological developments have affected the visual self-expression within all three faiths, as they have absorbed, adopted, and adapted imagery, symbols, and visual ideas from the pagan world of antiquity and from each other, and initiated new ideas and new interpretations that distinguish their respective vocabularies from each other. Images from common sources yield varied, parallel symbolic meanings in accordance with different, parallel spiritual needs. Moreover, the urge to express aspects of faith in visually symbolic terms has not waned, despite the fact that Western art has shifted toward a more secular point of view over the past three centuries or so. The need addressed by religion and expressed through visual language has remained to the present day. Abrahamic symbols of faith still reverberate within the broadest of time and space continua. They contribute a rich well of sacred signs, wedding human diversity to commonality, and endless particulars to universal ideas.

CHAPTER 1

SYMBOLS IN ANCIENT ART

Survival, Religion, Art, and Transformation

As far back as we trace it, art has addressed the *sacer*. As a visual concomitant of the verbal aspects of religion—prayer and myth—it has maintained a fundamental focus on the issue of survival. Survival is dependent upon a successful relationship with the *sacer*; it has created and therefore can destroy us; it can further or hinder us, help or harm us; it brings the rain and the sun in due or undue season and volume, and it supplies the game we seek in the wilderness (which *is* the *sacer*), as surely as it succeeds or fails to assist us in battling our enemies or traveling through the wilderness.

One sees readily how art assists the process of this relationship by examining one of the earliest works of sculpture from within the Mediterranean and European worlds: the *Venus of Willendorf*. Rather than presenting any individualized attributes, this tiny (4³/₈" high) figurine dating from about 24,000–22,000 BCE is a very concrete embodiment of the hope for survival by means of the abstraction of female fertility (see Figure 5). She is characterized by enormous thighs, a well-defined pubic area, a large belly with a prominent umbilicus, and large breasts, further emphasized by the placement across them of very rudimentary arms. Her head is devoid of a face; it is overrun by rows of "hair" that resemble the rows of a well-sown field. Indeed, that there are *seven* rows of "hair" may be construed as other than arbitrary, for *sacer*-related survival reasons that I explore below.

FIGURE 5   *Venus of Willendorf, oolitic lime-stone. ca. 24,000–22,000 BCE*

The placement of this figurine and others like her within the earth itself may be understood in one of two parallel ways. If the site was a cult site, then within the earth, mother of fertility, the *Venus* bespeaks a desire to connect us to that source of life. If the site was a grave site, then we may suppose that the desired consequence of the hoped-for connection to the *sacer* is rebirth—whether in an afterlife or in the sense of transmigration back to our *profanus* world one cannot say.

The connection to the earth—more specifically, to the realm beneath the earth, away from the *profanus* surface—is also seen in the earliest paintings in the Euro-Mediterranean world. The wall paintings found at Paleolithic sites such as Lascaux and Altamira, created deep within the *sacer*—and given the purpose of the work, most likely painted at night, during *sacer* time—include two primary types of image. One is the successful pursuit of game by hunters. In this *sacer* space at a *sacer* time, the powers of the *sacer* are intended to be visually inspired to assist the hunter "brothers" of the painters when they go out into the *sacer* the following day to bring back food to the *profanus*. The artists making these depictions function in a manner analogous to that of priests intoning prayers or poets reciting myths: they are inspirited to open a door between the *profanus* and the *sacer,* with the hope and expectation that the positive power of the *sacer* will enter and affect the *profanus*.

The second type of image that prevails among such cave paintings also pertains to survival but in the more indirect form of fertility. As always with symbols in visual art, the indirection can be two or even three layers removed from the literal and obvious. If the abstraction of "fertility" in its female aspect may be rendered by the image of a human female in which all fertility-related aspects are emphasized, then how would the male aspect be represented? The most direct means would be to offer a large phallus—and as we shall see, such an image appears often in the course of early art history. But more frequent is the image of a male animal associated with fertility. The bull, recognizable by his broad shoulders and long curving horns, is conspicuous among the images in the wall paintings of Lascaux.[1] It is not simply that bulls are powerful and fierce—virile—creatures. But as those living in a rural community would know well, they are virtuosi of fertility, capable of fertilizing an extraordinary number of cows without rest. The depiction of bulls symbolizes the abstract idea of fertility in "concrete" visual terms.

The importance of caves as sacerdotal points of contact between realms is underscored by an extremely early cave complex in the Nullarbor Plain in Australia. The Gallus site within the Koonalda cave complex includes wall decoration consisting of thousands of criss-crossing incised lines, some apparently handmade and some stick-made, together with the remains of wood torches, flint chips that had to have been brought in from the outside, and possible sculptural forms (these may be the incidental forms left as the detritus from flint flaking). These man-made elements date from between 50,000 and 20,000 years ago. The markings are found in the deepest cave as, entering from above, one descends through the triple complex deep beneath the surface, and the complex is far enough from the nearest possible point of human inhabitation that the journey today takes three days in a Land Rover. Why would a prehistoric people repeatedly journey such a great distance over such hostile terrain to arrive at a place where they—or some of them—would further plunge deep into the earth? The answer must be that they perceived this deepmost cave—a *sacer* space away from the *profanus* above ground, within the *sacer* of the wilderness, far from the *profanus* of human inhabitation— as a powerful and propitious point of connection between *profanus* and *sacer*. Hither the "tribe" made a pilgrimage, culminating with a descent into the depths of the earth itself, where the decorative elements that have survived reflect whatever ritual of *profanus-sacer* contact was exercised in this border space. Other Australian caves that are contemporary with this one include stylized faces and figures within their repertoire of parietal paintings and engravings.[2]

The notion of sacerdotal space and the type of images that dominate them (the Koonalda imagery, in its limited, nonfigurative vocabulary, is the exception) proliferate as we follow history and art history out of the Stone Age into the Bronze Age. Female fertility images abound—even as their style changes, tending from the robust to the svelte. In Syro-Palestine, the late Chalcolithic-early Bronze Age (ca. 3200 BCE) *Venus of Beersheva* exhibits attributes similar to those of the *Venus of Willendorf,* but in a slimmed-down version: emphasized thighs, pubic area, belly with pronounced umbilicus, and breasts accentuated by the placement of her rudimentary arms across the chest (the head is altogether missing). In the variously sized Cycladic figurines of the last few centuries of the early Bronze Age (ca. 2300–2000 BCE) one again finds such attributes, even as the style is one of simple lineation, reduced to smooth surfaces punctuated by angular geometries that seem sophisticated to our modern eyes.

One image illustrates the principle of symbolizing fertility in a particularly interesting manner. A figurine from Nahariya, on the central coast of Syro-Palestine, dated about 1800–1700 BCE—apparently a female figure, with slight but pronounced breasts and a clearly articulated pubic area—wears a headdress that rises as the horns of a bull. Between the horns is an erect phallus. Thus the figure incorporates female with male fertility symbolism and offers the latter with both direct and indirect imagery.

Female fertility figures abound in the art of the Bronze Age throughout the Near East and East Mediterranean, as does the image of the bull. Although these are found in various locations, none is more impressive than those at the site of Knossos on northern Crete. The image of the bull horns is repeated as a motif throughout the palace complex and even as a form associated with the main altar for offerings to the gods. This shouldn't surprise us: Zeus is understood by the Greeks, before the Minoan period of Knossos's heyday, to have been born and raised on Crete in a cave not far from Knossos, and Poseidon, Zeus's brother is the primary patron of the city according to the later Greek myths about the Minoan site. Both Zeus and Poseidon offer important avatars as bulls: the Bull of Heaven and the Bull of the Sea.

The significance of this becomes apparent when we consider one of the best-known of wall paintings at Knossos, the so-called Toreador Fresco, in which young men and women are shown somersaulting over the back of a powerful bull. Considering the later Greek myth of Theseus, this image is easy enough to understand. That story asserts that during the time when Minos ruled Knossos and Knossos maintained hegemony over the entire Aegean Sea, the Athenians were required to send seven youths and seven maidens as tribute to Minos's court every nine years—who never returned home, since they were fed into a maze to be devoured by the minotaur.[3] Until, that is, Theseus, prince of Athens, arrived among the tribute youths and destroyed the half-human, half-bull offspring of a bull and Minos's wife, Phasiphae.

The reality that underlies this narrative may reflect the principles that I have been discussing. It seems from the excavations in the Aegean that Crete—with Knossos as its main city—dominated the area during the middle Bronze Age, but that by the end of that era the mainlanders had asserted themselves. The palaces of the mainlanders were quite simple compared with the complex, maze-like palace at Knossos. Memory, the passage of centuries, and the transmission of tales that grow with each telling would explain how that maze, with a king who waited at its center in his throne room to greet the mainlanders, would become the famous labyrinth—a word combining Greek and pre-Greek elements, and meaning "the place of the double axe."[4] Double axes, their upturned edges recalling those of the horns of a bull, abound in the decor of Knossos. If we reasonably imagine that the king—Minos, in later Greek telling—was wearing a crown (perhaps it covered his entire face and head) adorned with the horns of a large bull, since as king he would be at least a relative of the God (in this case, Poseidon), one of whose avatars was a bull, then the memory of Minos would become the story of the Minotaur—the Minos-bull—which was transformed into the story of his strange illegitimate son.[5]

But why were the young men and women there in the first place and why did they seldom, if ever, return until the hero Theseus put an end to the minotaur and his labyrinth? The Toreador Fresco seems to offer a rite of passage, a puberty ritual, but a very dangerous one, in which both males and females participated. As a symbol of fertility on the grandest of scales—the image of the bull directly and indirectly (all of those double axes with upturned edges resembling bull horns) dominates the decor of Knossos—the bull offered a powerful centerpiece to such a ritual. But if we accord some truth to the Theseus story, then instead of risking the lives of Minoan princes and princesses, their surrogates, tributes from the mainland, participated in the bull-jumping. Thus those who entered the maze-palace of the double axes, received by a king who appeared part bull and part man, were utilized by him so that the rite of passage could be accomplished. Few of the surrogate princes and princesses would have survived such an exercise. The destruction of this system is associated in one thread of story with Theseus and in another thread of story with the volcanic destruction of Knossos.[6]

The survivors, in physical contact with the adolescent children of the Minoan nobility, would extend to the latter what they had gained by their contact with the bull: fertility. The ritual, a rite of passage into adulthood, would bring the Minoan children into the Minoan adult *profanus* by virtue of their now-official ability to contribute to the continuation of that community by being fertile. The tapestry of threads offering elements of this story is laid out centuries later in diverse works of Greek literature. But for our purposes the significant elements of it are the emphasis on the bull as a symbol of fertility and the varied ways in which that emphasis is visually (and otherwise) articulated.[7]

Nowhere is the notion of the king as a border creature and an avatar of the godhead more evident than in ancient Egypt. If the gods can be represented by bulls, then the pharaoh, as a representation of a god, might well be symbolized by a bull. It is therefore not surprising that one of the most important early works of Egyptian art, *Narmer's Palette,* represents the pharaoh of that name—who is conventionally credited with unifying the Upper and Lower Kingdoms for the first time—as a bull, among other ways. He is shown pushing down the wall of a city with his horns while trampling the city's protector to the ground with his hooves. The god within the bull resides within the pharaoh.

The bull, which is such a significant avatar of Zeus and Poseidon in the Greek tradition, of Dionysus in the Anatolian tradition (subsequently imported into Greece), of Apis and Buchis and even Amon in the Egyptian tradition, of Ba'al in the Canaanite tradition, and Marduk in the Mesopotamian tradition, is not the only animal that plays a major role with respect to suggesting survival through fertility and power. Rams and billy goats occupy an analogous position, often characterized by the synecdoche that yields images such as the double ax as symbolic bull horns at Knossos. Thus, for example, the development of the Ionic capital from the Aeolic capital, with the volutes that are its most definitive characteristic, may be understood as a stylization of rams' horns (see Figure 6). The less prominent but frequent feature of the egg and dart motif, in which swollen round areas alternate with upward-thrusting

FIGURE 6   *Proto-Ionic capital, Hatzor, Israel. ca. 1300 BCE*

rods usually tipped with arrowheads, may be understood as the alternation of female (swollen womb) and male (erect phallus) fertility elements. Both visual symbols of fertility and thus of survival personified by particular animals within ancient art variously represented, are clear.

The threat to survival comes in different forms. Our failure to produce offspring is one. The failure of our fields or livestock to thrive is another. Our enemies present another significant threat to survival, and unfortunately human history is in part a continuum of peoples making war against each other. In such a context, the lion is seen repeatedly as an apotropaic creature, particularly paired in a carefully ordered symmetry above or to either side of a monumental doorway. A bronze lion guarded the gate of the Temple of Dagon at Mari around 2000 BCE. At Hattusas, capital of the Hittite empire, which reached its peak between 1600 and 1200 BCE, the ruins of the palace complex reveal a monumental doorway flanked by lions facing toward anyone approaching. At late Bronze Age Hatzor, in northern Israel, monumental lions face each other on either side of the doorway of Temple 1A, embedded in the very walls (only one of the lions has been recovered). A procession of such lions, made of relief-carved and brightly colored ceramic tiles, leads toward the doorway of the seventh-century palace complex of Babylon. That the first and third of these structures are temples and the second and fourth are palaces underscores the manner in which both kinds of edifices, as habitations of priests on the one hand and kings on the other, are analogues of each other. Both serve as sacerdotal points of contact between aspects of *sacer* and *profanus,* presided over by two different kinds of *sacerdotes.*

Guardian lion figures are found in both monumental and more physically modest contexts throughout the ancient Near East and sometimes found in conjunction with other elements significant to the *sacer-profanus* relationship. Thus the cyclopean doorway at late-Bronze Age Mycenae is guarded by a pair of lions placed in rampant position above the entrance. The lions' bodies are carved in profile, and their heads—connected to the bodies by dowels and long since lost—would have faced toward those approaching. The two creatures flank a column with frond-like detailing for its capital. That detail reminds us that the column has evolved, both literally and metaphorically, from a tree trunk. (I shall return to this matter shortly.) In the context of this doorway, its role, together with that of the lions, may be understood. The tree stands at the center of reality and is essential to the order of reality; the lions, supported by and supporting the tree, are part of the process of maintaining that order. The king, whose gateway is protected by lions, is also represented by lions—but he is also the tree of life become a simple column; he is himself an establisher and protector of order, a *sacerdos* who stands between his constituents and the various forces of the *sacer,* whether wild animals, enemies, or dangerous as well as benign gods. Anyone approaching his gate would be well advised to do so with caution and a proper attitude.

The Sacer-Profanus *Border and Its Guardians*

Powerful creatures guard the border between realms. They *are* the boundary between *sacer* and *profanus*. The analogue of the temple as meeting point between *sacer* and *profanus* is the royal palace or the royal library, since the king and the scholar are both analogues of the priest in standing between these two realms. Even more logical as a creature to mediate between realms is one itself contrived of different realms, one whose very physical configuration suggests category intermediation. It is no surprise, then, that the rampantly disposed beasts on either side of the tree of life on an Iranian vessel from about the twelfth-century BCE are *winged.* These winged bulls are themselves contrived of two elements that do not co-incide in the *profanus* of our everyday world, though each element is part of our *profanus* experience. They are symbols of "border," and thus offer a unique and important form of guardianship between realms.

We can follow the trail of such creatures across cultures. The being that the Greek hero Oedipus meets at a crossroads separating the *profanus* of Thebes from the *sacer* of the realm beyond the city—whose riddle he solves, thus rescuing Thebes from the plague of the riddler—is called a *sphinx*.[8] The term refers to a creature with the body of a lion and the face of a human female; its variant form extends the human female at-

FIGURE 7   *Cherub figure, Khorsabad, Iraq. ca. 720 BCE*

tributes to the upper torso of the body and sometimes adds the wings of a bird of prey. In Khorsabad, protecting the great library of the Assyrian monarch Sargon II, enormous beasts sit astride either side of the entrance.[9] They have the bodies of lions *or* bulls, human heads, and great wings of a bird of prey (see Figure 7). One seeking to enter inappropriately—one seeking to cross the boundary from the *profanus* of the community at large into the *sacer* of the royal realm without the proper procedures—would be outwitted by the crowned head of such a beast, outchased by its enormous wings, and torn or trampled to death by its claws or hooves.

Such creatures are called *cherubs*.[10] When we understand what that term means in this context, we understand better what is meant in Genesis 3 when the text describes *cherubim* placed at the gateway to the Garden of Eden from which Adam and Eve are ejected, preventing those who should not enter from doing so—and we see how the images of bulls and lions move through transformation and complexity. Similarly, the tree at the center of reality—the tree of eternal life and order placed between a pair of lions or bulls, or winged lions or winged bulls—becomes a column or becomes a doorway that is the entryway into the realm of the king or his analogues. In other words, the king is the column, is the tree, and is implied at a site such as the palace at Khorsabad by the open space of the gateway that leads into the sanctum in which he resides. He stands between gods and men, and he is generally assumed to descend from both in the varied traditions of antiquity. At the very least, the favor of the gods rests on him.

Like the king, the pharaoh, or the shah, the hero is descended from god or favored by god—from Gilgamesh to Achilles to Aeneas. To see the continuous transformation of visual ideas, we might compare the inlay of the soundbox of a lyre from Ur to the images we have been discussing (see Figure 8). The soundbox—surmounted by the image of a bearded bull—offers a series of border-creature images: animals standing on two legs like humans and engaged in human activities, from carrying offerings to playing a lyre. These reflect various elements of the Mesopotamian mythic tradition, but the centerpiece of that tradition, reflected on the upper register of the soundboard, is the story of Gilgamesh. We see him with his arms around the upper torsos of two identical beasts with the body and horns of a bull and a human face. As such, he occupies the position elsewhere held by tree or column and functions as the order-maintaining center. The king as *sacerdos* is the hero as *sacerdos*. An analogous image, of which there are multiple examples in Minoan Crete, is that of the priestess, lushly bare-breasted, her skirt overrun with repeating triangle forms that we recognize as the fertility-symbolic pubic triangle, her arms upraised (like the upraised edges of a double ax or the horns of a bull). In her hands she holds a pair of serpents—phallic symbols of fertility both in their shape and in the manner in which they slither in and out of the openings into Mother Earth. As mistress of the beasts—*potnia theron*—she is the sacerdotal analogue of Gilgamesh or Sargon.

Different from these but analogous to them is the high-relief representation of Umdugud from 'Ubaid, Mesopotamia, in the middle of the third pre-Christian millennium. This relief dating from the early dynastic period—sheet copper molded over a carved wooden core—depicts the storm god himself presiding as the Master of Beasts. He is a border figure, with the body of a majestic eagle-like bird and the head of a feline; his wings are spread over a pair of wild stags with impressive antlers, disposed in perfect symmetry with their bodies in profile, backs to the center, and their heads turned toward the viewer. Thus the sacerdotal protector of the *profanus* and maintainer of order, be it god or king or hero or priestess, is depicted together with particular animals and symmetries to reinforce the symbolism of his or her position.

Border Structures and the Ordering and Reordering of Space

The varied sacerdotal characters emulate the god who breathes through them to the community, all of whose constituents thereby also possess an aspect of god-ness at some small level. The poet and artist are the analogues of those other sacerdotes, who are also inspired—in-spirited—to emulate divinity in creating the art. The same applies to architects of monumental structures, particularly religious ones. The act

FIGURE 8   *Sound box from lyre, Sumer (detail). ca. 2100 BCE*

of creating a temple is a microcosmic emulation of what the gods did at the beginning of time: superimposing order (*kosmos*, in Greek terminology) over chaos.[11] As we examine the pyramids—either the earlier step-pyramid style associated with Zoser (Neterkhet; ca. 2750 BCE) or the subsequent, canonical style associated with Cheops (Khufu; ca. 2570 BCE), Chefren (Khafra; ca. 2550 BCE), and Mycerinus (Menkaura; ca. 2500 BCE) and their three great pyramids at Giza—we realize that they offer a series of perfect, regularized geometries superimposed over the irregularities of the natural landscape around them. Diagonals, or diagonals contrived of horizontals and verticals, rising to a unifying point from the four directions of reality as we conceive it, contrast with the ups and downs and ins and outs of the Egyptian landmass.

If we turn to Mesopotamia and its great ziggurat at Ur (ca. 2100 BCE) (see Figure 9), we find that the same principle is operative. A progression of sweeping diagonals punctuated by horizontals and verticals, perhaps culminating with a perfect sphere, rises from the chaotic vastness like a perfect mountain to connect earth to heaven.[12] The long house temples of the northwest Semites—the northern Canaanites, as the Bible called them, or Phoenicians, as the Greeks would later refer to them—are contrived of horizontals and verticals. Adopted and adapted by the Greeks, such temples—the Parthenon in Athens, as it was rebuilt under Pericles, by Ictinus and Callicrates between 448 and 432 BCE, is exemplary—are paragons of this principle (see Figure 10). Over the irregular fastness of the rocky outcropping of the Acropolis is imposed a series of perfect, regularized horizontals (the layered stereobate, culminating with the stylobate), surmounted by a perfect, rhythmic pattern of verticals (the peristasis of columns, fluted to further accentuate the regularized pattern), surmounted by the layered horizontal of the Doric architrave, and crowned by a fronton based on that most stable of geometric forms, the triangle.

FIGURE 9   *Ziggurat, Sumer (artist's conception). ca. 2100 BCE*

FIGURE 10 *Ictinus and Callicrates: Parthenon, Athens, Greece. 448–432* BCE

In each of these cases, we recognize the principle of the architect's act emulating the gods who in-spirit him. The Parthenon, contrived by the geometries of the human mind, placed over the irregularities of the natural landscape, symbolizes just that: the ability of humans to be over/above (in Latin: *super*) nature (in Latin: *natura*). It expresses our desire to be *supernatural,* like the goddess it addresses, even as we must be careful not to commit the hubristic act of suggesting that the architect or his patrons are *too* god-like.[13]

In such an architectural context we observe the continuity of general principles together with transformation of the principle; ideas are adopted and adapted from one culture to another. The transformation of the principle of architecture as a bridge between *profanus* and *sacer* into a statement of the aspiration of the *profanus* to be like the *sacer,* in acting *super natura,* is visible in the contrast of the relative simplicity of the Egyptian pyramid and the more complicated funerary temple complex of Mentuhotep (ca. 2050 BCE) and Hatshepsut (ca. 1485 BCE), side by side at Deir el Bahri (see Figure 11). The complex's very designation

as both temple and tomb underscores the significant analogic relationship between these two institutions: each is a meeting point between
profanus and *sacer*. And we observe the principle of functioning *super
natura* in the profusion of horizontals and verticals punctuated by diagonals and rising to a pyramidal form that stands before a magnificently
wild and chaotic landscape. The idea of a natural growth transformed
into an ordered progression of columns is present, as it is in other
Egyptian complexes, such as the funerary temple of Amon-Mut-Khonsu
at Luxor. A close look at the capitals of the colonnade of Amon-Hotep
III within that funerary temple reveals them to be stylized lotus blossoms and papyrus fronds; nature has been reshaped as a perfect order
through the intermediation of human architectural intellect.

On the other hand, when we turn again to the Greeks we may observe a different aspect of synthesis and transformation. As the *polis*
took shape in the ninth and eight centuries BCE in the context of expanding Greek interchange with other cultures and the development of
her own culture, the Egyptians and the Phoenicians were two of the

FIGURE 11 *Deir el-Bahri. Remains of mortuary temple of Hatshepsut.
Eighteenth Dynasty, ca. 1480 BCE*

peoples who most impressed the Greeks, albeit in different ways. As we re-examine the Parthenon and dozens of other Greek temples, we recognize that they represent a synthesis between the long house temples of the Phoenicians—including a modified version of the tripartite interior division of these—and the continuous colonnade as a stylized, ordered forest pioneered as an architectural idea by the Egyptians. A variation of the rhythmic forest at Deir el-Bahri rings every Greek temple, instead of the mere pair of columns placed before a Canaanite (Phoenician) long house temple.

The Greek sense of all of this as an *order* is underscored by the very idea of architectural "orders" that achieve canonical form by the mid-fifth century BCE in Athens. At the heart of each order is the style of column and capital, again reflecting adoption and adaptation. Thus supplementing the geometric chasteness of the Doric capital, the Ionic capital of the Greeks evolves from the Aeolic capital of Anatolia and the Near East, with its fertility-symbolizing ram's horn volutes (see Figure 6). From Egypt, the acanthus leaves with their implications of immortality and rebirth—since the acanthus is somewhat of an evergreen—find their way into the shaping of the Corinthian capital.

The triple principle that we have been exploring—of art serving religion and thus focusing on issues that relate to survival, especially fertility; of borrowing from one culture and tradition into another; and of transforming either the specifics of the image, the specifics of its symbolic meaning, or both—is apparent again and again as one examines the art and architecture of pagan antiquity. Nowhere is this more apparent than in the last and most far-flung of ancient civilizations, Rome. Rome extends the various architectural forms and symbolic visual language of diverse ancient cultures one step further, completing the foundations upon which Western art and architecture are built.

The golden gate of the southern Italian Greek colony of Helia (subsequently, under the Romans, Velia) proves that the Greeks did, on rare occasion, make use of the technology of the keystone, but it was the Romans who pursued that technology to its logical conclusion. One such conclusion is the freestanding arch. Single and threefold arches of victory, celebrating aspects of the Roman ordering of the world, are found within Rome itself, in and around the old Roman forum, and all over parts of the Roman world. Either at the meeting of major crossroads, or on the boundary between a significant area within a city and the rest of the city, or between the edge of the city and the world outside, such arches are invariably festooned with inscriptions and relief-carved images that assert which Roman conqueror did what and when. The spandrels of such arches are decorated with winged figures, often shown trumpeting, which symbolize victory; they are thus referred to as *nikê* (in Greek) or *victoria* (in Latin) figures.

The stringing together of a succession of such arches, and the surmounting of one arcade by a second or a third, makes possible the reordering of the chaotic landscape of nature for the practical purpose of providing water from the distant wilderness (the *sacer*) to a city in need (the *profanus*), as if the hills and valleys across which such a structure— an aqueduct—extends were not there. It is thus a symptom of the Roman act of being like the gods who favor them—that is, of being *super natura*—and being able to draw (literally, *lead*) water across long distances.[14]

The stringing together of a succession of arches surmounted by a second and third arcade, not in a straight line but in an ellipse, yields the kind of structure of which the Roman Colosseum is the most famous example. Moving the half-moon-shaped Greek theater down from its place embedded in the hillside and doubling it, one face against the other, the Romans created amphitheaters—meaning "both theaters."[15] The Colosseum (so named because it was built near a colossal statue of the Emperor Nero depicted as the sun god) offers another symbolic statement of order over chaos, of the Roman subduing of nature. A succession of orders—colonnaded arcades that from the lowest level to the uppermost offer a progression of Doric pilasters surmounted by Ionic pilasters surmounted by Corinthian pilasters with their capitals— encompasses a space in which entertainments were offered to the Roman people. Battles between various kinds of wild beasts, beasts and men, and men against each other, armed variously with short-swords (a short-sword was called a *gladius,* hence *gladiator*), tridents, nets, and other weapons, were enacted over an arena contrived as an irregular landscape. The irregular shaping of the sandy surface by humans, as gods have shaped landscapes on the larger, worldwide scale, meant that the combatants couldn't see each other until the moment they finally met, while the audience, observing god-like from above, could see every moment develop before it happened.

The temple form of the Greeks is a synthesis of Phoenician and Egyptian elements; in Roman hands, this is further synthesized to specific aspects of Italic—particularly Etruscan—style. Roman temples absorb the essential form of Greek temples, together with their column and capital orders, particularly the Corinthian order, but adapt it to the Roman conception of how to shape space. Etruscan temples were elevated on platforms, with a distinct frontality defined by a porch supported by columns and stairs leading up to that porch; proportions were squatter and broader from left to right relative to the dimension extending from front to back than those of Greek temples, and side and back columns and stairs were not present. The Roman temple, as in the so-called Maison Carrée in Nîmes or the Temple of Fortuna Virilis in Rome, is habitually placed on a high base, with a front porch and stairs—but with pilasters around the sides and back, offering the illusion of the Greek *peristasis* and proportions more like those of Greek than Etruscan temples, but like the latter, commanding the space before it, not around it,[16] for as the Romans sacerdotally shaped and ordered virtually the entire space that they regarded as the world—beyond their far-flung imperial borders was *sacer* chaos—*within* that world, public and private buildings, from amphitheaters and temples to villas, governed spaces viewed as interior aspects of their ordered, god-emulating world.

A unique development of this principle is the ultimate Roman temple, dedicated to all the gods—the Pantheon—which is fronted by a Corinthian-ordered porch that by itself could pass well enough for a Greek structure. But the porch is actually attached to a very differently conceived body. Distinctly Roman, it is a perfectly circular dome, the first freestanding dome of any size in the Western architectural tradition. The dome may also be understood as an arch in three dimensions—another development carried beyond its predecessors by the Romans. On the interior, the dome of the Pantheon rises in seven layers, once vetted with glistening bronze, to an opening called an *oculus*—meaning "eye"(see Figure 12).[17] The seven layers correspond to a sense of divinity as sevenfold, which the Romans absorbed from the Greeks, who derived it from the Persians, who learned it from the Babylonians. The idea can be traced back even further to the Sumerians and the Egyptians (and perhaps as far back as the time of the *Venus of Willendorf*)—and so that aspect of the Pantheon decor represents nearly three millennia, or perhaps as much as twenty-five millennia, of continuity of a symbolic idea.

FIGURE 12   *Pantheon, Rome. ca. 120 CE*

The Sacer *Importance of Number*

The origin of the divine association with the number seven is not difficult to deduce. If one continuously observes the heavens, one may note that within the sphere of countless "fixed stars" that move in a constant spatial relationship to each other, there are seven heavenly beings that move with a reliable and recognizable periodicity across the heavens by night or day. These are the sun, the moon, and the five planets that we see with the naked eye (and are clearly different from occasional celestial visitors, such as meteors and comets). In antiquity, all seven of these were referred to as "wanderers" across the heavens—the word "planet" derives from the Greek verb *planeo,* meaning "to wander"—and were assumed to be associated with divinities governing various aspects of the *sacer,* to say nothing of influencing aspects of the *profanus* from the *sacer.* Each such wanderer, associated with one of seven heavenly spheres revolving around us, was called by the name of a god, as most still are today by way of Latin (Roman) names: Mercury, Venus, Mars, Jupiter, Saturn, the Moon, and the Sun.

This long tradition of seven as a *sacer* number—associated with completion and perfection and reflected in the seven-day week of the Mesopotamian calendar and in other ancient traditions—interweaves the concept of twelve as a *sacer* number. The heavens are divided into twelve areas of influence (the zodiac), and the gods that dwell on Olympus in the Greek and Roman and Etruscan traditions are, correspondingly, twelve in number. The lower walls of the Roman Pantheon are lined with niches for the Olympian gods. As the structure was dedicated to all of the gods, it not only offered a point of connection between all of them and the *profanus* but also echoed, on a microcosmic scale, the vault of heaven to which the Pantheon is connected by the oculus that permits light from heaven to enter the interior and move across the dome, as the eye of heaven moves through the day.[18] As Rome is self-conceived as the favorite of the gods, the center of the world ordered by Roman power connects to and echoes the world ordered by divine power.

There is another aspect of symbolic transformation that the discussion of architecture, particularly in conjunction with number, raises: abstraction. Where sculpted images from the *Venus of Willendorf* to the *Minoan Priestess* offer figurative representation as the mode of symbolic expression, the pyramids, ziggurats, temples, and tombs speak in the language of straight lines and angles and mathematical simplicity. Thus, not only geometry but arithmetic and numerology are instruments of addressing, accessing, and apprehending the *sacer*, and these are in turn repeatedly harnessed by visual forms. This is apparent not only in the configuration of tombs and temples but in what they contain. For example, in Egypt, the fact that four canopic jars contain the inner parts of the deceased (whose outer parts are mummified) is not arbitrary; four corresponds to the number of earthbound directions that are assumed to be repeated in the afterworld. Each of the four jars is governed by one of the four sons of the god Horus and is topped by the corresponding image. Hep, the ape-headed god, protects the small intestines; Tuamutef, the jackal, protects the heart and lungs; Amset, with the head of a man, guards the stomach and large intestine; and Qebhsenuf, with the Horus-resembling hawk's head, guards the liver and gall bladder. These border-creature lesser gods assure the safe passage of these essential internal elements to the *sacer*, wherein the soul of the deceased will be judged by their "grandfather," Osiris—who is both the father of Horus and indistinguishable from him, since Osiris was reborn *as* Horus after being killed by his half-brother Seth.

And as for the soul of the deceased, Egyptian tradition understands it to consist of seven aspects—the same as the number of *planetes*. Every dead man has a double, called his *Ka*, as well as an intimate little soul (we might call it, in the nonphysical sense, his heart) called his *Ba*, often depicted with the body of a bird and the face of the dead man. In addition, there is his *Khu*—corresponding to that glow within the mind that activates it when one is alive, but somewhat akin to his guardian angel.

His *Khaibit* is a sort of shadow of the deceased. His *Ren* corresponds to his Name (which identifies him in summary form as a distinct individual but is derived from the celestial waters and enters him at birth to help shape his character).

His *Sekhem* provided the power that animated his limbs while he was alive; its departure at death accounts for the stiff immobility of the body after death. Lastly, his *Sekhu* is the remnant part of his soul that inhabits his mummy when the other six aspects of it have dissipated—one might say that it enables the mummy still to be the remains of a distinctive individual in spite of the fact that all the distinguishing elements are gone. With this configuration of the soul in mind—that which connects the *profanus* mortal being to the *sacer* of immortality—it is not surprising that visual manifestations both of the individual components of the soul and of seven-ness should be an ongoing aspect of ancient Egyptian visual self-expression. Nor should we be surprised to find this sort of numerological focus both in the varied visual vocabularies of antiquity and in the Abrahamic visual vocabulary that grows out of it.

Religion, Art, and Politics

Among the more important Roman buildings were those in which administrators, legislators, and judicial leaders would meet. Such structures were often basilical in form; that is, they were longer than they were wide, and the interior presented a division into three longitudinal aisles separated from each other by two rows of columns. This idea also represents a transformation, both architecturally and linguistically. The term basilica is derived from the Latinized noun form of a Greek adjective—*basileios*—meaning "royal." In turn, that adjective was attached, in its traditional architectural context, to the Greek word for "porch," *stoa*. This last term referred to the kind of porch running along the edge of the *agora* (open-air marketplace and area of general social and political interaction for citizens of the *polis*), to protect those who might stroll under it from the hot Mediterranean sun. The *stoa basileios* referred to the long porch or that part of it reserved for individuals of particularly high stature. Such a porch resulted architecturally from the placement of a colonnade parallel to the outer wall of the agora (into which shops opened) and the overlay of a roof between wall and colonnade. The Romans doubly transformed this in order to engender a "basilica." The external colonnade became an internal one, running parallel to the outer wall of the structure. Two of these were placed across from and parallel to each other, each wall-colonnade pairing creating an aisle. And the space between the two colonnades created a third, middle aisle referred to as the "nave"—typically wider and with a higher roof than the side aisles, emphasizing them as separate, internal "porches." Complementing this architectural transformation was the linguistic one: the noun *stoa* was dropped and the adjective *basileios* was both Latinized and turned into a noun. The Romans usually used such buildings as administrative and judicial centers and occasionally as schools.

There is more. Most often the far end of such a Roman basilica was curved, rather than squared, yielding a large niche—an apse. Within that apse the chief administrator or presiding judge (or teacher) would sit, usually on a substantial seat, a throne of sorts referred to as a *kathedra*—a Greek term referring to a seat *(hedra)* with a back and arm rests designed to protect the one seated from exposure to an assassin. The seated individual would command the space before him, particularly if his throne were elevated on a platform, so that those seeking his attention would be looking up to him from a lower level.

The idea of such a niche at the end of an open space, from which the space is commanded from a raised position, recalls the siting of Roman temples and other public structures, commanding the spaces, such as fora, before them, from their raised platforms. Not surprisingly, that same idea attaches itself to the positioning of Roman statuary—as opposed to Greek statuary, which is intended to be seen from all sides, just as Greek temples are visually "entered" from all sides. The typical Roman statue is placed with its back to a wall or is ensconced within a niche. The ultimate example of this is the statue of Augustus at the villa at Prima Porta. The villa belonged to his wife, Livia, and as the viewer exited from the atrium into the back garden, from within its niche the sculpture commanded the viewer with upraised imperial hand. Across the cuirass of Augustus were the relief-carved representations of his triumphs on behalf of the Roman people. By his side, the image of Cupid (Eros, son of Aphrodite/Venus) astride a dolphin reminded the viewer of the emperor's descent from Aeneas, hero and son of Aphrodite.[19]

If such a statue was typically Roman both in its placement and its emphasis on decorative elements across its chest that are educative (that is, propagandistic), it nonetheless bears a direct compositional relationship with its Greek forebears. The *Augustus of Prima Porta* expresses

FIGURE 13 *Polyclitus: Doryphorus (Roman copy). ca. 440 BCE*

well the idea of *contraposto*—counterpose or counterpoise—with which Greek sculptors had continually experimented from the end of the sixth century BCE. In particular it emulates and transforms that principle as it was canonically expressed in the *Doryphorus*—the "Spear-bearer"—sculpted by Polyclitus in the 440s BCE, at the height of the classical period of Greek art (see Figure 13). That work expresses the idea of dynamic repose and ideal proportion that allied the human form to architectural form in the Greek (particularly the Athenian) mind just prior to and especially after the Persian wars.

Thus the *Doryphorus* not only offers a particular proportion of height to width and of head to body but also gives us a figure shifting weight. One leg tenses and extends as it receives the body's weight and the other leg relaxes and bends. Conversely, the arm that bends, on the same side of the body as the leg that bends, is tensed (because it holds the spear); the arm that extends, on the same side of the body as the leg that extends, is relaxed. The line between the ankles of the two feet is a perceptible diagonal, due to the motion of shifting weight; that angle is echoed by the knees but counteracted by an opposite diagonal described by the hips. The pectorals and shoulders offer a perfect pair of horizontals, and the slightly turning head presents a series of diagonals—chin line, nose line, eye line—that recapitulate the diagonal with which the visual ascent began. It is not that every viewer would analyze the work this way, but rather that unconsciously our eyes, in taking all of this subtle dynamism in, are intended to come away with the sense of a breathing being and not a stiff chunk of stone or vessel of bronze.

Works like the *Doryphorus*—the purpose of which is to express in visual terms what we might call a philosophical idea: perfect manhood, what the Greeks called "the beautiful and the good" *(kalos k'agathon)*—are the exception, not the rule, within ancient and medieval visual expression. Even in Greek sculpture this is hardly the starting point of visual thinking. The dynamic repose expressed by works like the *Doryphorus* evolves out of an earlier, stiffer presentation intended to express the eternal immutability offered by the *kouros,* the term (meaning "young man") that refers to the male statuary of the seventh and sixth centuries BCE (see Figure 14). In such sculptures, the figure is represented as barely striding forward; his legs are close together and perfectly parallel, just as his shoulders and hips, knees and ankles, chin and forehead are perfectly horizontal and his arms rigidly disposed in a perfectly balanced position to either side of his absolutely frontal torso.

Such a figure, with its stylized proportion—of hair, facial features, stomach muscles, knee caps, and shin bones—evolved over two centuries, connotes idealized and eternal stasis. Since *kouroi* may have been repre-

sentations of gods—or perhaps the ideal god of mature youth, Apollo—there is a logic to such hieratic representation, idealized and unchanging, which contrasts so emphatically with the more fully anthropocentric idea of dynamic repose that emerges in the fifth century BCE. In retrospect, of course, the Greeks also derived this visual idea from elsewhere, and then transformed it as the Romans would subsequently transform the Greek idea. The hieratic presentation of the *kouros* derives from the imagery of Egyptian pharaohs, striding yet not striding from within the confines of stone—false doorways and pillars as their framing context. This was an unchanging continuum within Egyptian sculpture for two millennia.

Whereas the Greeks carried the idea of how to render the human form rather quickly forward, the Egyptians responded to a different

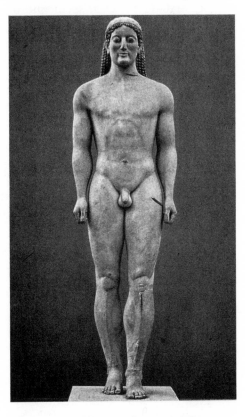

FIGURE 14   Kouros, *Anavysos,* Greece. *ca. 525 BCE*

set of concerns. Since their art represented pharaohs who were gods incarnate, their images expressed eternal and unchanging principles, like the gods themselves. The Greeks, on the other hand, evolved a growing interest in themselves—in humans as the measure of all things, as Protagoras put it—which caused them to transform their images into increasingly dynamic figurative representation.[20]

We are completing a circle back to the beginning point of our discussion, with the *Venus of Willendorf* and the symbolic use of the female figure to represent the abstraction of fertility, but facing in a new direction. Among the earliest sculpted figures of *males* in the foundations of Western art are those of the priests and votive offerings from Sumer. They present a hieratic and perfectly symmetrical positioning similar to that of Egyptian statuary, but their hands are clasped before them, across their bellies, not dropped to either side of their torso. The stylized, symmetrical positioning of the hands suggests that these figures intermediate between *sacer* and *profanus,* but the placement also recalls that of hands and rudimentary arms across the breasts or the swollen belly in earlier female figures, which were associated with fertility and thus survival. Perhaps that positioning for female figures, from the *Venus of Willendorf* to Cycladic art, came to be emulated and transferred to the image of priests who intermediate between *sacer* and *profanus.* That position in any case evolved as a convention for addressing the gods in many traditions. So, too, the fingers of the Sumerian figurines' hands are interlaced, as if the two realms—*sacer* and *profanus*—represented by two hands, are completely intermingled.

On the less specifically detailed scale, such figures, fully frontal and symmetrically disposed, their heads on a straightforward axis, with preternaturally large eyes—the eyes have been regarded as the windows to the soul for thousands of years—suggest an eternal and unchanging state. The role of the priest/votive is analogous to that of the king, shah, pharaoh—in short, the ruler—who plays a sacerdotal role, intermediating for his constituents with the varied aspects of the *sacer,* including the gods.

Thus we observe a progression of figurative representations of Mesopotamian rulers from the Sumerian to the Akkadian and Isin-Larsa and old Babylonian periods and continuing to the eras of the Neo-Assyrians, Chaldaean Babylonians, and Achaemenid Persians that exhibit the same essential presentation, even as specific stylistic details change: hair style, beard style (including lack of beard), nose shape, style of garment. They are frontal, symmetrical, their legs perfectly aligned (and barely apparent beneath the lower garment); their arms are either disposed to each side of the torso or bent so that the hands meet across the belly, or in another variation, one arm extends across the chest (generally exhibiting a weapon); and their faces are absolutely frontal, with enlarged eyes. They offer a stern, god-like, eternalizing aspect, which is the analogue of the representation of the pharaohs (which are clothed very differently, in only a wrapped skirt, so that the legs and torsos are exposed) and ultimately of the Greek *kouroi* (which are even further removed sartorially from their Egyptian counterparts, being completely nude).

Whereas Egyptian statuary is often framed by columns, the Mesopotamian statues, with their long garments marked by a stylized pattern of pleats that fall in regular flutes, *resemble* columns—as if the line between architectural and human form has been blurred. And if the Greek *kouros* begins at the point of the Egyptian figure but soon moves away from it, as dynamic repose and *contraposto* come to replace eternalizing hieraticism, the Greek *korê*—the female figure—emulates the Mesopotamian style of representing male *sacerdotes*. While head, arms, and feet are exposed, the torso and lower body of the *korê* are completely covered by one or more garments in a manner that, particularly early on, offers a strong dialogue between the architectural form of the fluted column and the sculptural form of the human figure.

The culmination of this dialogue came at the end of the fifth century BCE with the construction of the Erechtheion and its famous porch, held up by the figures of females *as* columns: *karyatids*. With this edifice, the blurring of category lines becomes explicit. The dialogue between sculpture and architecture is, in symbolic terms, one of the analogues of the ultimate dialogue between *sacer* and *profanus* in their varied manifestations. The presumably clear border between the two media, in being expressed in decidedly unclear terms, acts as a symbol of the complexly clear-unclear border between the two ultimate realms.

This was further expressed in the late fourth century BCE when full-scale nude female representation appeared, a form that had not been seen since the time of the Cycladic forebears of the Greeks, when a handful of stylized full-scale figures were crafted. Just as other issues were being explored by the fourth century BCE, such as proportion and the twisting of the principles of *contraposto* in increasingly unstable directions, so the divine nature of the *sacer,* in its aspect as the Olympian gods, came increasingly into question. In that context, Praxiteles' *Knidian Aphrodite* is one of several landmarks. It represents the goddess, born of the foam of the sea and washed up onto the shores of Cyprus, rising not from the sea but from the bath. She looks up at us, as if we have just entered and caught her in an exposed position: one arm extends across her breasts and the other attempts to cover her pubic area. But aside from the various ways in which dynamic repose is giving way to the moment, the goddess—who in earlier accounts would have simply turned us to stone with a glance or transformed us into beasts that would be torn apart by our own dogs—is reduced to inadequately covering herself up with a series of human gestures. And the sculpture was known by all to have depicted an actual human, for everyone knew that Phryne, the girlfriend of the sculptor, had modeled for it. Thus the goddess became a girl, and the girl an immortal goddess: the line between divine and human was blurred to the point of eradication.

A different sort of blurring is exhibited by a bell krater from Paestum dated to around 330 BCE. It portrays Zeus—whose seductive exploits are found throughout Greek mythology, including a number of instances when he assumes the form of a bull, a swan, or even a shower of gold to accomplish his seduction—as a pot-bellied, white-bearded old geezer. He is depicted with an equally decrepit Hermes (the messenger god and patron of merchants and thieves), who can barely keep his caduceus up. With a lamp to light the way, they drag a ladder to climb to a window where a woman's face appears—a prostitute, as the "woman at the window" motif means, going back at least as far as the Phoenician art of 1000 BCE.[21] The great Olympians had been reduced to a pathetic human state.

This analogue of Praxiteles' *Knidian Aphrodite* is echoed from the reverse perspective in coins from the late fourth century BCE depicting Alexander the Great with the ram's horns of Amon sprouting from his head to convey the message that he (who claimed descent from Heracles and thus from Zeus, and who subsequently asserted that he was adopted by Amon-Ra after his conquest of Egypt) is divine. Here the *sacer-profanus* border is blurred by a man become a god.

In the course of the centuries that connect the Greek to the Roman worlds by way of the Hellenistic age of cultural interweave and synthesis, many other works of sculpture offer variations of these same visual and conceptual themes. But no work more profoundly expresses the notion of transforming a visual idea to new symbolic purposes than the previously mentioned *Augustus of Prima Porta* in its relationship to Polyclitus' *Doryphorus*. If the *Doryphorus* is an idealized youth—the *kouros*-god become a god-like man, an athlete in his prime—the *Augustus* offers an idealized ruler, who has secured the borders of the empire (but, he would assert, saved the republic from *becoming* an empire) and brought prosperity far and wide. The figure dominates the space before him, so that in lieu of a bent arm holding a spear he presents an extended arm that commands the viewer. Rather than being a naked, muscled beauty, he is dressed in military garb, in order to provide the well-ornamented cuirass with its edifying symbolic narrative elements.

In this instance, Roman art synthesizes aspects of *form* from Greek art with *content* that is ultimately Egyptian in origin. Although the structure of the *Augustus of Prima Porta* echoes the *Doryphorus,* its details recall Egyptian works in which references to divinity and its imprimatur reinforce the power of the pharaoh. The interweave of religion and art with politics is paramount. In retrospect, every image of a king or pharaoh or shah in which the ruler's relationship to the gods is visually articulated is political in intention: the viewer is expected to be awestruck by that relationship and thus to accede to the ruler's authority.

Recall the pharaoh Chefren (Khafra; ca. 2550 BCE), seated on his throne with the outstretched wings of Horus wrapped around his head and shoulders (see Figure 3). The hawk is the symbol of the god whose patronage of the pharaoh is evidenced by the god's tangible presence upon him, conveying the message that Chefren rules as the avatar of the god, not merely in his own right. The *Augustus of Prima Porta* is accompanied by symbols that trace Augustus' bloodline back to the goddess Venus.

These rulers, like priests, prophets, poets, and artists, stand between realms, intermediating between *profanus* and *sacer* in a range of ways. The *sacer* refers not only to the gods but also to the wilderness and its bestiary and to the enemies of the state. This is not only apparent in the kind of statuary that I have been discussing but also in the relief carving and the painting that eventually threads its way through antiquity. Thus, a stunning bronze representation of Sharu-kin (Sargon) depicts the imposing figure who established the Akkadian empire, swallowing up Sumerian civilization and disseminating its most significant advances, whereas his grandson, Naram-sin, has visually survived by way of a relief carving.

The *Stele of Naram-Sin* presents the heroic warrior-king in the moment of divinely aided victory against his enemies. He ascends a mountainside, and the first thing we note is that he is larger by far than those around him—this is called significance perspective—and that those nearest him are aligned in order, whereas those below, representing the enemy, are in complete disarray. We notice next that he is adorned with a gigantic horned helmet—the horns of a bull, symbolizing male divine power—to underscore his position. This is further confirmed by the starburst that hovers above him. The image of Naram-sin conquering his foes with the starburst of divinity hovering overhead, conveys the idea that his conquest has been engineered through divine intermediation (see Figure 15). Finally, we realize that the landscape, like the defeated individuals within it, is rather chaotic below, but as it rises to the level of the hero and above him, it is stylized into an ordered shape, corresponding to the order within the landscape he is controlling. And all of this is also expressed verbally by means of the inscription that adorns its uppermost reaches.

FIGURE 15   Stele of Naram-Sin, *Iraq. ca.*
2400 BCE

A kingdom apart and over a millennium later, the painting on the coffin cover of Tut-Ankh-Amon tells a similar story. The young pharaoh is shown triumphing over his Syrian enemies. He towers above everyone else, but his troops and even the tiny Nubians who run alongside his chariot to fan him as he fights are all carefully arrayed; the Syrians tumble backward, in topsy-turvy chaos. Emblems of divinity hover over the pharaoh's head, and the hieroglyphs inform us of his great success. This work in particular reminds us of the intimate relationship not only between religion and art, but also between politics and art, for it is unlikely that Tut-Ankh-Amon, who became pharaoh at age nine and was dead by nineteen, ever went into battle, much less enjoyed a major triumph over his enemies. Nevertheless, future generations, viewing the information in the image, might believe otherwise.

The sacerdotal leader who protects us from our enemies (who are the *sacer* in the negative sense) is also the leader who protects us from wild beasts. He is the Master of the Beasts who controls them in an ordered symmetrical composition, and he is the action figure depicted slaying them in the wilderness. Thus a mid-

FIGURE 16   *Bowl with image of Sassanian king scattering wild rams. ca. 500 CE*

eighth-century BCE relief carving depicts the Assyrian monarch Assurnasirpal successfully killing the chaotic, uncontrollable lions whose fierce attributes become his. He who is king slays the king of beasts and drinks the latter's blood in an annual ritual of reinvigorating himself as a *sacerdos*. Twelve centuries later, we observe a Sassanian king depicted within a shallow relief-decorated gold and silver bowl, astride his horse in a perfectly ordered manner, scattering a carefully orchestrated disarray of wild animals—wild mountain goats, with their ram-like horns—before him. He is adorned with the bull horns of the moon and the glowing disk of the sun (see Figure 16).

The *Stele of Hammurabi* offers another kind of reminder of the triple alliance among art, religion, and politics. Above the lengthy cuneiform inscription offering the laws associated with the monarch's name is the image justifying the decree of those laws. It depicts Hammurabi receiving them from the sun god, Shamash. We see the seated divinity, crowned with a high horned helmet, extending his right hand to present to Hammurabi a scroll that contains the laws delineated on the stone below. The artist has had to solve a problem with his depiction: significance perspective with regard to two important entities. Hammurabi is connected to the god, but it would be presumptuous for him to be represented as the equal of the god, and yet the artist does not want to emphasize that Hammurabi is less important than the god, since the purpose of the depiction is to portray Hammurabi's authority and the justification for the laws he has decreed. Therefore, Hammurabi is depicted as precisely the same height as the god; their heads are on the same level. However, the god is sitting, and were he to rise he would tower over the king. Hammurabi both is and is not the same size as Shamash. Moreover, he is portrayed as a lesser figure by standing while the god is sitting, the way a servant or councilor would before a king.

We see the principle of significance perspective in use at another level when we examine one of the wall carvings of the Achaemenid Persian period in which the shah Dareius I is seated with his servants in attendance, as he receives gifts and obeisance from subject peoples. That he is larger than the servants is obvious. But more significant is the fact that his son and heir, Xerxes, also towers above everyone else—except his father. He and his father are at precisely the same level, above the others, but we recognize that were Dareius to stand, he would in turn tower above Xerxes. Thus we simultaneously see the son as equal to the father he will succeed and not equal to the father he has not yet succeeded, while both of them, god-like, are larger than those around them.

What all of the significant figures in these works of art have in common is the assumption made by their constituents that they are either part divine or imbued with a divine imprimatur; the favor of the gods rests upon them. The Greek word for favor is *kharis,* and so we might say that such individuals have *kharis*ma. That notion is expressed visually by various related means. The mark of divine favor might well be a sunburst or starburst element on or near them or a distinctive element in the cuneiform or hieroglyphic rendering of their name. Naram-sin's starburst exemplifies this. Later it will become common to wreathe the head of such an individual not with bull's horns but with the horns of the moon or the nimbus of the sun, as we have observed of the unnamed Sassanian king of the fifth century CE.

In rare instances, the divine connection carries beyond the ruler. As the Athenians of the fifth century BCE departed from the norm with statuary that represented idealized humans rather than gods or *sacerdotes,* so some of the relief carving on the Parthenon represents an even more extraordinary revolution. Formerly, the subject matter for pediments, metopes, and architraves on the upper reaches of Greek temples was either gods, or gods and giants, or Lapiths and centaurs, or Greek heroes and Amazons of the mythic past—in short, *sacer* or sacerdotal figures in time, space, and action. In a dramatic departure from this tradition, the Athenians placed depictions of themselves on the continuous frieze of the inner architrave of the Parthenon. Although the figures are engaged in a procession to honor the goddess who is the patron of their city, Athenians were effectively placing themselves as a community on a par with gods and heroes.[22]

There are further conceptual contrasts that parallel and thus symbolize the ultimate *sacer-profanus* contrast—or the blurring of it—in the imagery of Greek vase painting. In one noteworthy image, Heracles is shown wrestling the Nemean Lion in the first of his famous twelve labors. The line between hero and supernaturally powerful beast—parallel to the line between everyday men and everyday beasts—is accentuated by the distinctly different facial expressions of the combatants. The hero exhibits what the Greeks called *ethos:* a calm, aloof expression suggesting a divine-like distance from the moment and its consequences, as if, like the gods, he can see the moment as part of a larger intelligible, ordered whole. The lion exhibits what the Greeks called *pathos:* an intensely engaged expression, full of emotion and of focus on the isolated moment.

By the time Augustus had established peace across the Roman world, the Olympians had been restored to the pedestals from which they seemed to have slipped by the Hellenistic period. Nevertheless, scores of other gods came into focus as added patrons of the imperium, who could not be ignored lest they be offended and become antagonistic to the state. Augustus wanted to have himself shown attending to matters of spirituality. The most famous reliefs of this era underscore this. On the Vicomagistri relief we see Augustus as *pontifex maximus,* leading the communal sacrifices. On the inner casing of the *Ara Pacis* enclosure— the Altar of Peace commissioned by Augustus to confirm his success at having brought peace to the Roman world after more than a century of civil and other wars—there are relief-carved swags lush with vegetation and fruits, a symbol of the prosperity that Augustus' regime had brought about. On the outer casing that message is reinforced by the allegorical figure of Mother Earth suckling the infant twins, Romulus and Remus— the very earth suckles the empire of their descendants—as all manner of flora and fauna relax together contentedly, and gentle breezes (allegorical figures with their capes ballooning out) caress the entire assemblage.

On the *Ara Pacis*—underscoring the idea that Roman piety, led by Augustus, that is responsible for such success—is the processional echo of the Vicomagistri sacrifice relief, and also an echo of the Athenian processional on the Parthenon. However, there are crucial differences between the Athenian and Roman images. The Greek work offers an excited tension between textures—human and equine flesh, garment and flesh, flesh and hair—as between moods (the calm *ethos* of the riders, the worked-up *pathos* of the horses in the procession). The Roman work is a staid and serious narrative, and yet it is punctuated, as if to underscore the idea of family and community, by light touches: small children, arms upraised to be lifted by their parents in this meditative procession toward the offering of sacrifices to the gods—intended to express piety. It offers an emphasis on rhythmic verticals, and excitement is derived only from the virtuoso quality of the carving in various degrees of relief.

Within three-quarters of a century, the emperor's message to his constituents would shift from presenting himself as sacerdotal to asserting that he is *sacer*. Nero, one of the more hubristic of the Roman emperors, would have himself represented as the sun god. The colossal statue of the emperor rose to a height of sixty feet (a colossus that eventually gave its name to the amphitheater that would later be erected nearby). The figure was crowned by a sunburst; the same visual idea that had connoted a divine connection in Sumer over twenty-five centuries earlier now festooned the gilded head of the emperor, reminding his constituents of his uniqueness as a ruler with both feet firmly planted in the *sacer*.

While the portraiture we can clearly identify through most of antiquity offers the stylized and immortalizing images of kings, pharaohs, shahs, generals, heroes, and emperors to history, an important development emerges between the Hellenistic and Roman eras. An interest in "true" portraiture, which offers more than idealized individuals, is one aspect of it. The other is that the immortality of funerary portraiture begins to encompass everyday people. The culmination of this process is found in the encaustic funerary portraits on linen or wood found at the site of Fayoum, Egypt, during the late Roman imperial period, from the second through the fourth centuries CE (see Figure 17). Such images are startling in their naturalism and the vibrancy of colors that have survived so many centuries. And they conform to a pattern that we have seen in the art of many prior millennia: enlarged, staring eyes dominate the face, drawing the viewer in through those windows to the soul and enabling the deceased both to connect to the *sacer* and to intermediate for the living who view it.

Throughout this maze of images and ideas, several themes remain constant. The interconnected relationship among art, religion, and politics is one. A second is the continuity of symbolic visual language. A third is the transformation of the vocabulary of that language as it is adopted and adapted over the course of the millennia from one culture to the next. These three themes will be revisited as we turn to the Israelite-Judaean tradition that emerged from the ancient civilizations of the Near East and East Mediterranean and to the art of the Jewish, Christian, and Muslim progeny of that tradition.

FIGURE 17 *Funerary image from Fayoum, Egypt. ca. 400 CE*

CHAPTER 2

MONOTHEISM AND THE DEVELOPMENT OF THE ABRAHAMIC TRADITIONS

From Abraham to Exile

Near the beginning of the second millennium before the Christian era (BCE), a man called Abraham left the *profanus* of Haran for the *sacer*—the unknown—of Canaan,[1] divinely inspired by an understanding of the *sacer* that significantly distinguished him from his contemporaries: the *sacer* is not multifarious, visible, tangible, many-godded, or representable through statues or relief sculptures. Abraham conceived the *sacer* as singular, invisible, and intangible: one God, conventionally inexpressible yet, paradoxically, accessible through thought and word.[2]

Abraham's grandson Jacob—so caught up in wrestling with the *sacer* through the *sacer* of night, in the *sacer* of the wilderness, across the river border from where his family (his *profanus*) was encamped, that he awoke at dawn with a pulled groin muscle—was renamed *Israel* by the emissary of the *sacer*. The new name referred to Jacob's nightlong encounter; it means "one who has wrestled with God." Jacob/Israel's children would go into Egypt, their children's children would be enslaved there, and their descendants—the Israelites, tribal groups related to Israel's sons—would return, led by Moses, the ultimate *sacerdos*, to Canaan.

Along the road of return, in transition from the *profanus* of Egypt to the paradoxically *sacer profanus* of the Promised Land, in the *sacer* wilderness of Sinai, the Israelites engaged the *sacer* through Moses' intermediation. The engagement yielded a contract, or covenant, the acceptance of which would transform them and their descendants into a people like the land they sought: a *sacer profanus*—a people apart, a priestly people, an intermediating light toward and from the *sacer* among the *profanus* nations.

By about 1000 BCE, the Israelites were unified into a kingdom under Saul and David—perceived by their constituents as chosen to be kings by God and anointed (*mashiah* in Hebrew; *christos* in Greek) by God's *sacerdos* Samuel. In about 960–950 BCE, David's son Solomon had a great temple to the Israelite God built in Jerusalem (at a site selected by his father and that was undoubtedly an existing *sacer* Canaanite site).[3] Jewish, Christian, and elements of Muslim tradition locate the temple (commonly known as the First Temple) on Mount Moriah, where, according to Genesis 22, Abraham had offered his son Isaac to God.[4] The first book of Kings tells us that the craftsmen of Hiram— king of Tyre, capital of a realm the Greeks would later call Phoenicia[5]—designed and built the temple. Solomon paid handsomely for the services of Hiram's skilled craftsmen, who spent seven years on the project.[6]

We might expect that the Israelites' concept of the *sacer,* which is distinctly different from that of neighboring peoples, would have important implications for visual self-expression. Because the Israelites believed that God was invisible, unlike other peoples in the region, we might assume that the temple to the Israelite god would offer no visual relationship to the Canaanites—or the Egyptians, Mesopotamians, Anatolians, Greeks, or Romans among others. But this is not the case.

The temple, as described in 1 Kings 6:14–7:50, is a structure recognizable as a "long-house" edifice, similar to those associated with temples within the northern Canaanite world: a building longer than it is wide, fronted by a pair of columns and divided on the interior into an entrance hall, a main chamber, and a holy of holies (the innermost and most sacred chamber within the temple). The biblical text describes the edifice as possessing an outer foyer—with its entrance marked by two columns, referred to as Yachin and Boaz[7]—a large middle hall and a holy of holies (*sanctum sanctorum,* variant form of *sacer sacrorum* in the terminology that we have been using). The entrance to the latter was covered by a decorated curtain, called a *parokhet,* through which only the high priest, a descendant of Moses' brother Aaron, might pass to enter the holy of holies. Even he might do so only once a year, on the Day of Atonement.

Perhaps the long-house structure and elements aren't so surprising after all, given the Tyrian design and construction provenance. Nor should it surprise us that the temple was overrun with the kind of decorations along the upper walls mentioned in Kings: processions of lush flora and anthropomorphic figures, culminating with *cherubim*—winged lions or bulls with human heads—guarding the entryway into the holy of holies. Such manifestations of visual intermediation were rampant in the visual vocabulary of the Near East and east Mediterranean, in which the Tyrians were preeminent transmitters of cultural ideas.

Within the holy of holies were kept the Tablets of the Law, symbols of the covenant established between God and Israel at Mount Sinai during the journey through the wilderness from Egypt to the Promised Land. Outside the holy of holies, within the main hall of the temple, were lavers and basins, tables and implements of priestly service, and most prominently, a seven-branched *menorah*—candelabrum—the symbolic purpose of which was to remind the community of Israel of the covenant, with its ethical obligations and sacred promises.

Prominent among the commandments to their ancestors in the wilderness had been the injunction (in the Fourth Commandment) to keep every seventh day as a day of rest. This injunction was related to the biblical account of creation, in which after six days of shaping the world, God had rested on the seventh.[8] Accordingly, the Sabbath day of the Israelite religion reflected the aspiration to be like the *sacer* it worships.[9] This principle—*imitatio dei* ("imitating god")—is universal in the history and geography of religion, and it thus connects the Israelite religion to all other religions.[10]

The very idea of seven-ness had a long and significant place in the Mesopotamian grasp of the *sacer,* which may have been adopted and adapted by the Israelites. It is conceivable, indeed, that the sevenfold cycle of creation in Genesis derives from a sense of the significance of that number, even as the spiritual revolution of that narrative is clear: the number is harnessed to the process of engendering the universe by one God, *beyond* nature, and not to the struggles to shape our world by diverse gods that are *part* of nature. That transformation in significance having been established, the subsequent importance expressed in the keeping of the Sabbath, its various symbols, and the seven-ness of the menorah followed.

It was primarily their relationship with the *sacer* that had molded twelve tribes into a unity, tribes that remained fairly disparate in spite of their descent from a common ancestor.[11] But within half a decade of Solomon's death, the kingdom of Israel succumbed to forces pulling it apart. The northern part of the kingdom retained the name "Israel"; the southern part, centered around its capital in Jerusalem, came to be known by the name of the dominant tribe within it: Judah (*Yehoodah* in Hebrew). By 720 BCE, Israel (the north) had been swallowed up by Assyria, its tribes lost to history, having lost the unifying consciousness of their covenant with God. Judah would be devoured by Babylonia in 586, Jerusalem sacked, its temple demolished, its leadership carried off into exile. In this experience of destruction and exile, not all would be lost, however, for it was during the Babylonian period that the Judaean remnant of the original Israelite-Judaean kingdom began to grasp the universality of God, with whom their ancestors had established a covenantal relationship.

With the destruction of the temple, their thinking on that subject either had to move in a conventional direction—that the God of Israel had been bested by the Babylonian gods and was therefore hardly worth worshipping—or toward completing the spiritual revolution begun by Abraham. They chose the latter course, bringing toward full fruition an understanding of God as the maker of history, not one of the many players within it; as the author of the destruction and exile, meted out against them for their consistent failure to abide by the conditions of covenant, and not the defeated victim of Marduk and his cohorts. In exile the Judaeans came to focus more closely on the text of the Torah as a guide for everyday life. They began to address God through the reading of God's word and through prayers wherever groups of them convened—for they realized that God was everywhere and could be addressed anywhere, rather than only through sacrifices brought to a centralized temple and through sacerdotal offices mediating between the people and God.

The return from exile came sooner, perhaps, than anyone but inspired prophets would have imagined. Less than fifty years after the destruction under the Babylonian Nebuchadnezzar, the Judaeans witnessed the destruction of Babylonia by the Medo-Persians, whose leader, Cyrus, invited the Judaeans to return home and rebuild the destroyed temple in 538 BCE. This proved both that God's power is far-reaching and that God would forgive and restore those who turned their hearts back to God. But the return also proved to be more troubled than half a century of hopes had anticipated. The Babylonians had taken only those of threat or use to them; their grandchildren, imbued with that new sense of God's universality, returned to a Judah populated by those who had not gone into exile, and whose sense of God had not changed from the ethnocentric viewpoint that had predominated in previous generations, in addition to those who had been on the fringe of Judah, in Samaria, since the time when the Northern Kingdom had been destroyed by the Assyrians. The two parts of the community—those returning and those who had never left—were at spiritual odds with each other.

The source of disagreement was not only the nature of God but also the nature of Judaean leadership. Should that leader be a descendant of the house of David, a political leader in the conventional (even if God-anointed) sense? Or should he be a descendant of the house of Tzaddok, high priest in Solomon's temple and descendant of Aaron, the brother of Moses—a spiritual leader? The answer differed depending upon whether or not one had been in exile or had reviewed one's sense of God. Socioeconomics also defined the fault line separating parts of the community. The profundity of this schism is clear from the pained reconstruction of the central communal shrine: it took twenty-three years to build the Second Temple—more than three times longer than it had taken Solomon to build the first one—with all of the resources of the Persian Empire at the Judaeans' disposal.

Crisis and Transformation: The Era of the Second Temple

The goal in the reconstruction was to have the second structure mirror the first. The rebuilt temple was thus modeled on Solomon's temple, to the extant that memory and tradition would permit, or so we may infer from what we take to be its description in Ezekiel 40–43. The basic threefold structure was repeated, but the details must have been Perso-Babylonian in style, with frond motifs and glazed tiles and a style of guardian *cherubim* somewhat different from those in Solomon's temple. Again the menorah occupied a prominent place. But it, too, may well have now acquired Perso-Babylonian detailing, for the Judaeans returning from Babylon under Persian patronage surely would have been influenced stylistically by forms that prevailed across a Persian Achaemenid Empire that extended from Egypt to India.

Such an assumption receives oblique reinforcement from two pairs of "evidence." The description in the biblical text is quite generalized— although the specification of different courtyards in Ezekiel 40 at least suggests that the outer configuration of the temple precincts was different from that of the First Temple. Visual rather than verbal reinforcement comes from the occasional piece of jewelry that has turned up in Israeli excavations exhibiting Achaemenid style. From this we can at least infer that Achaemenid art was present in Judaea, even if we cannot assume definitively that its presence extended to the temple.

More compelling is the evidence from imagery depicting the Second Temple menorah, although that, too, is oblique. The Second Temple would stand for six centuries, until destroyed by the Romans in 70 CE as the culminating act of suppressing a five-year-long revolt by the Judaeans. We may infer from the details of the menorah portrayed on the Arch of Titus, recording the defeat of the Judaeans and the carrying to Rome of the most significant appurtenances of the temple, that it is a fairly accurate image. It is not a Roman-styled candelabrum, and it possesses two distinctive features that tie it to the period during which the Second Temple existed (see Figure 18).

The first is a frond motif at the bottom of its stem, a motif characteristic of the style of furniture and column decor of the Achaemenid Persians. The fronds reinforce the notion of the menorah as a tree-like entity, a symbol of life in that it is associated with the covenant between God and the Israelite-Judaeans that guarantees eternal spiritual life. If, on the one hand, we use this motif as a reference point for the larger matter of the Second Temple décor, on the other, we use it to help us conclude that the depiction on the Arch of Titus is a true-to-life image of the menorah and not some Roman stylization: why would they maintain that motif in their depiction if it had not been there?

Moreover, below the stem one observes a base made up of twelve rectangular lozenges framing zodiacal symbols. The symbols of the heavenly realms were particularly popular as decorative motifs of cosmic—*sacer*—import during the Hellenistic period from the time just after the death of Alexander (323 BCE) through the era of Roman domination. It would most likely have been during the time of Herod's refurbishments of the temple precincts between 19 and 9 BCE that such a Hellenistic-Roman-style base would have been added, its symbolism transmuted, for only Herod would have had the temerity to add to the unalterable menorah, and we are well aware of Herod's taste for the Hellenistic-Roman style.[12]

Numbering twelve, the zodiacal symbols would have lent themselves effectively to absorption as motifs in Judaean art, where their symbolism would be recast as the twelve tribes of Israel, ideally reconstituted in full array. The menorah, symbol of the covenant between Israel and the *sacer,* is the heaven-pointing object that rests on a twelve-part, tribes-of-Israel base, its flames as intangi-

FIGURE 18   *Arch of Titus, Rome (detail: Menorah from destroyed temple in Jerusalem). ca. 85* CE

ble but as visible as the pillar of fire that led Israel through the wilderness between Egypt and the Promised Land, a "portrayal" of God's intangible, invisible presence.

But this matter has carried us half a millennium beyond the return from exile and the rebuilding of the temple. By the time the temple menorah had assumed the form visible on the Arch of Titus, the Persian Empire had yielded to Alexander the Great, Alexander had perished and his empire had been divided, and a descendant of one of Alexander's successors, Antiochus IV, had attempted to introduce images of his gods and of himself *as* a god into the temple in Jerusalem in 168 BCE. The three-year-long struggle against Antiochus, led by a family traditionally called the Maccabees,[13] that began as a struggle for the right to address the *sacer* according to the dictates of the Israelite-Judaean tradition had evolved into a war for political independence. That political independence was largely facilitated by an eventual alliance with Rome.

A century after the death of Simon, the last of the five Maccabean brothers—a century of Judaean political independence—Rome would throw its weight to a non-Judaean and his quest to wipe out the descendants of the Maccabees and possess the Judaean throne himself: Herod.[14] Herod was favored by Rome but detested by the Judaean subjects he came to rule by 37 BCE. He attempted to please the pagans among them by building theaters and temples to their gods. He sought to please the Judaean Jews he ruled by expanding the platform on which the temple rested—the temple mount—while refurbishing the temple itself, including, perhaps, the seven-branched menorah.[15] Everything that has survived archaeologically suggests that Herod's expansion was overwhelmingly characterized by Hellenistic-Roman style.[16]

These varied projects failed to achieve the popularity that he so desperately—at least initially—sought, while his fear of assassination grew so severe that over time he put to death most of his sons and scores of family and court members, including the last descendants of the Maccabees. Not surprisingly, anarchy followed his death in 4 BCE; not surprisingly, Rome absorbed Judaea (no longer to be called "Judah," the anglicized rendering of its Hebrew name) as a subprovince within its empire, ruling it through subgovernors called "procurators"; and not surprisingly, Judaeans became increasingly angry over Roman domination, as decade followed decade—finally revolting against Rome in 65 CE. And it was that political revolt that led to the Roman destruction of the Second Temple.

There are still other issues from the era of the Second Temple that are important for this discussion. Eventually, more than three-and-a-half centuries after the return from exile, as Judah developed into an independent kingdom and then grew larger and larger, and as increasing numbers of Judaeans became involved in commerce with their non-Judaean neighbors, rather than farming or herding, the temple became, for some, an increasingly distant structure, one that it was inconvenient to visit other than during the three annual pilgrimage festivals. No doubt, some were unable to make the journey even for those important occasions.

Some time in the course of the Second Temple period, the institution of the synagogue evolved and became formalized to meet the needs of the faithful.[17] Structures were built and the form of prayers to be conducted within them was codified, including the division of the Torah into sections so that it could be read week by week throughout the year (and reread year after year). The earliest synagogue remains found to date are from the last pre-Christian century, to the north, at Gamla on the Golan Heights and toward the Dead Sea, at Massada. In the first case, the location offers an obvious logic: the great distance from Jerusalem and its temple. In the second case, the logic is different. King Herod built Massada as a fortress (but also as a pleasure palace) where he could take refuge should the need arise, and he included in that complex a synagogue.[18] Later, in the early 70s CE, Massada would become the refuge, for three years, of the last Judaean rebels against Rome, at which time its synagogue would undergo some reconstruction.

These two early synagogues share a number of significant features in common. The first is the seating arrangement. It is clear from the series of benches that wrap around the periphery on three sides that these are houses of gathering for prayer and discussion and not edifices where offerings are made, intermediated by a priest who alone has access to its more interior parts. The structure is a rectilinear version of the bouleterion, the small semicircular structure layered with benches used by the leadership (the *boulê*) of the Greek *polis* as a meeting place in which to discuss matters of importance to the community. Thus, one might infer that the increased contact with the Greek world during the Hellenistic period yielded a significant architectural development, and that this development represented both adoption and adaptation of an idea.[19]

The second distinctive feature is that there are no benches on the side facing Jerusalem; that side is left "open." The seating is thus oriented toward the Judaean capital and its temple, toward which those praying would direct themselves. Both synagogues are rooted in the sensibility articulated in 1 Kings 8:12–53 by King Solomon, when he dedicated the First Temple, that God's attention be most intensely focused on that site and thus that the most potentially successful address to God would come about by way of that site. This accentuates the role of the synagogue as a secondary rung on the sacerdotal ladder that connects the *profanus* community to the *sacer* through the primary rungs, which are the temple, on the one hand, and the text of the Torah, on the other. The implications of this for the future development of Judaism and Jewish art (as well as for Christian and Islamic art) are significant.

As for the decor details of these two structures, what little survives at Gamla and Massada suggests the kind of emulation of Hellenistic-Roman decorative style offered by the temple itself. Corinthian capitals—the symbolism of their acanthus leaves either still in place or the style merely passed along as part of the dominant decorative vocabulary of the last pre-Christian century—may have topped the columns that held up the roofs, for example. How might we infer this? Although too little remains of the synagogues themselves to offer us a strong decorative picture, we can infer some details from what can still be observed at Massada in the rest of Herod's fortress/palace complex. Given the significant adherence to Roman decorative canons in Herod's palaces, it is reasonable to assume that such decorative self-expression existed in the synagogue that he built there.[20]

—⁂—

The difficulties of the Second Temple period, which began virtually with the return from Babylon and had become so pronounced by the time of Herod, were spiritual as well as political and are well expressed early on in the texts associated with the return and its aftermath; the narratives of Nehemiah and Ezra are dense with internal communal strife. It would be seventy years after the completion of the Second Temple that Ezra's arrival from Babylon would temporarily reunify the community. Ezra was called the *Sofer,* meaning "book-man." He arrived from Babylonia (whose Jewish population was still substantial) in the middle of the fifth century BCE. On the one hand, his methodology of reasserting a sense of unified Judaean peoplehood, as reported in the book that bears his name, was extreme, calling for the breakup of families and communities. "Put away your foreign wives and children," he enjoined them, promoting ethnic purity as a basis for a proper covenantal relationship with God.[21]

On the other hand, he who narrowed the franchise of the covenant broadened it immeasurably. Ezra is said to have written down and read out to the people the entire Torah at the conclusion of the harvest festival in the year 444 BCE, causing Judaeans to weep as they recognized their covenantal failures. Except by the literalists who argue that the totality of the Torah was received by Moses at Sinai, Ezra is credited with redacting the book of books: weaving together various strands of text that had evolved during the previous thousand years since Sinai. In any case, he made the Torah accessible to the people by providing a standard written version of it. In so doing, he cemented a book-focused foundation for the peoplehood of Israel-Judah and shaped another in the series of transformations that define the history of their ancestors and descendants.

Ezra effected a *nomocratic* revolution. Previously, the leadership of the people had been a function of direct divine connection to prophets and priests, conduits through which God instructed the Hebrew-Israelite-Judaeans on their behavior toward both God and humans. Such leadership constitutes theocracy.[22] Once divine instruction was cast in a final written form, that situation changed; the Torah offered the definitive word of God as a guide for how to live, obviating the need for prophetic conduits. In Greek, the word "*nomos*"—law—is used to render "Torah." Nomocracy is thus "rule by law"—the law of God's word in the Torah, rather than by God's word through prophets and priests. The history of the Judaeans following Ezra's redaction was largely governed by the Torah's words—and by the scribes and scholars who devoted their lives to studying it in order to elucidate it.

The scribes and scholars debated and discussed what beyond the Torah might also be recognized as the word of God. For the people of that book, other books were added in the centuries that followed Ezra: prophetic books, of course, but also books recounting the history that led from Moses to Ezra (including the books of Ezra and Nehemiah) and poems of praise to God as well as works of philosophical and theological reflection—on the nature of good and evil and reward and punishment—or worldly observation. Books of mourning over exile and destruction, such as Lamentations, were added, and books like Jonah and Ruth that undercut the ethnocentric emphases of Ezra (for the first reminds us that God's interest is in all peoples and not only the Israelite-Judaeans, and the second goes even further by concluding with a genealogy of its heroine—a Moabite, one of the traditional enemies of Israel—that presents her as the grandmother of King David). Within six centuries of the nomocratic revolution the entire Hebrew Bible—the *Tanakh*, an acronym for Torah, *N'vi'im* (Prophets), and *K'tuvim* (Sacred Writings)—had shifted into place.

Whereas prophets and priests are born, scribes and scholars are made; anyone, in theory, can become one. Thus, Ezra's nomocratic revolution not only affected the nature of Judaean leadership but also broadened the potential sources of that leadership. Prophets and priests lead by revelation, but once they are gone and the text of that revelation is recorded in a definitive form, questions arise as to its interpretation. At times, the meaning of the words of the Torah (whether or not they were all recorded by Moses at Sinai) may appear opaque. Thus, scribes and scholars seeking to illuminate textual obscurities labored over questions ranging from whether heaven or earth was created first (examining the opening line of Genesis, "In the beginning, God created the heavens and the earth," we ask, but which *first?*); to how, exactly, Moses died (Deuteronomy is decidedly minimalist in the information it offers us); to what the phrase really means in Exodus 23:19 that enjoins us not to "seethe a kid in its mother's milk" (how does that eventually come to mean, for a traditional twentieth-century Jew, that one may not eat a cheeseburger?).

This flow of literary development was not a simple one reflecting a straightforward and smooth evolution for the Judaean community. On the contrary, it was a community that continued to be torn by political, religious, and socioeconomic schisms through the centuries between the building and the destruction of the Second Temple. The literature that began to reappear from around the Dead Sea in 1947 does not merely reflect an outer edge of the Judaean *profanus* of two millennia ago. Those associated with that outer edge apparently saw the various viewpoints expressed in the literatures referred to above[23] and the leadership associated with those viewpoints as dangerously *off the mark* with respect to a covenantal relationship with God. In this regard, the Dead Sea scrolls remind us of two issues. First, and specifically, the community and its leadership remained factionalized throughout the Second Temple period; within the "mainstream," Sadducees, Pharisees, and other groups contended with each other, as well as with outsiders. Second, and more broadly, intense concern about the *sacer* underlay the factionalism; many asserted that failure to live up to the covenantal relationship would result in disaster.

Thus, a range of texts defined a community as ideologically splintered as it was theoretically unified by the assumption of a common covenantal history, as we follow that history forward to the time of Jesus and its aftermath. Indeed, the most significant Judaean schism would finally set in, by the late first century CE, with respect to the figure of Jesus, and regarding the nature of God. To the earlier question of whether God is universal, as opposed to ethnocentric, would be added the question of whether God does/would/could assume human form, with all of the concomitants of that question. By the early second century, the Judaean community had begun to tear itself into two increasingly distinct and divergent sects: Judaism and Christianity. What divided them was not only the question of God but also the term "anointed"—*mashiah-christos* (whose English versions are "Messiah" and "Christ")—and the matter of which day should function as a Sabbath and what festivals and life-cycle events (in particular circumcision) should or should not be celebrated. What divided them, too, were divergent perceptions as to what constitutes God's written Word.

Part of what lay at the heart of such issues was the question of whether Ezra's nomocratic revolution had been legitimate—had it been *real?* Had God truly ceased speaking to the descendants of Abraham and Sarah directly through prophets? If so, then the "Divine Word" can only be that which is understood to have been written before Ezra; anything written after his time cannot lay claim to such a source. The answer was clear for each group. For Jews, prophecy had unquestionably ended with the bona fide nomocratic revolution. For Christians, that revolution was false, for prophecy had continued beyond Ezra at least through the time of the apostles of Jesus. Thus, the Tanakh was viewed by Christians as the record of an *old* covenant—the Old Testament— valid and important, but only a forerunner of more important texts that carry beyond its time frame. Later material, particularly anything pertinent to the life and time of Jesus (who was God in human form for the purpose of human salvation), could be and was included in the record of a *new* covenant—the New Testament.

Internal issues crossed external concerns as the revolt against Rome proceeded midway between the death of Jesus and the schism yielding Judaism and Christianity. The Romans, expecting to spend a few weeks suppressing a revolt in a province as much in the throes of factionalized struggle within as with Rome, were surprised and frustrated to spend five full years engaged in that effort. Jerusalem finally fell in the summer of the year 70; Roman soldiers, stung by the humiliation of such a protracted struggle and reeling from the heat, burned the temple, from which the most precious appurtenances were carried off, along with Judaean prisoners, to Rome.[24] That triumphant procession would be portrayed by the Romans twenty-five years later on the inner side of an arch erected to honor the deceased emperor Titus. Titus had been a general in the year 70 and had completed the suppression of the Judaean revolt and the sacking of Jerusalem. The interior of his eponymous arch shows him on one side, riding proudly into Rome in a quadriga—a chariot drawn by four horses. Across from him (on the other side of the arch interior), the conquered Judaeans are shown being led into Rome, accompanied by trumpets and carrying objects from the destroyed temple, the most prominent of which is the seven-branched temple menorah (see Figure 18).

Competing Progeny:
Judaism and Christianity

These historical, theological, and art historical developments have re-verberating significance for the visual symbols of the Jewish, Christian, and Muslim traditions in the nearly two millennia that follow. By the early second century CE—more than a century after the death of Herod and within less than a generation of the erection of the Arch of Titus—the schism within the Judaean tradition yielding Judaism and Christianity also began to yield different interpretations of visual symbols. The two progeny of the Hebrew-Israelite-Judaean tradition began to clarify their differences and engage in a sibling rivalry that, as with the issues of the parent tradition, was informed by both internal and external matters.

As Judaism took the shape that we would recognize today in terms of texts, prayers, ceremonies, rituals, and customs—and its condition of being dispersed as a far-flung archipelago of islands in diversely non-Jewish seas—one can identify four foundational elements that anchor it. The first is the belief in a single, all-powerful, all-knowing, and all-good *God,* creator of the universe and author of all that resides within the universe. The second element is the concept of *peoplehood:* Jews, as heirs to the covenantal tradition that evolved from the time of Abraham forward, are unified by accepting the principles of that covenant with God, which militates against all of the aspects of their history and geography that pull Jews and Jewish communities in various directions. The third element, which defines the covenantal relationship, is the *Torah,* the umbilicus connecting the people to God (the *profanus* to the *sacer*). Its core is the Ten Commandments, but more fully, the term Torah (meaning "teaching" or "enlightenment") refers to the Five Books of Moses, which, Jewish tradition asserts, contain 613 commandments. The fourth foundational element is the *Land of Israel,* the most central element of which is Jerusalem, of which the essential center is the temple, with the holy of holies as its conceptual center—the ultimate point of divine-human connection. The Land of Israel is the ideal space in which all aspects of the *sacer-profanus* relationship can be most fully and ideally worked out.

In the history of Judaism, stretching across scores of cultures and civilizations, these four elements have been ever-present, even as they also evolved. "Torah" evolved to refer not only to the Pentateuch but also to the entire Hebrew Bible; later still it came, in parts of the Jewish world, to encompass all of the interpretive literature that developed over the centuries.[25] Peoplehood became both narrower and broader. It became narrower in the sense that, for various historical reasons, it became an exclusive concept: one cannot easily enter into Jewish peoplehood after the fourth century. It became broader in the sense that it became increasingly difficult to specify what Jewish peoplehood meant: religion? nation? ethnic group? body of customs and traditions? The concept of God remained constant, except that in the past two hundred years the role of God in the world has increasingly been questioned by some Jews, particularly in the half century since the Holocaust. Yet many who do not believe in God still consider themselves Jews. Similarly, as the definition of Torah has broadened over time, its role, in the past two centuries, has diminished in the lives of many who nonetheless have called themselves Jews. In our own era there are secular Jews and cultural Jews who assert no connection to the Land of Israel and believe neither in God nor in the importance of the Torah, beyond acknowledging that it is an interesting work of literature.

One might add a fifth element that has played a role in the history of Jewish thinking: the *messiah*. For most of diasporatic history, Jews have considered themselves to be in a state of exile and have believed that with the advent of the messiah—a divinely anointed descendant of the house of David—the exiles would be gathered in, the Holy Land would be reclaimed and the temple rebuilt as "the mountain of the Lord's house shall be established as the top of the mountains, And it shall be exalted above the hills; And peoples shall flow unto it" and "all the nations of the earth shall recognize that God is God."[26] However, with the advent of Reform Judaism in 1810 in Germany, this idea was rejected by some Jews. The designation of Reform synagogues as *temples* was not arbitrary but ideological: it implied that Jews were not in exile, waiting for the messiah, but that they were secure anywhere in the world, and therefore their houses of worship were not temporary structures to serve until the advent of the messiah and the rebuilding of the temple in Jerusalem, but were every bit as valid in their time and place as the temple in Jerusalem was in its time and place.

Christianity is an edifice built on four pillars analogous to those of Judaism. The significance of the *Holy Land* is present, with Jerusalem as the center, but also significant are Bethlehem and Nazareth and other sites essential to the narrative of Jesus and those around him. The concept of *peoplehood* also parallels that of Judaism, but whereas the Jewish concept eventually became exclusive, the Christian concept has always been inclusive. From its beginnings to the present, the Christian religion has actively sought new adherents. Both faiths share the concept of *election,* but over the centuries, Judaism has more often associated the chosen with birth; Christianity's focus has been on choosing to live one's life as a Christian. Therefore, Christianity avoided the ambiguity that came to apply to Judaism; Christianity is defined by its religious principles, not by ethnicity or nationality.

The primary texts connecting the Christian *profanus* to the *sacer* are the *Gospels* (meaning "God's word" in Middle English). The term is intended to underscore the notion that these texts *are* God's word, that the Hebrew Bible forms a prelude to the Gospels and the rest of the New Testament—a concept by definition rejected by Judaism, for which the entirety of God's direct spoken word is found in the Hebrew Bible. *God* is also conceived of as all-powerful, all-knowing, and all-good. But where Judaism asserts that God is invisible, Christianity defines God as simultaneously singular and threefold (as the Trinity) and presents an aspect of God as visible and tangible—indeed in human form.

The concept of *messiah,* an element that is less than central to Judaism, is at the heart of Christianity. The very word is built on the Latinized version of the Greek *(christos)* translation of the Hebrew word, *mashiah.*[27] Whereas for Jews the term has always referred to a mere mortal descendant of King David, for Christians messiah connotes much more than a *sacerdos*—prophet, priest, king, poet. *Christ* is not merely an individual with a foot in each realm. He is the absolute meeting point of *sacer* and *profanus,* heaven and earth, God and man. That article of faith is so central to Christianity that its name reflects belief in that aspect of faith. Whereas Jews have been waiting for the messiah to arrive for two millennia, Christians await his return—the Second Coming.

As with Judaism, aspects of Christianity's essentials have evolved as it has spread far afield. Most apparent is its textuality. The Gospels are merely the centerpiece of the larger New Testament, which is the most important part of the Christian Bible, but the Hebrew Bible, as Old Testament, is considered its essential forerunner. For some Christians (Catholics, for instance), texts like the Wisdom of Ben Sirach, Maccabees 1 and 2, Judith, and Susanna and the Elders are part of the divine word; they are known as intertestamental texts. For others, such as Protestants, these are not regarded as canonical. On the contrary, they are to be hidden away, lest they be read and mistaken for divinely inspired texts by the untutored. Thus, they are called *apocrypha* (meaning "hidden away" in Greek)—which is precisely how Jews also view them. So, too, a vast body of interpretive literature—patristic and scholastic writings—has evolved in forms parallel to that of Judaism.

Over the course of their respective histories, both faiths have been fraught with internal conflict, schism, and accusations of heresy, although this is more apparent for Christianity, as a religion that came to dominate Europe after the fourth century. It appears that monotheistic faiths require not only belief in one God but an assumption that there is only one proper understanding of, and path to, that God. We often forget that we stand on layer upon layer of historical interpretation—that the revelation came centuries or even millennia before us and that therefore we might humbly consider the possibility that none of us possesses an exclusive sacerdotal conduit to the *sacer.*

The spiritual struggles within both Judaism and Christianity and the sibling rivalry between them were complicated by external factors. The pagan polytheistic Roman Empire had officially recognized the legitimacy of the Israelite-Judaean tradition in the 60s BCE when Pompey the Great passed through that part of the world. The Romans were willing to tolerate any form of spirituality that didn't interfere with the rendering of taxes or other civic responsibilities. As believers in many deities, the pagan Romans abided by the principle that it would be better to honor yet one more aspect of the *sacer,* even if it proved false, than to risk offending a legitimate aspect of the *sacer* by banning or even merely ignoring it. So Pompey recognized the cult of the god worshipped in Jerusalem.

The Roman legal term for this is *religio.* In this context the term referred to any form of addressing the *sacer* that the Romans accepted with the conviction that it was at least harmless and at most potentially beneficial to the state. The opposite term in Roman law is *superstitio,* meaning not only a false faith but a dangerous one; "politically subversive" is an appropriate translation of the term. In the second and third centuries, Judaism and Christianity each claimed to be the legitimate heir to the *religio* status granted to Judaeans by Pompey and confirmed by Julius Caesar, Marc Antony, and Octavian (later known as Augustus Caesar) in turn. Each saw itself as the legitimate child of the Israelite-Judaean parent and the other as the bastard child, and each sought to have the Romans accept its version of that understanding. The Romans saw Judaism as the true heir to the Judaean *religio* (perhaps because of the name, which in Latin or Greek was identical to what in English we might call "Judaeanism"). Christianity was labeled *superstitio,* which meant that it was outlawed. This, in turn, forced Christians to practice underground, reinforcing the Roman view that they were indeed subversive. Christians were intermittently persecuted because of that political assumption, culminating with the attacks on the faith by Diocletian, the last Roman emperor (r. 284–305) who saw Christianity as a menace to his desperate efforts to hold the overextended empire together.[28]

This situation changed in the course of the fourth century. Diocletian's adoptive son Constantine, unlike his father, saw Christianity as glue that could *help* hold the empire together. In 313 he issued the famous edict at Milan that finally granted Christianity *religio* status. More than that, he encouraged and supported its expansion and participated personally in the great debate on Christian belief at Nicaea in 325. It is likely that Constantine's support of Athanasius and the bishops who argued for the validity of the triune concept of God was instrumental in making it the cornerstone of Christian faith. As a result, Bishop Arius and his followers (Arians), who believed in the separateness and superiority of God the Father, who is eternal and unchanging, over the Holy Spirit and more importantly, the Son, who is born, grows up, and dies, were deemed to be heretics. By the late fourth century, under Theodosius, Christianity—triune Christianity—had become the official religion of the Roman state, and all other systems of belief, including Judaism, Zoroastrianism, Mithraism, and the old Greco-Roman polytheistic systems, began to be labeled *superstitio.*

This would have enormous consequences for the medieval European world toward which the late ancient Roman world was rapidly spiraling. Both the internal developments of and the relations between Judaism and Christianity would be affected. The laws against Jews seeking converts, for example, would help drive Judaism inward toward the exclusivity discussed above. The emergence of and wrestling with internal misbelief—heresy—would depend on being in the majority or the minority, of tolerating or persecuting.

Nor does this collision of contending absolute truths end beyond Theodosius—and we must never forget that the notion that a proper relationship with the *sacer,* based on a proper understanding of it, is regarded as essential to survival throughout most of human history. Barely had Christianity asserted itself as the dominant *religio* in the European, Mediterranean, and Near Eastern worlds, when a third offspring of the Abrahamic Hebrew-Israelite-Judaean parentage stepped onto the stage of history.

The Third Child: Islam

Along the western coast of the Arabian peninsula, in an area known as the Hijaz, Muhammad was born in the trading city of Macca in 570 CE.[29] In 610, at the age of forty, while out in the *sacer* wilderness on a spiritual retreat—specifically on Mount Hira—Muhammad perceived a single, invisible, all-powerful God communicating with him. He returned to Macca a changed man and began to preach a faith different from the polytheistic paganism practiced by most of those around him. By 622 Muhammad was either driven out of Macca or chose to leave, establishing himself in a city to the north, named Yathrib, where he would make his mark as an adjudicator among warring tribal factions. This city would eventually become so significant within his lifetime that it would be called simply *al'Madina*—"the city." By the mid-620s he had both solidified his political-military base and begun to shape the principles of the new faith of Islam—meaning "submission (or "commitment") [to the will of God]."

By the time of his death in 632, Muhammad had returned to Macca as a conqueror and gathered a large number of adherents to his teachings and preachings—ultimately recorded and redacted a generation after his death as the Qur'an (meaning "recitation")—which, he asserted, were the words of God through him as the Seal of the Prophets. Islam rests on five "pillars," or obligations. The first of these is *shahada,* or credo: the belief in one, invisible, all-powerful but merciful, all-knowing God; in the ultimate prophecy through Muhammad and in scores of other prior prophets, including Abraham, Moses, David, John the Baptist, and Jesus; and also in angels and demons, the predetermination of good and evil, and heaven and hell, where reward and punishment for one's actions during life are meted out. The second pillar is the obligation to pray formally *(salat)* five times a day (in the beginning, like traditional Jews, Muslims prayed three times daily; some time before the death of Muhammad they began to pray five times daily). The obligation to help others through *zakat* (a prescribed rate of charitable giving—analogous to the informal or formal tithing practiced by Christians and Jews) constitutes the third pillar. The fourth pillar is the obligation to fast *(sawm)* from sunrise to sunset during the ninth month of Ramadan (Jews fast on the tenth day of the seventh month—as Muslims once did—for twenty-four hours). The obligation to make the pilgrimage to Macca and Madina—the *hajj*—at least once in one's lifetime, if at all possible, is the fifth.

There is a sixth duty that is particularly important in Islam: *jihad*, which means "struggle." The most important level of *jihad* is within oneself, being as pure a *Muslim* (submitter/committer to the will of Allah) as possible. The second most important level of struggle is to make the *dar al'Islam* ("realm of commitment") as pure as possible— for schism and division beset the *dar al'Islam* soon after the death of Muhammad; within a generation there was a split between those who followed the Prophet's nephew and son-in-law, Ali—calling themselves Shi'ites—and those who asserted that the proper path of Islam should include traditions *(sunna)* that had emerged since Muhammad's death but were consistent with his teachings and consistent with his dictum of folding the people's prior traditions into Islam as far as possible. They called themselves Sunnis. Thus *jihad* within the *dar al'Islam* has often meant a struggle between these two factions—but many more subgroups developed within Islam over time, as with Christianity and to a lesser extent, Judaism. The third level of *jihad* is the obligation for Muslims to proselytize, spreading the word of Islam through the rest of the world, the *dar al'Harb*.

Islam has four elemental foundation stones, which are the analogues of those in Judaism and Christianity. The concept of an invisible, intangible, all-powerful, all-knowing, and ultimately merciful God— *Allah* is the Arabic word for God—is virtually identical to the Jewish concept of God, while differing significantly from Christianity's belief in the Incarnation.

A concept of *peoplehood* is second—*umma:* the word is linguistically related to the word *'am* in Judaism, but the inclusiveness of the Muslim concept is closer to the Christian idea of peoplehood than to the exclusive shape of peoplehood in traditional Jewish thinking as it evolved after the fourth century.

God and people are connected by a *text*, the Qur'an, in which the speeches and teachings of Muhammad in Macca and Madina, from the beginning of the revelation to him in 610 until his death, are recorded.

Beyond the Qur'an, the *hadith,* sayings about or attributed to Muhammad are not as canonical as, say, the Prophets and Hagiographa are for Jews or the Acts of the Apostles, Epistles, and Book of Revelation are for Christians, but they are closer to the Qur'an than rabbinic or patristic and scholastic commentaries are to their respective textual traditions. Over the centuries Islam also developed entire seas of commentary on the Qur'an and *hadith,* organized into various schools that are the analogue of Jewish and Christian commentaries.[30]

The concept of sacred land for Islam focuses on three places: Macca, Madina, and Jerusalem (called in Arabic *al'Kuds*—"the Sacred"). While the veneration of Macca and Madina derive from the long-term roles they played in the life of the Prophet, Jerusalem's sanctity is based both on inherited pre-Islamic traditions and on one extraordinary moment. For many Muslims, as for Jews and Christians, the sacred city is revered as the site where Abraham offered his son to God and as the site of Solomon's temple.[31] But more importantly, it is the place from which Muhammad is said to have ascended to heaven on his steed Buraq (lightning) and to which he descended after an audience with God, in the extraordinary night journey, called the *isra',* that began and ended in Macca. Thus, in a literal sort of way, Jerusalem is the meeting point between heaven and earth—between *sacer* and *profanus.*[32]

Over the course of Islamic history, in some parts of the *dar al'Islam* there also developed a messianic element. The *mahdi,* a caliph who disappeared from the community of his followers, is expected to return to initiate an age of perfection in the future. This idea is thus more closely related to the Jewish concept of messiah than to the Christian one, as the future it anticipates is less extreme (and less clear) than the one anticipated by Christians. Moreover, the *mahdi* is not universally accepted throughout the *dar al'Islam.*

Over the course of its history, Islam developed guidelines for relations with Jews and Christians. A pact—*dhimma*—was established by Muhammad with the Jewish minority that he simultaneously despised for its failure to recognize him as the corrector of errors in the God-human relationship recorded in the Bible and respected for the foundations of that relationship set down by Judaism. The *dhimma* later extended to Christians and others, like Zoroastrians, who focus on a text as an essential part of their faith. All such peoples, accorded a prescribed form of respect, are thus referred to in Arabic as *dhimmi,* "People of the Pact." The *dhimma* limited what such groups could be and do within the Islamic world, even as it accepted the continuity of their lives and institutions. The phrase "People of the Book," also used by Muhammad, reflected his appreciation of the textuality of Judaism, and it eventually was applied to other peoples whose spirituality was centered on a book.

Over the centuries, visual self-expression within each of the three Abrahamic siblings—Judaism, Christianity, and Islam—has been characterized by three overlapping patterns derived from the constant commercial and cultural interchange among them and their birth in a common milieu: (1) they share with each other inherited visual terms from the worlds of antiquity that defined the contexts from which they all sprang; (2) they have absorbed, adopted, and adapted imagery, symbols, and a range of visual ideas from each other; and (3) they have initiated new ideas and new interpretations that distinguish their respective vocabularies from each other.

CHAPTER 3

CHRISTIAN SYMBOLS FROM CATACOMB TO CATHEDRAL

Early Christian Imagery

One of the common misconceptions regarding the direction taken by the Hebrew-Israelite-Judaean tradition around the time of Jesus is that it simply evolved into Judaism. As we have seen, history is more complex than that. Both Christianity and Judaism derive from the Hebrew-Israelite-Judaean tradition, as two siblings from a common parent. The problem of theological sibling rivalry was multiplied by the larger pagan political Roman context, and that rivalry in turn impacted how Jewish and Christian art developed.

Given its at-risk status during the second through early fourth centuries, we should not be surprised that the earliest Christian art was produced in and around the catacombs.[1] Contrary to popular belief, nobody dwelled there underground (the air would have been too unbreathable for long-term residency). But it makes sense that both the early Jews and Christians buried their dead well outside the city limits, in the first case to avoid pagan pollution in negotiating the transit between *profanus* and *sacer,* and in the second because the rites of passage to the *sacer* (death) as well as the general engagement of the *sacer* (God) could be more safely conducted by a *superstitio* away from disapproving eyes.

The earliest Christian symbols found in the catacombs share a common theme of salvation. Thus the repeated image of the dolphin, with its reputation as a savior of sailors lost at sea, represents Christ as the potential savior not only of those afloat in the sea of life but, more importantly, those tossed overboard from the ship of life into the eternally stormy seas of death. Cognate with this image is the ship's anchor, suggesting Christ as the mechanism that can secure safe harbor for a soul that might otherwise be lost catastrophically at sea.

The ultimate sea image is the fish. Like the dolphin, the fish long predates Christianity as a symbol of the positive possibilities that the *sacer* may yield. Both symbols are found, for example, in Nabataean art of the third century BCE.[2] The fish is a symbol of well-being and of survival because there never seemed to be an end to the supply of fish, and thus it was always available as a source of food. In the catacombs the image is layered with more specific Christological significance. The fish recalls two miracles recounted in the Gospels: the miracle of the loaves and fishes and the miracle of the draft of fishes. But at a more esoteric level, one that more educated Christians would recognize, the Greek word for fish—*ichthus*—is an acronym. It stands for the words *iesos christos theou uios soter:* "Jesus Christ Son of God Savior." Word becomes image and vice versa.

Human-shaped but just as oblique is the repeating image of the Good Shepherd. There is an array of variants of this subject within the Christian catacombs. Each differs slightly from the others, but they share the same idea: a young man carries a lamb or a young goat—or in some cases, a ram—on his shoulders. As a visual idea, we can trace this back to a key Greek sculpture from the late Archaic period, the Calf-Bearer, from around 525 BCE. We can follow the conceptual basis of that visual idea forward into the Hellenistic period, in which there are several sculptural versions of an old woman carrying a sheep or lamb to the marketplace on her shoulders or under her arm.

By the time we have arrived at that point, the intention of the image is to evoke our sympathy for the old woman who is either protecting her charge or desperate enough to carry it to its destruction in the marketplace so that she may survive. That intention has been reversed with the idea of Christ as Good Shepherd, keeper of the flocks. Far from sacrificing the lamb for his own survival, *he* is the lamb who sacrifices himself for *our* survival. The image yields that conceptual transformation by melding visual pagan underpinnings to Hebrew-Israelite-Judaean narrative underpinnings. In the latter we recognize the Good Shepherd as Moses journeying to the edge of the *sacer* to bring back a stray lamb from among his father-in-law's flocks.[3] In that context he encounters God in the burning bush and with it, the call to become the shepherd of the Israelite flock.[4]

The Good Shepherd as Christ offers a synthesis as well as a furthering of both the Greek imagery and the Israelite narrative. This is layered still further when, in some catacomb images, the animal in question is a ram. That image would further evoke the text of Genesis 22, in which, at the last moment, Abraham, instead of offering Isaac, substitutes a ram in sacrifice, provided by God. In Christian thought, the account of the offering by the father of his son to God, in which the son is redeemed at the last moment, is the forerunner of the offering by God the Father of God the Son as a sacrifice for the redemption of humankind.[5]

Such an interpretation is sometimes further underscored by additional details. Thus, on a sarcophagus from the catacomb of Praxiteles, the Good Shepherd image is repeated three times—once in the center and once at each side—as if to underscore the triune nature of the salvational figure symbolized by the image. These figures frame a composition in which little putti—Eros-cupid-angels, symbols of divine love—cavort among thick, winding vines, lush with bunches of grapes. We are thus reminded of several ideas simultaneously: Christ's blood sacrifice, of which wine and thus grapes are a symbol;[6] the notion that Christ is also the vintner who cares for the cosmic vineyard, in which we are all branches and grapes (thus the compassionate shepherd is synthesized to the compassionate vintner); and the fact that, in order for a vineyard to grow in a healthy manner, the careful vintner cuts away the rotting vines (and thus we are warned not to be among those who get cut away through unrighteous thoughts, words, or acts). Not to be cut away is to achieve salvation in the world to come, into which the sarcophagus is a doorway.

The entire composition is so tightly wrought that there is no empty space within it. It exhibits *horror vacui*—a fear of empty space—which in both pagan and post-pagan art historical contexts refers to the notion that every act of art-making, by invoking the *sacer* (the artist is in-spirited by the *sacer* to create the artwork), opens up the possibility that something negative might enter the *profanus*. Thus the painter or sculptor covers every inch of the surface on which he works, leaving no space through which negative aspects of the *sacer* might enter our realm. That practice is probably amplified in this case, as that surface is the side of a *sarcophagus*—a doorway between *profanus* and *sacer*.

Thus, apparently simple images lend themselves to a startling array of complex syntheses and transformations. An image in the third-century catacomb of Domitian depicts the Good Shepherd as Orpheus. Once again a pagan narrative underlies the image. Orpheus was the musician so skilled that he was able to charm death itself into allowing him to bring Eurydice back from Hades. He may be seen as a symbol of death and resurrection, who entered and returned from the realm of death, but also as a symbol of and warning about failed faith, because his turn around at the last moment consigned his beloved to death again. But we also recognize a synthesis between this story and a biblical narrative. David was the consummate shepherd before he became King of Israel. In that capacity he protected his flocks from wild beasts with his sling, but he also entertained them with his harp, just as later he would rescue Israel from the Philistines with his sling and King Saul from his demons with his harp. And if Jesus is the descendant of King David, anointed by God, then this image of the Good Shepherd is not only a metaphor for his shepherding of his Christian flocks but also a reminder of the human lineage that, in conjunction with his divine lineage, makes him what he is.

The imagery symbolizing the journey back to life from death is found not only in the pagan story of Orpheus but also in the biblical story of Jonah—whose story we also find in the catacombs. Jonah's two most crucial moments were when he was swallowed by a sea creature—and subsequently regurgitated—and when he fell asleep under a gourd, which withered in the sun, so that he awoke parched. In the first case, we see a symbol of descent into and return from the underworld. In the second, we recall God's instruction to Jonah that he ought to be more concerned about saving the sinning Ninevans, who are part of God's beloved creation, than about the shriveled gourd. Both are forerunners of the heroic salvational adventure of Christ, who descended and returned, carrying us with him, and who shows concern for all humans who hearken to him.

That nearly all this imagery is found in the context of passing from life to death is logical; it conveys the promise to those undertaking that journey of transit and transformation—and to those left behind—that it is a journey of hope, not despair. It asserts that, in the context of faith in Christ, death is not a curse but a blessing, the beginning of eternal life for the soul.

Other symbols are even more indirect, and not all of them are found in the catacombs. The floor of a villa at Daphne, from about 400 CE (by which time Christianity has emerged as the *religio* of the empire), is decorated with the mosaic image of a phoenix on a stylized hill. Such an image might be understood as a pagan symbol of immortality through eternal rebirth, since an old pagan tradition regards the phoenix as a unique creature that lives for a thousand years, builds its own funeral pyre, incinerates itself, and then emerges anew from the ashes. But the emphatic halo—although the halo idea also predates Christianity[7]— perforated by five rays suggests that the image has been appropriated to Christian symbolism. This singular creature whose death is self-directed but is reborn into immortality represents Christ. He dominates Golgotha, the five rays of light standing in for the five wounds in his self-sacrificing body.

There are other winged creatures that engage the passage from pagan to Christian significance. None is more interestingly transformed than the peacock. A second mosaic floor from the same villa offers a pair of peacocks, disposed in a manner that recalls the myriad of pre-Christian images of paired border creatures positioned on either side of a tree of life or its analogues (pillar, hero, priest) (see Figure 19). In this case they are placed to either side of a basket filled with bunches of grapes; vines swirl around both basket and peacocks. The basket symbolizes the Christ who, in his self-sacrifice, is the ultimate tree of life, flanked by birds whose flesh, according to an old Egyptian tradition, does not rot.

FIGURE 19   *Mosaic floor, Daphne, Greece (detail: Peacocks flanking basket of grapes).*
ca. 400 CE

Thus peacocks evolved, within the early Christian tradition, as a symbol of eternal life.

Moreover, within the Greek tradition we may recall the story of how the eyes on the peacock's tail came from the thousand-eyed monster, Argus, set to guard Io (one of the unhappy human recipients of Zeus' lustful attentions). She was rescued by Hermes, who told story after story until each of Argus' eyes closed in sleep; as Hermes plucked them all out and tossed them below, the peacock passed by, catching the eyes on its tail. In Christian thought, those eyes symbolize the all-seeing church. Furthermore, Hera—queen of heaven, wife-sister of the supreme god—took on the peacock thereafter as her own symbol. Since the queen of heaven in Christian thought is the Virgin Mary, the peacock also symbolizes her intermediating presence. Finally, early Christian thinkers likened the strange call of the peacock to the cries of the early Christian martyrs, who died for their faith. On the other hand, the strutting carriage of the peacock also associates it with pride and vanity. Thus, like the vines, it offers both positive reassurances and negative warnings to the devotee.

A similar message is portrayed on a fifth-century sarcophagus from Ravenna, on which the central image is a pair of peacocks flanking and drinking from a fountain overflowing with water. The tree of life as source of life has been transformed into a container from which life-sustaining water bursts forth. Moreover, as much as we might understand the fountain to symbolize Christ as the source of eternal life, it is also associated with the Virgin Mary as the source of that source, by evoking passages from Song of Songs 4:12: "A garden shut up is my sister, my bride; a spring closed up, a fountain sealed"; and 4:15: ". . . a well of living waters"; and Psalm 36:10: "the fountain of life in [whose] light we see light." And in drinking thirstily from it, the peacocks add another layer to their symbolic content. The bird, in general, is a symbol of the soul—this idea, too, can be traced to ancient Egyptian imagery—shown eagerly deriving sustenance from the source of eternal life.[8]

—⚭—

Early Christian art offers diverse figurative subjects as symbols of salvation. A mosaic dating from around 430 CE from the pilgrimage church of Santa Maria Maggiore in Rome offers the saving passage of the Israelites through the Red Sea. Led by a youthful Moses, who taps the waters with his stick, the ordered rows of the saved are arrayed on the left bank of the sea. On the opposite side the well-armed Egyptians pour out of their city (dominated by the kind of arch that Roman art repeatedly uses as a synecdoche for major cities), their ordered rows starting to collapse into chaos as they approach the sea, where several are shown being swallowed up—including the white-bearded figure of the Pharaoh.

Moses is a frequently depicted Hebrew biblical character. Others also appear, such as Abraham. In a second mosaic in Santa Maria Maggiore, he receives the angels who will announce to him the miraculous (given his and Sarah's old age) birth of Isaac (see Figure 20). In a manner frequently found in late ancient and medieval art, in one register we see a series of actions that, in the *profanus,* would be offered in a linear sequence, but in the *sacer* are presented all at once. Not surprisingly, there are *three* acts in the same register—Abraham greeting the strangers, ordering Sarah to prepare food for them, and serving them—since that number underscores the Christian understanding of the *sacer* as triune. Christian thought emphasizes the fact that the passage in Genesis describes a visitation of *three* figures.[9]

Whereas the angelic halos suggest the divine connection of these figures, Abraham also has a kind of halo around his head—but only in two of the three representations of him, and more to the point, his is a dark, imperfectly formed one, whereas the angelic halos are bright white and perfectly rounded. His connection to the *sacer* is different from theirs. As Abraham instructs Sarah regarding the preparation of fine food for these visitors, he gestures with his first two fingers held up, his two outer fingers held down with his thumb. We understand from writings on rhetoric by

FIGURE 20 *Mosaic, Church of Santa Maria Maggiore, Rome. Fifth century* CE

the late first-century Roman teacher, Quintillian, that such a gesture is a rhetorical one: when making a point in a court of law, one punctuates one's remarks with such a gesture.[10] Abraham is making a point to Sarah—but that gesture will eventually evolve into a benedictory one, a rhetorical gesture of salvational intention.

Still earlier in the Hebrew Bible is Noah, whose story of survival in the world-consuming flood offers another logical opportunity for salvational imagery. On a wall in the third-century catacomb of Saints Peter and Marcellinus there is a painting of Noah in the ark, but his gesture of releasing the raven to investigate the possibilities of dry land has been confuted with the early Christian gesture of prayer. His is the *orans* position, with the arms thrown up and the hands held open as if to receive the Holy Spirit from above.[11]

That gesture is exhibited by any number of individuals who stand on the border between *profanus* and *sacer*. A carved pyxis from the first quarter of the sixth century tells the story of St. Maenus, who stands in a doorway with his arms and outstretched hands upraised. Both St. Maenus and Christ, depicted enthroned, on the side of the marble sarcophagus of Bishop Liberius (d. 387), are attired in the Roman *togatus* style. The manner of representing significant figures in pagan Roman art has been appropriated to rendering important men of the spirit in Christian Roman art. So, too, the Christ depicted on the sarcophagus is beardless.[12] There are two overlapping explanations for this. If Christ is depicted holding forth among the apostles, he is simply heir to the depiction of glorious young Greco-Roman Gods, such as Hermes/Mercury and Apollo. The one is the ultimate messenger for the Greco-Roman pagan world—and Christ is the ultimate messenger of salvation to the Christian world. The other is the ultimate symbol of light, reason, order—just as his opposites, Pan and his associates, are associated with darkness and chaos. As the image of Satan and his son, the Anti-Christ, grows out of the bearded imagery of Pan, with his horns, hooves, and other goat associations, the image of Christ derives initially, in the Western visual tradition, from that of Apollo.

The second reason for a beardless Christ is action-context specific. In renditions of the passage in which he is debating with the learned men in the temple—presumably just prior to, or in the process of, attaining his bar mitzvah[13]—he would obviously be young and therefore beardless. That is almost certainly the case on the high-relief-carved sarcophagus of Junius Bassius (ca. 359 CE). There we see a very young, large-headed

Jesus (as the eyes are the windows to the soul, the head is the dwelling place of the soul), enthroned and engaged in a serious discussion with two older, bearded men. He seems to be gesturing (but his hand is broken off). We recognize the politician/orator/philosopher's toga and the scroll, in his surviving hand, of what we might take to be his New Thinking (as opposed to the scroll of Old Thinking in the hand of one of his interlocutors).

Christ's foot virtually rests on the head of a bearded figure holding up a garment almost as a "roof"; such a depiction is typical for senior pagan gods, particularly those representing forces of localized nature.[14] Thus, Jesus not only holds his text, which will supercede the text held by his interlocutor, but his faith doctrine will crush beneath the heel of his spiritual sandal that associated with the old pagan gods. A pair of columns flanks the three figures. Just as an arch can be a synecdoche for Rome, a pair of columns would become increasingly common in both Christian and Jewish art as a synecdoche for Jerusalem and its temple. Seated before or between these columns, these figures carry on their discussion exactly where the Gospels say they did: before the temple in Jerusalem.

Christ is only gradually depicted in early Christian art, and gradually his image acquires a bearded countenance. There is a range of ways in which we see him, reflecting both passages from the Gospels and narratives outside them. The mosaic of the Good Shepherd adorning a lunette in the sixth-century mausoleum of Galla Placidia in Ravenna offers Christ as a young, beardless shepherd embellished with a halo around his head and the upper part of his shepherd's staff as a cross: the shepherd who is also the lamb is the Christ who will be sacrificed on the cross. Another relatively early kind of representation places him as a child on the Virgin Mary's lap. On a wall in the Roman catacomb of Comodilla a painting dated to 528 shows them flanked by a pair of saints, Felix and Adauctus, and the donor Turtura, who paid for the work (see Figure 21). The work reminds us of certain details from the prior pagan artistic tradition as it anticipates certain developments in the Byzantine tradition to follow. Thus we recognize, in the size relationship between Turtura and the others, the principle of significance perspective so frequently seen in Mesopotamian and Egyptian art; her presence with the saints and the Virgin and Child underscores the sense

FIGURE 21 *Wall painting of Virgin and Child,*
Saints Felix and Adauctus and donor, Turtura.
Catacomb of Comodilla, Rome. 528 CE

of *sacer* timelessness and layers the border between *profanus* and *sacer*: Turtura is closer to our reality as the others are variously closer to pure *sacer* reality.

The sense of timeless time is balanced by the sense of space-less space: although the Virgin and Child are "seated" upon a throne, they seem to hover as much as to sit, and the overall space in which the group poses has a spaceless quality to it, just as the figures possess a distinctly flat quality. This does not reflect lack of skill in rendering volume as much as desire to emphasize the spiritual and the metaphysical rather than the material and the physical. It is analogous to the eternalizing stiffness of Egyptian statuary that remained virtually unchanged in its conventions for thousands of years. The early Christian figures are also rigid, frontal, eternalizingly static, with en-larged eyes looking as much through us—to that Other realm—as at us. In this regard, they are also reminiscent of the late Roman portraits of the dead from Fayoum. While the Christ Child holds the scroll of his New Covenant, the Virgin Mary holds and indicates the Christ Child, the donatrix indicates them, and Saint Felix holds her as if presenting her to them. St. Adauctus offers the rhetorical gesture that derives, like his *togatus* garb, from Roman visual vocabulary. As the gesture is shift-ing toward being benedictory, it doesn't lose its rhetorical nature: we (the viewers) are blessed.

The overall emphasis on the spiritual and metaphysical side of the Virgin and Child never wanes in the varied visual traditions of the East-ern churches, whether they are shown seated on a throne-like structure, or whether, as in the renowned icon The Virgin of Vladimir (ca. 1125), we are shown only the upper part of such a composition within a gold spaceless space that offers no contextual elements whatsoever. Two details in this work make it distinctive, in different ways. The first is a pair of starburst elements on the Virgin's garment—one on her shoulder, the other above her forehead—that we can trace, as a visual expression of a *sacer* connection or imprimatur, back to the Sumerians and Akkadians. (One thinks, for example, of the starbursts that hover over the head of Naram-Sin on his stele.) The second is the way in which the artist has started the slow shaping of a humanistic perspective: the mother and baby press their cheeks against each other. Her gaze out at us pulls on a different set of strings from those attached to color symbolism: "Behold my little baby who will die for you," her eyes seem to say. But the attenuated figuration and adult-like form of the baby Jesus that all icons share in common distinguishes them from the style of imagery taking shape in Western Christian art.

Also typical of the East is a thirteenth-century Byzantine icon with stylized, hieratic poses and, in lieu of shadows lineating the garments, gold leaf, underscoring the supernatural quality of the two figures. Their garments yield the blue of his Truth, the red of his impending self-sacrifice, and also the green of spring, resurrection, and eternal life (see Figure 22). He holds the scroll of his Testament in his left hand and gestures benedictorily with his right; her fingers are positioned to allude to the Trinity. There is an attenuated quality that defies physicality; Jesus looks very much the miniature adult, which underscores the seriousness of his message. Two angels hover in tondi that are both plaques on the wall of that spaceless space and windows within the wall that marks the border between *profanus* and *sacer*; the angels peer in at this pair of border creatures, at whom we peer from the other side.

Nonfigurative symbolic vocabulary in early Christian art also continued

FIGURE 22 *Virgin and Child (Byzantine icon). Thirteenth century*

to evolve. One observes, for instance, on the sarcophagus of the Archbishop Theodorus, from sixth-century Ravenna, the familiar image, in yet another variant expression, of a pair of animals flanking a tree of life. The animals are peacocks, and sprouting from behind and around them are vines. But the central image is a medallion—a perfect circle—within which are two interwoven images. One is a pair of Greek letters: *alpha* and *omega*. The first and last letters of the Greek alphabet symbolize the statement by Jesus, "I am the beginning and the end"—the totality of reality. Those letters flank the second symbol: *khi rho*. The "x" is the Greek letter *khi,* and what appears to be a staff with a little pitcher at its peak is the Greek letter *rho.* These are the first two letters of the word *Kh-rh-i-s-t-o-s.* Moreover, in the Greco-Latin bilingualism of the early Christian world, the fact that the two letters look like Latin "P" and "X" enables the combination simultaneously to symbolize *pax*—"peace."

So Christ, who is the hero/priest/pillar/tree-of-life, is represented by the first two letters of the word Christ and by the letters that sum him up: first and last, beginning and end. That configuration is repeated on the lid of the sarcophagus, this time ensconced within a circular wreath—a symbol of fertility, peace, perfection—a Roman visual idea cognate with the swags on Augustus' *Ara Pacis.* Moreover, this wreath

FIGURE 23   *Sarcophagus, Istanbul. ca 600 CE*

proves to be one of *three,* and in the two on either side, in lieu of the *khi rho,* the cross is shown.

The cross is only beginning to reach its full stride as a symbol around this time, for the Romans crucified tens of thousands of individuals deemed politically subversive. That Jesus was believed to be a subversive is suggested by the inscription said to have been placed above his head and repeated in endless numbers of representations of the Crucifixion: "Jesus of Nazareth, King of the Judaeans." This "title" written in the operative languages of Judaea at that time—Aramaic, Greek, and Latin—indicated that his execution was due to political opposition to Roman authority. It would hardly do, particularly when the faith was still regarded as a *superstitio,* to memorialize him by means of the humiliating instrument of his execution.

Later, as that memory faded and Christianity ascended toward hegemony, the Crucifixion became a logical symbol of Christ, whose form of death came to be treated as unique to him. By then, the term Christ had ceased to mean merely "anointed"; it offered the connotation of savior—a unique savior who is no less than God Itself become one of us, who suffered and died in the most horrible manner and thus experienced human reality at its most painful. In that context, the cross is also a perfect symbol because, as a horizontal beam intersecting a vertical beam, it symbolizes the meeting of opposites: heaven and earth, divinity and humanity, *sacer* and *profanus.*

Images of the cross became increasingly frequent over time. One sarcophagus shows a pair of apostles flanking it on the side and the *khi rho* symbol within a wreath on its front (see Figure 23). There the two flanking figures suggest angels, but we recognize them as allegorical figures of victory derived from those embellishing the spandrels of Roman victory arches.[15] In presenting the Christ monogram within a circular wreath of perfection, these figures present Christ as the source of true victory—victory over evil and over death itself.

The cross is the central image soaring in the stylized heavens in the cupola of the mausoleum of Galla Placidia (ca. 450 CE), where it emerges from a blaze of stars that yield, in the four spandrels of the cupola, four images representing the four evangelists. By the eighth century, a profusion of large crosses had invaded the British Isles. One of these, the Ahenny Cross (from south Ireland, near Tipperary), is an eleven-foot tall, mid-century work that synthesizes Christian with traditional Celtic visual elements. Its horizontal-vertical meeting point, symbolizing the meeting of realms, is enveloped by a circle. In pushing out in four directions, the cross also represents the four-directional, finite *profanus* reality of which Jesus was part, while the circle represents the perfect, infinite, complete *sacer* reality of which he was also part. Five high-relief spheres adorn the arms of the cross and its centering point, corresponding to the five wounds in Christ's self-sacrificial body. Finally, the entirety is overrun by a series of stylistically contrasting motifs that derive from the rope-like Celtic decorative vocabulary, suggesting an endless flow of reality.

On an early eighth-century marble balustrade dedicated to Saint John the Baptist and associated with the Patriarch Sigvald, from Civitate, Italy, is a complex series of reliefs, the upper central motif of which is the cross (see Figure 24). Where the two beams meet is an eight-pointed star. We are reminded that this is the tree of eternal life, for on the eighth day after entering Jerusalem, after being put to death on the cross, Jesus rose from the dead. That it is the tree of life is made more apparent by the fact that it is flanked by a pair of cypress trees, thus making it the center of a triune configuration and the emergent tradition of three crosses on Golgotha, symbolizing Christ and the two thieves who are his antitheses. Moreover, the cross rises from its sibling on the lower register, a stylized vegetal form. That element spreads its

FIGURE 24 *Balustrade relief of Patriarch Sigvald, cathedral baptistery, Civitate, Italy. 762–771*

upper "branches" as griffin-like heads, and as birds—symbolizing souls—consuming bunches of grapes; the lower part is flanked by a pair of border creatures, their body parts from different realms.

The composition introduces us to another element that will become increasingly prominent in the symbolic vocabulary of medieval Christian art: the representation of the four evangelists by figures that reflect aspects of Christ that each Gospel text is said to emphasize. Thus, imaginatively deformed upper body elements, with the lower bodies or legs shriveled into the most minimalist of representation, offer us Mark in the lower right, Luke in the lower left, Matthew in the upper right, and John in the upper left quadrant. The first is represented by a lion because the Gospel according to Mark is said to emphasize the royal aspects of Christ and his descent from the Davidic house (according to a hagiographic tradition dating from around the late sixth century). The second is represented by an ox (or bull) because the Gospel of Luke is said to emphasize the sacrificial nature of Christ (the ox and bull are preeminent sacrificial animals). The third is represented by a man-angel because the Gospel of Matthew is said to emphasize most strongly the human qualities of Jesus. The Gospel of John, separated in time, style, and key aspects from the others (which are thus called the synoptic Gospels),[16] is remarkable for its soaring oratory and is thus represented by an eagle. On Sigvald's balustrade, each of these four creatures carries a tablet identifying who he is.

By the eighth century, moreover, the naked cross with geometric and vegetal embellishment is beginning to yield to the image of Christ himself on the cross. Contemporary with the two previously discussed images is a representation of the Crucifixion worked in repoussé bronze on the cover of a book in the National Museum of Ireland in Dublin. Celtic rope motifs adorn the lower parts of the Christ figure, with a watery element covering his torso, as if to underscore the fact that he is the source of everlasting life.

The Expanding Symbolic Language of the Medieval Period

Over time, the powerful symbol of the cross also entered Christian architecture. The idiom often used for entering a church is that we "enter the body of Christ." In the architecture of the church this metaphor began to be shaped by structures conceived as cruciform. The symbolic intention is

FIGURE 25   *Church of Haghia Sofia, Istanbul. ca. 532–537* CE

that as one enters such a space, one enters the instrument of Christ's self-sacrifice, where his body is implied. The Greek cross (all four arms equal in length) dominates the eastern topography of Christian ecclesiastical architecture, and the Latin cross (the lower arm longer than the other three, offering a longer nave than transept arms and apse) the western.

Whereas the threefold doorway that often leads one into a church—particularly larger ones—connotes the Trinity, larger structures are often accessed by *five* doorways. This extends the metaphor: one enters the body of Christ by means of the five wounds in his body. Fiveness is often addressed in the Eastern tradition by a different means: the four arms, equal in length, are surmounted by cupolas, and a fifth, dominating the others, rises over the space defined by the meeting point of the four arms.[17]

The first freestanding domed structure is the Roman Pantheon.[18] The perfectly spherical cupola of that edifice was designed to emulate the dome of heaven, to which it was in turn connected by the opening—the *oculus* (eye)—at the peak of the sphere. In the sixth century, Justinian the Great, arguably the most important Byzantine emperor, rebuilt the Church of Holy Wisdom (Haghia Sophia), in Constantinople.[19] That structure was dominated by a dome that emulated the Pantheon cupola (see Figure 25).

There are two major differences between the two structures, however. The dome of the Haghia Sophia is much flatter than that of the Pantheon. More important, instead of possessing a single oculus, the dome of the Haghia Sophia rests—or seems to float above—openings that completely ring it and connect it to, as they disconnect it from, the edifice below. Perhaps this helps account for the flatter structure of the dome: it helps promote that sense of lightness. The division between *profanus* and *sacer* is more pronounced in the Haghia Sophia as the dome begins its rise above a high wall line (in the Pantheon, the seven "layers" of the dome begin virtually at ground level). Moreover, the extreme emphasis in Christianity on the soul, connecting us to the *sacer,* is addressed by an interior ablaze with the light of heaven that streams through myriad openings, rather than moving starkly along the dome interior as the light does in the Pantheon. If the eyes are windows to the soul, in the Haghia Sophia the windows are the eyes that in their multiplicity suggest the all-seeing presence of God, filling that interior with the light that connects those within to the *sacer* without.

The lower parts of the Haghia Sophia assume a basilical form, the nave flanked by side aisles accessed through a pair of colonnades. Within the structure of most basilical churches there is an arch that separates the nave from the apse, which terminates the building, just as columns separate the nave from the side aisles. An arch such as that in San Paolo fuori le Mure in Rome reveals a formal structure similar to that of the freestanding victory arches that once abounded throughout the empire. Just beyond the arch, the *sacerdos* performs the ceremonies before the altar that connects the community to the *sacer.* Thus, the arch connects our world, with death as its end point, to the next world of Christian eternal life—yielding victory over death. Not merely its structure, but its decorative elements remind the devotee of its triumphant role. The arch in San Paolo is dominated by the figure of a haloed Christ who offers a rhetorical—benedictory—gesture to all who approach. Soaring in the blazing golden spaceless space around him are the winged symbols of the four Gospels, and below them a pair of angels leads surging bands of the beatified toward him. On the spandrels, against a rich blue—the color of the sky and thus of Truth— Saints Peter and Paul gesture to us to carry our attention up to the fierce face of God.

Beyond the arch, the bulbous apse presses the end of the structure away from us—usually the eastern end, facing toward Jerusalem. In the case of the apse of San Paolo, the hint of a second arch leads us in, and the spandrels are decorated with winged creatures that directly recall the winged victory figures on Roman arches of victory. The apse form has a dual source. On the one hand the semicircular termination of a building—often a basilica—was not unusual for Roman judicial and legislative structures. The relationship between such a form and a church apse becomes apparent in the case of a cathedral—the seat of a bishop—where the episcopal throne (Greek: *cathedra*) is placed along the back wall of the elevated space of the apse.

But the second source for the apse is the Torah niche of the early synagogue, a small recessed area in the wall that faces Jerusalem. The Torah niche was invariably decorated with scenes that portray God's redemptive role in human affairs, which is the theme absorbed and developed by the church apse (see Chapter 4). In San Giovanni in Laterano in Rome, the apse mosaics were added to the evolving structure by Jacopo Torriti in the late thirteenth century (see Figure 26). The area is visually divided into upper and lower parts. In the upper realm, ensconced in a deep sky-of-Truth blue across which wisps of clouds (the clouds of doubt dispersing before the sun of Truth), God the Father is framed by a blazing halo. He is surrounded by nine angelic beings, symbolizing the nine choirs of angels.[20] The uppermost of these represent

FIGURE 26   *Jacopo Torriti: Apse mosaics, Church of San Giovanni in Laterano, Rome. Thirteenth century* CE

the six-winged seraphim, referred to in Isaiah 6 as intoning "Holy, holy, holy, the Lord of Hosts; the whole earth is full of his glory!"

From that uppermost register a dove, symbolizing the Holy Spirit, swoops down through the golden spaceless space of the lower register. In pagan Greek terms we follow her from the *aither* to the *aer*. In the center of that realm is a cross, flanked by the figures of the Virgin Mary (identified by the Greek abbreviation for "Mother of God") and John the Baptist (labeled in Latin, but also recognizable by the rough-hewn garment and unkempt, hirsute appearance that always marks him, reminding us of his time in the wilderness). Farther from the center are not only the figures of Saints Peter and Paul (on the same side as the Virgin) and John the Evangelist and Andrew (on the same side as John the Baptist) but also—smaller, in accordance with significance perspective—the figures of Saints Francis and Anthony, scions of Western monasticism and its renewal in the thirteenth century. Smaller still, and kneeling by the protective Virgin, is Pope Nicholas IV, who sponsored the mosaics. In an act of some modesty he is the only figure without a halo. We recognize the scene as a timeless moment within spaceless space.[21]

The cross itself is marked at the meeting point between its vertical and horizontal elements by a scene in which John the Baptist anoints Jesus with water from the River Jordan. In a splendid act of conceptual continuity, the rays of light emanating from the dove of the Holy Spirit become water by the time they flow over (visually behind) the cross. These waters are gathered into a pool at the base of the cross, where two deer are symmetrically disposed facing toward the pool, as if about to drink from it—recalling both many pagan images and the passage in the psalms likening the soul to a swift deer in its eagerness for God.[22] The water—third of the four natural elements (after *aither* and *aer*) in the Greek tradition—spills from the pool into four streams that flow into a rich garden, which becomes the ground upon which all of these figures stand (except for the pope, who kneels). The four streams represent the four streams of God's Word flowing through the four evangelical texts, but they are also labeled as the four rivers referred to in Genesis 2 that flow through the Garden of Eden: the Tigris, the Euphrates, the Gihon, and the Pishon. Thus, this fourth element, earth, both is and is *not* of our world: it is Paradise (where the sainted, the beatified, and the morally upright stand), and yet it is merely the gateway to Paradise—the Holy Land through which the River Jordan and its baptismal waters flow.

The four rivers terminate within the soil of this garden, and flowing along its lower edge—closest to where *we* stand—the Jordan is labeled, connected and *not* connected to the four rivers, populated by ordinary fish but also phantasmagorical little putti. Below the point where the waters part into four streams we can discern a tiny gilded gated cityscape—guarded by an angel with a sword of fire. This is an allusion to the Cherub(im) guarding the portal back into the Garden of Eden from which Adam and Eve have just been ejected (described in Genesis 3). Within the walls stand Peter and Paul, and surmounting the tree growing within the enclosure is the haloed phoenix. Every part of these intricate mosaics is packed with reminders of God's salvational presence, of which baptism—rebirth into the community of Christendom—is the first step.

Variations of the themes expressed in the apse at San Giovanni can be seen in different materials and formats elsewhere. The twelfth-century apse mosaics of the upper basilical church of San Clemente in Rome, named for the third successor to the seat of Saint Peter, are dominated by a cross. But in this case, the cross is embellished with the figure of the crucified Christ, as well as twelve doves, symbolizing the twelve apostles, and flanked by the figures of the Virgin Mary and John the Evangelist, gesturing in counterpoint. That the cross is the tree of eternal life is underscored by the fact that it rises not merely from a "tree" but from an acanthus tree. The acanthus is an evergreen and had been a symbol of eternal life from the time of the ancient Egyptians, who were the first to make use of its symbolism in the capitals of their columns, to the time of the Greeks and Romans, whose Corinthian capitals continued that tradition.

In the apse of San Clemente, the acanthus grows as an endless vine, reminiscent of the garland motifs on the *Ara Pacis*. Below it flow the waters of a four-forked river toward which a pair of deer incline their antlered heads to drink, and beyond them a pair of peacocks struts in watchful symmetry. Below the entire composition, poised in the spaceless green of spring and rebirth are the figures of a haloed lamb—the self-sacrificing *agnus dei* ("lamb of God")—flanked by the twelve sheep that repeat the allusion to the apostles on the cross above (see Figure 1). These are all motifs that we find repeated in myriad places across Christendom through the centuries.

The pattern of intermediation between *profanus* and *sacer* in the Christian tradition has a distinctly ladder-like quality to it. The church may in its entirety be the meeting point between heaven and earth, but within it, the apse with its altar and its officiant are closer to the *sacer* than the nave with its congregation. Just as the art within drives us toward the apse and toward the offices that will yield heaven to us, we are urged to enter the church by the plethora of visual and other symbols on the exterior that remind us of the risk of remaining outside and the rewards to be derived from entering.

A soaring bell tower serves to locate a church visually and aurally from any place in town—and the more soaring it is, the more awesome and emphatic the statement regarding the power of the institution to intermediate between us and the vastness of the universe. But such towers were not initially associated with churches; they served a more mundane purpose. With the approach of some danger (more easily discerned from such a height) the ringing of the town tower's bells would warn the local inhabitants that they must hurry inside protective walls or risk injury, capture by an enemy, or even death. Placing the town tower close to the church—and eventually attaching it to the body of the church—served a double purpose. Aside from the role just described, that clamor warned the inhabitants, when the time for prayer arrived, that they must hurry inside the spiritually protective walls of the church or risk a far more profound injury than that threatened by marauding bandits or attacking soldiers: injury to one's immortal soul.

Moreover, as the Western architectural tradition evolved from the Roman to the Romanesque to the Gothic, it progressed along not only a particular aesthetic trajectory but also a continuously evolving symbolic one.[23] The extreme verticality that emerges for the Gothic tower in most of its classic manifestations suggests an intended heavenly emphasis: the spirit, as the eye, is driven upward.[24] So, too, the rising of the Gothic arch toward an ogival point (which causes it to resemble a pair of hands coming together in prayer) emphasizes a heavenward focus. Furthermore, the structure of the Gothic church—vastness of space and surface visually divided into myriad details of both figurative and abstract conception, with details that range from biblical narratives to grotesques to crockets and sprockets—suggests it as a microcosm of the vast and well-ordered world that God made. Smaller details are typically arithmetic fractions of larger details.

Often this notion takes further turns. Thus, for example, in the program of the stained-glass decoration of the thirteenth-century Cathedral of Leon, Spain, there is a threefold structure: the natural realm, the human realm, and the divine realm. Aside from the triune implications of a threefold scheme, the universe in miniature is depicted on those translucent walls that simultaneously separate and connect the world outside and the world within the church. We are both raised up toward the upper world to which we aspire and reminded about the dangers endemic to the lower world of which we are a part. Moreover, the fact that the medium of this message is a series of windows recalls the double principle of continuity and transformation: what began with the oculus of the Roman Pantheon and proceeded toward the windows of the Byzantine Haghia Sophia now arrives, by way of smaller Romanesque apertures, as vast and colorful swatches of Gothic glass.

Around the outer church walls and around and above their doorways are analogous visual patterns of reminders, encouragement, promises, and warnings. Many churches tend to offer pairs of lion figures before their doors (reminiscent of the so-called Lions' Gate at Mycenae, but usually crouching at the bottom of pillars holding up the porch before it) or lions subduing or destroying serpents (symbolizing Christ the Davidic king slaying Satan). So, too, the arched space—the tympanum—above doorways, such as the south portal into Moissac's Abbey Church of St. Peter (ca. 1120), might be dominated by the figure of Christ seated in glory on the Throne of Heaven.[25] At Moissac he is surrounded by the symbols of the four evangelists and a pair of angels, together with twenty-four beatified elders, reconstituted as a heavenly orchestra, referred to in the Book of Revelation. Significance perspective is emphatically in use: Christ is huge in comparison with the angels and apostles, who are nonetheless quite large in comparison with the twenty-four elders.

Among the many interesting elements of the composition is the rhetorical-become-benedictory gesture made by Christ, balancing the gesture of indicating the book of his New Covenant. A feature new to this discussion is the form of the halo around Christ's head. Impressed within it are the upper three arms of a cross. The three visible arms remind us of the Trinity. But simultaneously, since we know that, were his head not blocking it, we would be able to see the fourth arm of what we know to be a cross, we are also reminded of the sacrificial act that has yielded our salvation as surely as it led to the enthronement we see before our eyes. Only the Christ figure displays this kind of cruciform-inscribed halo (though he is not always so adorned).

On the tympanum over the main door at the Chartres cathedral (ca. 1200), not only is Christ haloed, but his throne is enveloped by a mandorla—an almond-shaped halo that surrounds the entire body. In Christian iconography, the mandorla is reserved for Christ (usually in depictions of him sitting in final judgment; thus his figure is both welcoming and warning)—and occasionally for the Virgin Mary in Assumption. Further variations on the same themes may be observed on the tympana of many other churches and cathedrals. Some include scenes with tiny figures of those approaching judgment and those who, having been judged, are directed either to heaven or hell. Scales are typically held by the angel Gabriel who is balanced by a demonic, serpentine counterpart, as tiny humans who have sinned irremediably are plucked by their heads or caught by creatures emerging from slavering jaws.

FIGURE 27   *Apse painting, Church of Sant Angelo in Fornis, Italy: Christ in Glory (detail). ca. 1090*

The image of Christ Enthroned naturally carries into the church, where the image is most frequently found dominating the apse. One impressive example is in the church of Sant' Angelo in Fornis in southern Italy (see Figure 27). There a Christ in Glory is seated on an exquisitely decorated throne and enveloped in a highly stylized garment; the whole is set within a deep blue-of-Truth background. A blazing cruciform halo emanates from behind his head with his enormous and riveting eyes that bore through the viewer. With his left hand he holds open the book in which we read (in Latin): I am the beginning and the end (spelling out, in order to symbolize this, the first and last letters of the Greek alphabet, *alpha* and *omega*); I am both first *(primus)* and renewal *(novissimus)*. With his right hand he gestures. However, as with his thumb he presses down the third finger, thus emphasizing the Trinity, the last finger also points up—thereby emphasizing the Trinity a second time, by holding up three fingers. The notion of a Christ who, while merciful, is also a stern judge is particularly evident in the representations of him as *Pantocrater* (All-powerful; Creator of All) that often soars above us on the cupolas of Eastern Christian churches. In these we recognize a fierce visage very different from the early beardless face of Christ derived from the pagan images of Apollo and Hermes; the fierce, bearded image derives from images of Near Eastern gods.

Subtly different details may be discerned, such as eyes that look up and away to represent the connection to the *sacer,* an expression that can be traced back to second-century pagan Roman representations of philosophers and, eventually, even emperors with a strong *sacer* connection, like Constantine. Fingers may simultaneously symbolize the Trinity—the three lower fingers, clinging together—and the dual nature of Christ as God/Man—the two remaining fingers, each separate, one pointing in a horizontal direction, the other vertical. Variations of finger gestures recall patterns of variation in the image of the cross and the Crucifixion. During the eighth through tenth centuries, images usually depicted Christ's head in an upright position with his eyes wide open. Such a pose accentuates his victory over pain and death: the *Christus triumphans* reminds the viewer of the eternal life made available through Christ. Subsequently, it became more common to represent his head lolling to one side, with his eyes closed: this *Christus patiens* ("Suffering Christ"), in accentuating his pain, emphasizes his self-sacrificial nature. This tension between Christ's suffering for humanity and his triumphant victory over death, analogous to the tension between his human aspect and his divine aspect, is found throughout the depictions of phases in Christ's life.

FIGURE 28 *Giotto:* Virgin and Child, *oil on panel. 1321*

From Renaissance to Baroque

As nineteenth-century art historians looked back at the Western artistic traditions taking shape in the fourteenth through sixteenth centuries, they took their lead from the sixteenth-century painter and biographer of Florentine artists, Vasari, and came to refer to that period as the Renaissance.[26] By that they meant a rebirth of aesthetic and conceptual values that we associate with the Greeks and Romans and that were abandoned by a Christian world struggling to divest itself of the pagan side of its parentage. By the fourteenth century, an interest in expressing the physical reality of the visual world and not only its spiritual aspects stepped to the front of the stage of Western art, first in Italy and subsequently in other parts of Europe. More broadly, the central role of God shifted somewhat from the center to the side of the stage of human activity. Humanism meant that humans were at the center, bearing an increased responsibility for shaping their world, and in art, it meant a greater emphasis on the human side of Christ. The Renaissance represents both a continuum of key concerns and familiar symbols from the medieval period and the introduction of new ones.

We may observe these issues in summary form if we turn back to the image of the Virgin and Child. Giotto's *Enthroned Madonna and Child* (1321) offers a strong sense of Renaissance humanism (see Figure 28). Christ is the ultimate symbol of the connection between humanity and God, and both Eastern and earlier Western representations of the Christ Child and his Virgin Mother tended to emphasize the divine side of both by dematerializing them. But Giotto exhibits interest in the human side of Christ. All hint of stylization is gone from the garments filled out by fleshy beings: Mary is a robust Tuscan mother (she even has milk-filled breasts pressing out against her inner garment) with her robust Tuscan child. Like a baby he grasps one of the fingers of her left hand that holds him; with his other hand he reaches for what is in his mother's other hand.

Giotto's depiction does retain archaic elements, such as the gold-leaf ground and the Gothic intricacies of the throne where the pair is ensconced. Symbolic colors are still in place and what Mary holds in her hand is a white lily that both symbolizes her virgin purity and alludes specifically to the phrase "Lilly of the Sharon [Valley]" from the Song of Songs with which the Virgin is associated by Christian tradition. A closer look suggests that the image may be that of a rose, albeit a white one. Since the biblical Hebrew of the Song of Songs can be rendered by either flower, lily or rose, that aspect of the flower's allusiveness can be considered unchanged. On the other hand, a rose is often used as a symbol of Christ's passion, with its blood-red color and its thorns. A *white* rose would not lose the force of these ideas but merely cross them with the reference to virgin purity and add the further suggestion of unique-ness: there is only one white rose, *this* one, as there is only one Christ, *this* one. The baby reaches both toward her purity and toward his fu-ture martyrdom.

The symbolic emphasis on the Virgin and Child developed in various ways—as near us because they are like us, rather than distant from us because they are so different from us, as those who evoke our love more than our awe or even our fear. If we jump forward another century and to the north, where the Renaissance was developing in the Netherlands, Belgium, and Germany, we can observe this development in Jan Van Eyck's *Lucca Madonna* (ca. 1433). The manner in which the Virgin holds her right breast toward the mouth of the suckling babe could not be more humanizing, even if there is a stylized stiffness, particularly in the emotionless infant that suggests something beyond the natural. The throne is a textile canopy (like a marriage canopy under which the Eternal Bride sits) and carpet, overrun with images of fruits and flowers (like paradise), setting the Virgin and Child off from the rest of the image and thus from us, as the light of heaven from the window to their right illuminates them.

The canopy is flanked by four *trompe-l'oeil* figures; in their fourness they suggest the four evangelists, but the figures appear to be lions, re-minders of the description of Solomon's throne in 1 Kings 10:18ff, and therefore a reference to the Virgin as *Sedes Sapientiae* ("Seat of Wis-dom"). On the windowsill sit two apples; a third rests in the hand of the Christ Child. This confirms the layered symbolism that the fruit is intended to offer. The apple has come to be understood as the fruit eaten by Adam and Eve in enacting the Original Sin.[27] Christ's entrance into the world had as its purpose to assuage that sin; thus he grasps the fruit of evil firmly in his infant hand (like Heracles grasping and stran-gling the serpents in his crib). The fruit of sin has become the fruit of salvation.[28]

Another century forward and back in Italy, and any of Raphael's splendid Madonnas, such as the *Small Cowper Madonna,* (ca. 1505), yields an even more emphatic humanization of the *sacer*-connected Mother and Child. The latter is a chubby baby, and everything about his gestural language and hers underscores that notion. They are set in a completely natural landscape, and gone from it is nearly every super-natural element: only the halos remain, but so faintly as to be nearly in-visible. Such a work is at the opposite end of the spectrum from what

Byzantium offers with respect to symbolic statements of *sacer-profanus* focus.

Raphael's work is part of the High Renaissance, a phrase encompassing works created around 1500–1520 that yield the most complete fulfillment of the principles of humanism, of dynamic repose by means of stable yet energized composition and sweetness of detail. By the end of the second decade of the century, the crisis for Western Christendom of the Protestant Reformation has begun to take shape, and by the 1530s there is a reflective crisis in Western art—particularly in Italy. That visual crisis, called Mannerism, expresses itself by means of strange distortions of body and gesture, compositions that are deliberately off-kilter and colors that sometimes shock the eye with their vehemence.

Among the more interesting painters associated with the Mannerist crisis was Francesco Mazzola of Parma, known as Parmigianino,

FIGURE 29 *Parmigianino:* Madonna with the Long Neck, *Florence. ca. 1535–1540.*

whose figures are often attenuated, almost Byzantine, in both torso and limbs. One of Parmigianino's more stirring works is *Madonna with the Long Neck,* (1534–1540) (see Figure 29). Her preternaturally sinuous neck is matched by startlingly long and thin fingers. The atmosphere is strangely charged with sensuality, from the diaphanous covering of the Virgin's belly and its umbilicus—emphasizing that source of salvation— to the long exposed leg of the child extended from among the crowded group of angelic figures who push in on the Mother and Child. The Infant is asleep, but its overly long body with its slightly swollen belly, its bald head that looks more shaved than not yet grown in, and most of all, its drooping left arm, convey a sense of death, suggesting a *pieta;* it presages Christ's death and the mourning over him by his Mother.

FIGURE 30 *Jan Van Eyck:* Madonna with Chancellor Nicolas Rolin ("Autun Altarpiece"), *panel. ca. 1433 or 1437*

The Christ's future is further symbolized by the cold, uncapped marble column that is the visual foil for the tall Virgin and her column-like neck—alone it would presage that moment in Christ's Passion when he was bound to a column and whipped. But the small background figure with the extended scroll and the exposed leg that counterbalances the large, exposed foreground leg of the child-angel intensifies this. If, as some have suggested,[29] he is Isaiah declaiming a "voice crying in the wilderness" then his presence alludes both to that past prophetic moment and forward to the moment in the future when the words of not hearkening to Christ (but killing him instead) will be fulfilled.

By the late sixteenth and early seventeenth century, Michelangelo da Caravaggio was carrying the humanizing revolution to an extreme that shocked many of his contemporaries. In a variation on the combined theme of the Virgin and Child and the Adoration of the Shepherds, Caravaggio's *Madonna of Loreto* (1604) offers an exquisite Neapolitan woman standing in her doorway, barefoot, with a large infant in her arms. Their flesh glows with a resplendent light for which there is no obvious external source—it is the bright light of preternatural goodness that illumines them—and their respective haloes, offered in perspective, are barely visible circles. Kneeling before them on—or just above—the ground and steps leading to the doorway is an old peasant couple. Most disturbing to the artist's contemporaries, right before the viewer's face are the dirty bottoms of the filthy feet of the peasant man. Thus not only have the Virgin and Child been rendered unequivocally as a mother and child from the lower classes, but the sacred scene has been soiled by the most earthbound of *profanus* elements.

The significance of Caravaggio's conception can be underscored if we step backward in time to compare it to the *Madonna with Chancellor Nicolas Rolin ('Virgin of Autun')* of Jan Van Eyck (1437) (see Figure 30).[30] Nicolas was the powerful administrator of Burgundy at that time (his son, Jean, had just become bishop of the Cathedral of Autun, to which the painting was donated). He is shown kneeling at a *prie-dieu* within the Virgin's own *sacer* chamber, with his hands clasped in a devotional gesture. Without the traditional saintly patron, he has gained admission to this other-worldly space. The entire interior is distanced from both the outside world seen through the threefold windows (and beyond the parapet) and us, even as the hierarchy of intermediation to connect us to the ultimate *sacer* is contained within the image, offering the Christ Child, Virgin Mother, and an angel on the one hand, and the chancellor who is both more than we are and yet one of us, on the other. The Christ Child gestures benedictorily toward the chancellor; the angel crowns the Virgin with the crown of heaven, which transforms her seat into the throne of heaven and alludes to the future when she will be seated next to her son on that throne as his bride. It also confirms the idea that the chancellor kneels within a *sacer* space, interweaving the politics of his position with religion.

The garden between the windows and the parapet—a double allusion to the *hortus conclusus,* the closed garden of the Song of Songs ("A closed garden, my sister, my spouse") that is interpreted as an allusion to the Virgin and the Garden of Paradise to which we may be returned through the sacrifice of her Son—is laden with carefully chosen symbols. Peacocks strut. Blood-red roses with their thorns anticipate the Passion. Irises and lilies allude to aspects of the Virgin—for the iris, or sword lily, is most specifically a symbol of the Virgin in her sorrow at the suffering of Christ, whereas the ordinary lily is a symbol of her purity. As much as the world beyond the parapet is our world, it too has qualities that suggest otherworldliness: the sparkling Meuse River that dominates the central opening symbolizes the "pure river of water, clear as crystal," flowing through the New Jerusalem of the messianic future. Even the historiated capitals have their pedagogic role to play, drawing from both the Hebrew biblical and Roman pagan traditions. Thus, to the left the stories of the expulsion from Eden, Cain and Abel,

FIGURE 31   *Coronation of William II by Christ, Cathedral Monreale, Sicily, mosaic. Twelfth century* CE

and the drunkenness of Noah all focus on sinful moments, while on the right the justice of Emperor Trajan is drawn from Roman historiography.

All of which leads in an important direction: the interweave of religion and art with politics. The mosaic Virgin and Child (ca. 1120), in typical Byzantine style on the east wall of the south gallery of the Haghia Sophia, are flanked not by the saints we might expect but instead by the figures of Byzantine Emperor John II Comnenus and Empress Irene, seated to either side of the sacerdotal pair, as if participating in a *sacra conversazione*. We might simply construe this as a humble spiritual statement of drinking at the fount of eternal life, were the royal couple facing toward the Virgin and Child. But instead they face out at us, as frontal and hieratically disposed as the Virgin and Child. There are two slight differences between the central and side figures: the eyes of the two mortals focus sideways toward the center and, *symmetria*-style, each holds a different object pushed toward the center (she the scroll of imprimatur and he the bag of money for the upkeep of the faith and its structure). So, too, their height is rendered slightly lower than that of the Virgin and Child, and the outline of their haloes is of a different hue— but the fact is that their heads are surrounded by haloes not one whit smaller than that of the Virgin. Thus the viewer receives an unequivocal message not only of their support of the church but of divine approval— to the extent of sanctification—of the royal couple.

In some cases, divine approval of political leadership is direct, and in others, subtle. In the small church popularly known as La Martorana, in Palermo, Sicily, the sweep of twelfth-century mosaics includes a rendering of the Norman king Roger II being crowned by Jesus himself.[31] It is true that the figure of Christ is much larger than that of the king, offering a good instance of significance perspective, and seems to hover above the ground line. On the other hand, not only is the king far more sumptuously arrayed than his patron, but he *is* being crowned by *God,* offering a far more important visual statement to the viewer than the small matter of significance perspective provides. The hand of God the Father is also seen, reaching down from heaven with its fingers held in a rhetorical, benedictory—confirmatory—gesture. This is a Christian equivalent of the imagery and message on the Babylonian Code of Hammurabi: the *sacer* is envisioned approving the actions of a sacerdotally conceived political leader.

The identical idea is expressed a stone's throw away, in Monreale, where, on a wall of the cathedral, Roger's grandson, William II, is also represented being crowned by Christ (see Figure 31). His right hand, rather than offering to us a benedictory gesture, is placed on William's crowned head. William, in turn, gestures to Christ in a manner reminiscent of the Virgin or John the Evangelist at the Crucifixion, as if to draw our attention to Christ, but also to Christ's gesture of imprimatur.

The figure of Christ on a throne is one that would have been familiar to most of Christendom. He typically holds his text, opened or closed, as a book or a scroll, in one hand, and gestures benedictorily with the other. Occasionally, instead of a text, the *orbis mundi*—the sphere of the world—rests on his knee, supported by that left hand. It is difficult to imagine that this kind of image was not intended to resonate with the

FIGURE 32 *Simone Martini:* The Annunciation, *tempera on wood panel. ca. 1333*

constituents of Otto II, who is shown on an illuminated page of the *Registrum Gregorii* (ca. 983) (see Figure 4). Otto is enthroned, with a scepter in his upwardly extended right hand and the *orbis mundi,* adorned with a cross, cradled in his left. Flanked by four allegorical figures of the nations doing him homage—they offer similar circular objects (but without crosses or other marks)—he surely would have been at least unconsciously associated by the viewer of that era with the image of the enthroned Christ attended by angels or the four evangelists or various saints.

⎯⎯⎯ ✹ ⎯⎯⎯

Christ and the Virgin Mother bring us back to the beginning of the Renaissance in an *Annunciation* (1333) by Simone Martini and his student, Lippo Memmi (see Figure 32). The spread of gold leaf across the spaceless space and crocketed and cusped gothic architectural framework present a distinct medieval flavor. Nor has numerological language been forgotten, from the triune composition that separates the main scene from the side panels to the simultaneous emphasis on five offered by way of the five ogival arches that articulate the upper part of the frame. So, too, the viewer *sees* (seeing is believing) the words—*Ave gratia plena dominus tecum* ("Hail, [thou who art] full of grace, the Lord is with thee")—issuing in embossed gold from Gabriel's mouth toward the Virgin's ear. Soaring within the central arch, the dove of the Holy Spirit swirls within a circle of seraphs. But below, a marble floor that terminates at the gold background "wall" suggests naturalistic space, the centerpiece of which is the vase of lilies of Mary's purity. And the garments of the angel are still floating from the realm above whence he has arrived, even as he kneels so that his action and the words issuing from his mouth move antiphonally upward; both his garments (which billow out) and those of the Virgin (which tense inward), as well as those of the side figures, are delicately webbed in the kinds of shadows that bespeak an interest in the *profanus* naturalism of garments on bodies in space.

Gabriel's wings are bird-like, conveying a naturalistic rather than supernatural feathered quality to them. Crowned with the olive wreath, the angel also bears an olive branch to underscore the news he brings of the birth of the Prince of Peace. Most charmingly, the Virgin positively recoils at the news—her face is an encapsulation of shock, with its upturned brows and puckered lips—in a powerful representation of the dismay suggested in the Gospel statement that the spirit was disturbed within her. The whole thus offers an explosive moment that draws us in by its highly emotive quality, particularly with regard to the response to that moment by a very human, young girl filled with *pathos*. This is the earliest known large altarpiece for which the Annunciation is the central element; thus it is artistically transitional from a number of viewpoints.

One of the loveliest renderings of the same subject, a century later, is the *Annunciation* (ca. 1428) now in the Diocesan Museum in Cortona by the Florentine Dominican friar Fra Angelico. The painting is divided into three parts by the slender front columns of the portico where the Virgin sits—or rather, appears to be rising, neither yet standing nor any longer sitting—and greets the annunciating angel who, in dynamic *symmetria,* genuflects as he gestures toward her; his bent knees push down as hers push up. The leftmost third leads the eye, by way of the lush garden with a closed gate—the *hortus conclusus*—to a background scene in which the cherub of Genesis 3 is shown expelling Adam and Eve from the Garden of Eden. The Pauline principle of Christ as the new Adam and Mary as the new Eve is articulated in a visual context that is medievalist in its *sacer*-symbolic transcendence of normative time/space. The Virgin's gesture suggests simultaneous surprise and beatific acceptance; the dove of the Holy Spirit hovers in a golden glow above her head and a *trompe-l'oeil* image that might be taken as that of God the Father (some have interpreted it as the Hebrew biblical prophet Isaiah) gestures from the medallion in the portico spandrel.[32] Both she and the angel are molded with just enough chiaroscuro to suggest flesh-and-blood creatures like us, yet little enough to suggest that they may be part of another, more perfect reality than ours.

Perhaps the most interesting archaic element is the inscription of phrases extending from the angel's mouth to the Virgin's ear and back from her to him. Yet here, too, Fra Angelico has followed a slightly new course of action. The words from the angel are from Luke 1:35—"The Holy Spirit shall come upon thee, and the power of the Highest shall overshadow thee"—rather than the more traditional "Hail Mary, full of Grace . . . ," and the Virgin responds, "Behold the handmaiden of the Lord; be it unto me according to thy word," from Luke 1:38. Her words are written upside down, visualizing the words going from right to left, from her to him. We are both in the midst of tradition and in the throes of visual revolution.

One may, once again, observe the parallel rather than identical direction taken by that revolution in the north by a comparison with a contemporary Annunciation scene that forms the center of the triptych

FIGURE 33   *Robert Campin (Master of Flemalle):* The Merode Altarpiece, *tempera on wood panel. ca. 1425*

known as *The Merode Altarpiece* (ca. 1426–1428) by the anonymous Master of Flemalle (see Figure 33). Typical of the Flemish sense of everyday place, and of a northern conviction that "corporeal [objects may be] metaphors of things spiritual," the event transpires in a homey setting.[33] Even so, body language is stiff, garments are lushly overflowing, perspectival concerns are more awkwardly expressed than in Italy—and the entire work is overrun with symbols. This Virgin of Humility sits on the floor before a pewlike bench, with a sacred book in her hands. The naturalistic emphasis includes the way in which the whoosh of the angel's arrival has blown out the flame of the candle on the table—its bright whiteness a symbol of the Virgin herself, who is about to be transformed, like the candle. But at the same time, Christ is represented by the candle, transformed, and his mother is represented by the candlestick that holds the candle. We recognize the almost complete absence of supernatural elements: no haloes, no words across the picture plane, natural illumination occasioned by the windows from left and rear that allow the light of heaven to fill the room. But in observing them we see an exception to the *profanus* atmosphere: the tiny, barely noticeable figure of an infant Jesus bearing a cross in his arms, who swoops like a bird in a flood of golden rays from the leftmost window into the room, at a diagonal angle that will carry him just over the genuflecting angel's head toward the ear of his mother.

We are reminded not only of the dove that traditionally plays this visual role but also that the dove symbolizes the Holy Spirit and that its swooping is intended to call to mind the "spirit of the Lord [that] swoops over the face of the waters" in Genesis 1:2. This, in turn, reminds us that we are witnessing the new creation and the beginning of a new covenant. The word has already been transformed into flesh, and given the lack of a fire in the fireplace, we may infer that the season is late spring, the season of rebirth—nine months prior to the winter-time Nativity that will follow. Spring is far enough along not only for the home fires to be extinguished but for flowers to flourish—those on the table are pure, white lilies. Do we also recognize in the hanging towel and laver nearby not only another reference to Mary ("a fountain of gardens" and "a well of living waters") and to her purity, but in the flanking of the towel by two bright red textiles the coloristic juxtaposition of her purity and his blood: an allusion to the Crucifixion to come? We certainly recognize this in the rich redness of her garment. We also notice that her womb is subtly emphasized by the star-like pattern of illumination on that part of her garment covering her belly. This is an allusion to the *Revelations of St. Brigitte,* in which Christ said to her: "I took a body without sin or lust, entering the maiden as the sun shining though a clear stone. For as the sun entering the glass hurts it not, so the Virginity of the Virgin abode uncorrupt"—and it completes the circle of symbolism begun by the sweeping Christ child and furthered by that blown-out candle, for St. Brigitte also refers to physical illumination being "reduced to nothingness" by the radiance of divine light.[34]

That we see only sky through the windows of the Virgin's room suggests that the setting is tower-like, which, together with the shower of gold bringing Christ toward her ear and womb, reminds us of the Greek story of Danae who, imprisoned in a tower, was visited and impregnated by Zeus in the form of a shower of gold. The result of that divine-human encounter was Perseus, a hero who would destroy the evil Medusa with her hair of snakes and rescue Andromeda from the jaws of a sea serpent. Danae's tower became, in the medieval period, a symbol of chastity, and the visitation from Zeus a symbol of the Annunciation as early as the thirteenth century in Italy; here it has been carried north. The notion of her chamber being above ground level is reinforced by the two wings of the triptych: the donors who financed the work kneel (in a closed garden in which a rosebush grows) before the stairs leading up to her space; on the other side, Joseph plies his carpenter's trade (by the fifteenth century he is

FIGURE 34   *Piero della Francesca,* Baptism of Christ, *Sansepulcro, Italy, tempera on panel. ca. early 1450s*

depicted frequently as a craftsman providing for his family by good work) in a workshop also above the level of the donors, for beyond his window the city stretches out *below.* The object placed on his windowsill to advertise his skills (there's a second one on his workbench) is a mousetrap—an allusion to St. Augustine's comment that the marriage of the Virgin and the Incarnation presaged by the Annunciation were a trap set by God to catch the Devil by fooling him as mice are fooled by bait in a trap.[35]

The Christ and Marian narratives interweave and encompass the Joseph narrative in the varied story of the Nativity.[36] One interesting visual aspect of that story is its physical setting: the tendency in Eastern Christian art is to place the holy family in a cave, whereas Western art tends to locate them in a manger, an idea brought into Italy by Giotto from the French Gothic tradition. Duccio, for one, often combines the two traditions, keeping the cave of the Byzantine tradition but embedding within it a wooden structure. An *Adoration of the Magi* from after 1482, by Sandro Botticelli, places a shed structure within the massive but crumbling stones of an earlier building: the old order is crumbling, in all of its pride—that old order, while it ordinarily refers to the old covenant, given the obvious Roman nature of the architecture, also suggests the old pagan order—to be supplanted by a new order and a new covenant that emerges in a humble structure. In Botticelli's painting, the figures in the painting who lead from the two sides toward the holy family form both a dynamic X-form when seen compositionally together with the lines of the manger architecture and also an incomplete circle. The part missing, left open so that we have an unobstructed view of the holy family, is the part where we, the viewers, stand, completing the circle of figures in attendance by our presence. The painting therefore carries the notion of time-transcendence one step further than previous works of art. Viewers in every age who stand there and look at the *sacer* scene are invited to see themselves as spiritually *present* at it and thus to be part of its consequences. This inclusion is reinforced by the self-portrayed artist on the lower right who turns to look out at us over his shoulder.

Within the chronology of Jesus' life, an obvious next stopping point is his encounter with John the Baptist. Among the most stunning Baptism of Christ scenes is that by Piero della Francesca (ca. 1450) (see Figure 34). The strident visual humanism of the mid-fifteenth century is evident in the solid Tuscan peasant figures of Piero's Christ and John, with their broad faces and scraggly beards and hair. We are reminded, particularly where Piero's Jesus is concerned, of the biblical comment regarding the Anointed One, that "he hath no beauty that we should desire him." But there is more. Christ's glowing columnar body, his solidly rooted legs and feet are visually echoed by the luminous tree trunk that, also rooted, extends its branches with their lush foliage into the heavens. There is no halo for this Christ, in this naturalistic portrayal, but the simple earthenware bowl from which St. John pours water over the Lord's head is placed precisely to play that visual role. We might also almost miss the dove fluttering directly above Christ, its wings outspread, so similar is its configuration to the wisps of cloud fluttering across the sky, which in its rich, radiant blueness symbolizes God the Father. Thus all three elements of the Trinity are present but symbolized by means of completely *profanus* elements. That Christ is the central figure is not only a matter of composition; he is the connection between heaven and earth—literally, since his body is submerged by the earth of the background, while his head is surrounded by the heavens. Moreover, a gentle light emerges toward the heavens from behind the earth: it is the light of dawn—of a new era, a new covenant—of which Christ is the embodiment.

⁂

The beginning of the earthbound end of this narrative of a new covenant is the Last Supper, perhaps the most famous version of which was painted by Leonardo da Vinci in 1495–1498 for the refectory of Santa Maria delle Grazie in Milan. It was placed there so that the monastic diners would always have this gastronomic moment looking over their shoulders as they ate. Leonardo diverges from tradition, in placing all the figures, including Judas, on the same side of the table,

FIGURE 35   *Leonardo da Vinci:* The Last Supper, *fresco from Santa Maria delle Grazie, Milan, (detail). ca. 1495–1498*

grouped in four sets of three around the central figure of Jesus (see Figure 35). That "natural" breakdown of twelve in Renaissance thinking accords well with Christian numerological symbolism: three as trinitarian and the number of theological virtues, and four as the number of the Gospels as well as the cardinal virtues, the times of day, the seasons of the year, and the rivers flowing through paradise. Moreover, together, three and four equal seven, which corresponds to the number of the gifts of the Holy Spirit, the joys as well as the sorrows of the Virgin, the days of creation and of the week—and of completion and perfection. Multiplying them back to where we began yields not only the number of apostles but the hours of the day and of night and the number of gates in the walls of the New Jerusalem of the messianic era.

There is thus a dynamic tension between an extremity of order and the chaos of the moment, as there is between medieval thinking and Renaissance style. We understand from everyone's body language that the Master has just announced that "one of you shall betray me"—thus Leonardo has chosen an earlier moment in the Gospel narrative than was traditionally shown—as, in one way or another, eleven of the apostles either lean or gesture toward Christ ("and they . . . began everyone to say unto him, 'Lord. Is it I?'"). Judas, however, recoils backward, distinguished from the others by that bodily gesture and by the way in which he alone is enveloped in deep shadow; he offers no protest, knowing what the others do not, and reaches instead for the not-yet-blessed sop.[37] Although no halos appear, the head of Christ is centered in the middle of three windows, beyond which a lightening sky suggests an imminent dawn—but the light might just as well be emanating from the head of Christ.

This Last Supper is the prelude, then, to the betrayal in the garden, the coming before Pontius Pilate, the various experiences of suffering (the Passion) that lead to the Crucifixion. In this subject, too, we can discern a predilection for the figurative robustness of a human-emphasized Christ as we move within the Italian Renaissance. Andrea Castagno's frescoed *Crucifixion* (ca. 1445), painted originally for a cloister of the monastery of Santa Maria degli Angeli in Florence and later moved to the Convent of Sant'Apollonia, offers a powerfully muscled Christ—a big-boned man of the woods and fields—suffering stoically and heroically for his adherents, his fingers curling in pain; his mother is a toothless old peasant woman placed in counterpose to a solid-featured St. John. These are figures whose feelings we *feel,* even as they retain archaic plate-like halos (albeit angled in perspective). There are no other supernatural elements. Space is both natural and beyond natural: an evident ground-line landscape and a dark blue sky, but so dark that its shape is not discernible (the light has gone out of it; that light is the luminous Christ who glows within the lunetted space). Time is collapsed, since saints Bernard and Romuald are also in attendance. Between time and space are the skull and bones lying at the foot of the cross—simultaneously a reminder of the mortality of the body that awaits us all and a continuation of the tradition according to which Adam's remains lay buried beneath the hill of Golgotha. The redemptive blood of Christ, seeping into the earth, washed over the bones of the aboriginal sinner, cleansing them and him and thus making paradise possible for him as well. The second Adam redeems the first.

That second Adam's uniqueness resides in being as fully *sacer* as he is *profanus,* and so earthly death is merely the prelude to resurrection and heavenly ascent. Within the narrative that encompasses his journey from *sacer* to *profanus* and back to the *sacer,* Crucifixion, Deposition, Lamentation, and Entombment are ultimately followed by Resurrection. There is no more stirring version of this moment than that by Piero della

FIGURE 36 *Piero della Francesca:* Resurrection of Christ, *San Sepulchro, Italy, fresco. ca. 1455*

Francesca, whose *Resurrection* dates from the late 1450s (see Figure 36). The sky that emerges from the earth as Christ emerges from the tomb is even more explosively predawn than in Piero's *Baptism*—and is balanced, below, by the soldiers guarding the tomb who, in their awkward poses, have fallen asleep. They have missed the rising of Christ from the tomb and are about to miss the dawn of the new era and all that it implies. We are warned, by implication, to choose whether or not to be like them; one figure leans back against the tomb while another leans out toward us, including us in the completed sphere of space. The choice is also underscored right to left across the picture plane: winter and trees without leaves are depicted on one side, while spring and trees richly adorned with foliage are depicted on the other. That choice recalls the two trees in the Garden of Eden associated with the wrong choice by our aboriginal ancestors: the tree of knowledge of good and evil—the eating from which brought about death for humanity—and the tree of life, from which they didn't manage to eat before being cast out of the garden. That is the tree to which Christ will lead his constituents.

Certainly the most remarkable aspect of the fresco is Christ himself, who again connects heaven to earth by his placement, as he connects the dark figures below to the bright skies above. On the one hand, Piero has reverted to the use of a halo barely hidden among the wispy morning clouds. On the other, he has outdone himself with respect to a Christ that is both classically beautiful of body and as unclassically ugly of face as the most earthbound of Tuscan peasants, with wiry beard and mustache, broad nose, low forehead—and deep circles around eyes that stare out at and through us in an almost ghoul-like manner. He has, after all, just risen from the dead, and there can be nothing elegant about that. The dark physical elements of the moment underscore both the human reality of which Christ was part and the supernatural spiritual brightness that is this moment's conceptual antipode.

⸺∞⸺

This handful of examples of how the symbolic vocabulary of Christian art expanded even farther in the Renaissance than in the previous millennium could easily be multiplied with regard to subjects, artists, and media. One important instance of a slight move outward in subject is the frescoed image in the Sistine Chapel in the Vatican of *The Giving of the Keys to St. Peter* (1481) by Perugino. The setting in which the apostle kneels before the Master, the center of an undulating line of foreground figures, is the courtyard of the temple in Jerusalem. It is there that Jesus hands over the keys to Heaven and Earth, in referring to Peter as the rock upon which the New Church shall be built. Peter's name is thus punned upon, since in Greek *Petros* means "rock." The work is part of a papal program that interweaves religion and politics as much as any imagery does, for each pope is the successor to St. Peter. The image of Christ bestowing upon the apostle his imprimatur speaks implicitly of the extension of that imprimatur to the wearer of the papal tiara. The side structures that dominate the background of the fresco are distinctly Roman arches of victory, of which several are still visible in Rome. This pair is modeled on the Arch of Constantine, that bridge figure between pagan and Christian Rome, and each is decorated with three candlesticks. This is the number of the Trinity, but combined, the arch candles offer the number of candlesticks typically placed on the altar at High Mass, and the number of the days of creation and of divine perfection (symbolizing power, majesty, wisdom, love, mercy, and justice).[38]

In spite of the handling of space to give a sense of natural depth, the timelessness of the moment is expressed by the double group of figures in the middle ground: to the left, the moment when Jesus says, "Render unto Caesar that which is Caesar's," and to the right, the stoning of Christ. The temple—the New Church—that dominates the background, is not the temple as it had been nearly fifteen centuries earlier, but the idealized structure of the perfect reality-to-come. And yet it *is* that temple as it was believed to have looked, its faceted domed appearance a variation on the visual reference that was a constant throughout medieval Christian representation. This was, interestingly enough, the Dome of the Rock, the late seventh-century Muslim edifice devised by Abd'al-Malik on the presumed site of the Israelite and Judaean temples, which to this day dominates the landscape of Jerusalem (see Chapter 4). Both the Jewish and the Christian visual traditions came to view the destroyed temple as architecturally similar to that structure. Centuries of architectural hegemony dominated the visual imagination for generations of Europeans visiting the City of David and returning with that domed image embedded in their memories.

The Christian rendering ranges from absolutely domed to quasi-domed; Perugino's is actually eight-sided, whereas, for instance, in the panel painting done by his most illustrious pupil—Raphael—of *The Marriage of the Virgin* (1504), the "temple" is circular. The eight-sidedness of Perugino's dome underscores the birth of the new covenant signified by the passing of the keys to St. Peter, for eightness relates to renewal and rebirth into perfect life. The new covenant marking the new creation begins with the eighth day (the first creation cycle having been a seven-day one). It also relates to Christ's resurrection on the eighth day after he entered Jerusalem. Perugino's image synthesizes elements drawn from Filippo Brunelleschi's dome for the cathedral in Florence (1420–1436), with its eight-faceted reddish roof. Not only had Brunelleschi studied the Roman Pantheon, which served as an inspiration, but one might reason that the notion of the Jerusalem temple lurked within his mind.

There certainly can be little doubt that such a thought was in the forefront of the bevy of architects, culminating with Michelangelo, who recreated St. Peter's Church in Rome in the course of the early sixteenth through mid-seventeenth centuries. Given the failure of the rapprochement agreement signed by the pope and the Greek patriarch—in the Florence cathedral, beneath Brunelleschi's dome, in 1439—to heal the schism between the Eastern and Western churches, and given the complications of the Western schism that had exiled the pope to Avignon between 1308 and 1378 and until 1415 maintained a split between pope and antipope, the desire by the middle of the century to assert papal leadership of the Christian world is no surprise. In 1506 Pope Julius II commissioned Donato Bramante to completely rebuild St. Peter's, which would, among other things, assert the basilica's position as the New Temple and Rome as the New Jerusalem. The project would eventually engage twenty popes and fourteen architects.

For our purposes the most important of these are Bramante, Michelangelo, and Gianlorenzo Bernini. The first two shared the vision of a commanding dome rising above the point where nave and apse meet transepts. This form would confirm the structure as the spiritual center of the world, emulating and succeeding the domed temple in Jerusalem (as the latter came to be pictured), even as it reinvigorated the position of Rome as the political center of the Western world, a position the city held when the Pantheon's dome was designed and built. An oblique confirmation of the architectural aspect of this notion may be found in Raphael's 1512 fresco in the Vatican apartments depicting *The Expulsion of Heliodorus from the Temple*, in which the spaces between the receding arches suggest the rounded swelling of the lower part of a cupola—in particular the "space" closest to the forefront arch. Raphael shared the sense of the Jerusalem temple as domed.[39]

The pope's commission to Bramante to rebuild the church was followed a few years later by an invitation to Michelangelo and then Raphael to paint the papal chapel and apartments. As these projects within the Vatican proceeded, the architecture of St. Peter's was placed in a succession of hands, but by 1546 Michelangelo took it over. He reinstated Bramante's original Greek-cross plan—Bramante had decided to change it to a Latin cross—but raised the height of the dome and, rather than Bramante's hemisphere, designed a ribbed dome. The play between rectilinear and circular elements, together with play between tetra-partiteness and penta-partiteness, is powerful and apparent, the entirety dominated by that dome, which in turn dominated the Roman skyline in a manner distinctly related to the manner in which the Dome of the Rock dominates the Jerusalem skyline.

FIGURE 37   *Gianloranzo Bernini*, Baldacchino, *St. Peter's Church, Rome, bronze.*
1624–1633

Within the basilica, Bernini would mark the meeting of the nave, apse, and transepts—and below, the grave and putative place of St. Peter's martyrdom in what had once been Nero's Circus— six decades after Michelangelo's death. Bernini's structure, a canopy, or baldachin, was sought by Pope Urban VIII as the centerpiece of the interior of the recently completed building (1623). What was needed was no ordinary baldachin but one visually significant enough to draw the viewer's eye all the way from the entrance to the enormous nave (Michelangelo's Greek-cross conception had ultimately been supplanted by a Latin cross). The eye-catching bronze canopy— the bronze torn from the revetment within the portico of the fifteen-hundred-year-old Roman Pantheon—wraps vines around a quartet of twisted columns, gigantic versions of the twisted early Christian columns that had stood before old St Peter's, which were, in turn, an allusion to the destroyed temple in Jerusalem (see Figure 37). Tradition held that St. Helen, mother of Emperor Constantine, found the remains of the temple columns on her pilgrimage to Jerusalem and that they were twisted. These were brought to Rome and erected before the doors of the new church of St. Peter then being built and now, thirteen centuries later, were commemorated by Bernini, further emphasizing St. Peter's Church as the temple of the New Jerusalem.

A close look at the vines reveals that they are laurel, associated with the Barberini clan of which Pope Urban VIII was a member. But no plant derived as a symbol from the pagan past could serve more effectively as a statement of transformative redemption. The laurel, after all, was the nymph Daphne, pursued by Apollo and changed by her river god father into a plant and thus rescued from Apollo's clutches. It symbolizes not only spiritual transformation but redemption, as well as the condition of partaking of two distinct realms (Daphne, like Christ, had both human and divine parentage); it also signifies Apollo himself, who after the event made the laurel wreath his personal emblem and a symbol of victory. And Apollo, god of light and healing, is an obvious pagan forerunner of Christ. The victory of which the laurel wreath speaks here is that of eternal life over death.

The project occupied Bernini for nearly a decade (1624–1633). The master devised four large volutes rising from the twisted columns and joining over the center to support the symbolic orb and its cross (the *orbis mundi*). The totality offers a stunning visual intermediary between the individual and the cavernous enormity of the basilica, a combination of tomb-marker, symbol of continuity with the early church, and statement of Roman Catholic and papal resurgence in the midst of the by-then century-long struggle with Protestantism. Bernini's recreation of the piazza outside the church, which he began under Urban's successor, Alexander VII, in 1656, also joined that struggle. It creates a microcosmic space (the conceptual mirror of the microcosmic space within the basilica) in which crowds could gather for the papal benediction given *Urbi et Orbi* ("to the city and to the world"). The pope would speak forth from the loggia, beyond which the soaring roof, and beyond it, the dome, and beyond that the vast sky, rise. The huge oval piazza, held between double rows of columns, suggests the outflung and inward-pulling arms of a living, loving organism. The colonnade is crowned with an army of saints, who peer down encouragingly as the arms of Mother Church gather in the faithful to be blessed by God through God's vicar, the lineal descendant of Christ's chosen deputy.

∞

In the context of the Renaissance and the subsequent baroque and rococo eras, an expanding circle of subject matter not only encompasses a broad range of straightforward Christian issues but pagan mythological subjects turned around in esoteric and complex symbolic Christian directions. In backtracking in time to Botticelli's *Primavera* (ca. 1478), we encounter an allegorical painting of spring that is also an exercise in the Neoplatonism popular among the intellectuals of Botticelli's era (see Figure 38).[40] The foliage and light coming through it are arranged around the shoulders and head of the central figure to create a large circular halo, hinting that the allegory also contains Christian layers.

FIGURE 38   *Sandro Botticelli:* Primavera, *Florence, tempera on wood. ca. 1482*

After all, spring is the season of rebirth, and the Christ narrative is the ultimate account of rebirth into eternal life. Thus the central figure with the demurely tilted head (tilted as Christ's head is, so often, on the cross) appears as much like the Virgin Queen of Heaven as the pagan Aphrodite, her belly glowing as if a light were shining on it, and the cherubic Eros above her a symbol of mystical, spiritual, divine love and not frisky springtime lust. The lush, dark trees that fill the upper part of the painting are orange (or golden apple) trees, a symbol of chastity, purity, generosity—in short, of the Virgin, but also of the fruit of the Fall and the Redemption.

The nymph Chloris, pursued by the wind god, Zephyr, is transformed before our eyes into Flora, the flower-bedecked and blossom-strewing personification of spring, so that before us a rich and fabulous paradise opens up. Such simultaneity of what in the *profanus* would be sequential moments shouldn't surprise us: this is, after all, the *sacer* realm. But Chloris' transformation also alludes to poetry by Ovid, with whom the late fifteenth-century Florentine Neoplatonists were so familiar, in whose *Fasti* (V, 193–212) the transformation from maidenhood to womanhood is effected by the successful suit of the man who becomes a maiden's husband.

On the other side of the painting, Hermes, messenger god, raises the staff (from which the usual serpent is missing) that heralds his messages. Apollo, god of light and knowledge, of medicine, poetry, and music, gave the caduceus to Hermes in exchange for the lyre. Thus a pagan symbol of both death-dealing and life-giving (the caduceus) has intersected the Christian symbol of the Fall (the serpent twined around a tree trunk) within the garden of redemption. Near the upraised caduceus the oranges or golden apples are small clouds. Hermes raises his staff to dispel them, as the Guide of Souls into the *sacer* (the realm of death but, for the righteous, the realm of eternal life).[41] His cloak is decorated with falling flames; fire both destroys and cleanses, and can also be associated with divine love.[42]

Hermes is also the leader of the Graces, who share the left side of the image in Botticelli's painting. While the three Graces offer a trinitarian significance (separate figures, they are joined hand to hand and are dissimilar yet strikingly similar in face and form), there is more to them. As the pursuit of the chaste Chloris by Zephyr transforms her into Flora (the personification of Beauty), so that triad of figures finds its contrapuntal opposite in the figure of Chastity (the central Grace) who intermediates between the flamboyant figure to her left—Voluptuous Pleasure—and that of Splendor (or Beauty) to her right.[43] It is toward the central figure that Eros aims his arrow, but the three, to repeat, are joined together, the hands of *voluptas* and *pulchritudo* upraised directly over the head of *castitas,* toward the *sacer,* in a gesture that echoes the gesture of Hermes. In contrast, all of the hand gestures of the right-hand trio of figures are in the opposite direction, from the *sacer* downward toward the *profanus.* And at the center, the figure of Aphrodite recapitulates both directions: her left hand gestures downward and her right hand upward, as if partaking of both realms, the *sacer* and the *profanus,* heaven and earth. She bridges all realms as the goddess of love, for that element is the ultimate center around which the world revolves and the ultimate connector between God and humans. In Christian terms, that center is personified by Christ, the God who comes from the *sacer* and, in sacrificing himself, returns to the *sacer,* out of his love for humankind.

This complex and esoteric pattern of thinking is furthered in the painting that parallels Botticelli's *Primavera,* his *Birth of Venus,* in which, rather than being chastely if alluringly garbed, the goddess is completely naked (like an unvarnished truth).[44] At first glance we understand the image as a visual distillation of that moment described in Hesiod's *Theogony* (190–195) when Aphrodite—born of the foam (Greek: *aphros*) of the sea, coalesced around the castrated genitals of Ouranos harvested by his son Kronos, the Titan—arrives, as a beautiful young girl, onto the shores of the island of Cyprus. It is a gruesome account of creation out of destruction: the birth of the goddess of love from an act of strife symbolizes the paradoxic tension in the universe between love and strife.[45]

But the Renaissance Neoplatonists, who were Botticelli's literary counterparts, looked beyond the horrific in more complex and esoteric directions, which include not only a wide range of classical sources but also biblical sources that are understood to coincide with them not by accident but by divine intention. Pico della Mirandola had asserted that the phrase in Genesis 1, "the spirit of the Lord hovers over the surface of the waters," alludes to the spirit of Love *("spiritus amoris")*.[46] This is what we see—Love incarnate—being swept ashore by the gentle Zephyrs, as the Hour of Spring (herself a figure of contrapuntal chasteness) greets Love with the flowered mantle that she is in the act of throwing onto the goddess's naked body. The goddess herself, while naked, covers herself in a double gesture; she is simultaneously chaste and sensuous: the embodiment of opposites. (She also recalls—is modeled on—Praxiteles' *Knidian Aphrodite* in her gesture of naked modesty.)

The exquisite creature that Botticelli sets before us is ushered forward by the foamy waves of the sea and also by a shower of rose petals that flutter from above out of the mouth of the wind. Thus heaven (Ouranos), far from expressing the dismay that would derive from a Hesiodic reading of the destructive event that preceded this moment, offers an approving response to the daughter who has taken solid and definite shape from the amorphous sea into which his seed has been spilled. The transformation of the destructive act into personified creative impulse receives a shower of approval from the victim of castration. Thus the unified Ouranos has succumbed *willingly* to the self-sacrifice of dismemberment that transforms the One into the Many and whose parts will ultimately be regathered into eternal resurrected life as One. Dismemberment or self-sacrifice as death leads to creation and eternal life.

Joy is expressed by the mystical rain of roses that accompanies the zephyrous spirit swooping over the waters.[47] Moreover, Pico asserted a threefold distinction among celestial, human, and bestial love, in which the fully realized human form is recognized as a reflection of the first, and both human and celestial are noble (whereas the bestial sort is dross). The naked Aphrodite is the unadorned celestial love taking apparent human form (perfect and yet paradoxically and strangely imperfect). And to tighten that circle, she and her clothed twin *(Primavera)* can be construed as symbols of the twin aspects of that personification of Christian love who is transformed in the descent from heaven to earth, self-sacrificed, and then unified with his source, and whose death yields eternal life to his constituents.

Such complex symbolic thinking abounded in the mind, as in the visual world of Botticelli and his contemporaries, and in those artists who followed him. Titian, for example, painted an allegory of *Sacred and Profane Love* (ca. 1515) in which, one might say, the synthesis in Botticelli's *Primavera* has been taken apart again (or on the other hand, the pair of Botticelli's canvasses has coalesced into one): the symbols of two forms of love are clothed and unclothed before us in one frame.[48] Both the discussion of Titian and of other artists' esoteric paintings could easily be multiplied. Interest in oblique and even obscure pagan-sourced Christian symbolism proliferates during the fifteenth and sixteenth centuries and beyond.

One of the more effective expressions of esoteric thinking from later in this era is the renowned *Burial of Count Orgaz* in Toledo, Spain, painted in 1586–1588 by El Greco. Before the viewer a miracle takes place: the appearance of Saint Augustine and Saint Stephen at the translation of the count's body in 1327 from its initial burial place in the Monastery of the Augustinian Friars to a sepulchre in the Parish of Saint Thomas. The moment is full of allusions to the contemporary world, as well as to other works of art by El Greco himself. The scene of Saint Stephen's martyrdom, painted elsewhere by the artist, is depicted on the chasuble of Saint Thomas, for instance.

The painter has depicted himself among the nobles and stares out at us. A Franciscan friar is shown in profile on the far left. A figure counterbalances the friar, to the far right, reading the funeral service. That is Pastor Andres Nuñez Madrid, patron of the painting, who commissioned it to celebrate his court victory over the Toledanos with respect to the continued fulfillment of the contents of the count's will.[49] Since that victory and the commission came more than 250 years after the event being depicted, we understand how fully we stand before the timeless time and spaceless space of the *sacer*.

Near Andres Nuñez Madrid, a figure with his back to us is positioned as we the viewers are, to imply our inclusion in witnessing the miracle.

However, his view is less fixed on the appearance of the two saints shown below, lifting the count's body, than on what is happening in the upper half of the painting. There we see the soul of the count, represented as a baby, being received into heaven through a series of curtain-like, cloud-like, flesh-like elements, as if being passed into and through the spreading orifice of a birth canal. That canal leads to rebirth into eternal life. The count's soul is raised by an angel, presented by John the Baptist and the Virgin Mary and received by Christ himself. Angels, saints, and prophets witness the moment, echoing the noblemen who witness its counterpart moment below.

The totality offers simultaneous miraculous occurrences in the mirrored realms of the *sacer* and the *profanus,* above and below, with regard to the soul and the body—and also potentially encompasses those within the painting and the viewers outside it as simultaneous witnesses to both occurrences. Where the count's soul is assumed, his fellow nobles can hope and expect to go, and so can the viewer who leads a virtuous life and whose faith is strong enough. The voice said to have been heard at the time of the miracle asserted that "such is the reward for those who serve God and His Saints."[50]

⸺⸙⸺

So, too, in the sixteenth and seventeenth centuries, particularly in the Netherlands, there is further branching out toward the *profanus* world and its elements, but with a *sacer* significance. Thus an ostensive religious painting may overflow with profane elements, and genre paintings may include visual symbols familiar from religious subject matter. In the work, *Christ in the House of Mary and Martha* (ca. 1550) by the Amsterdam painter Pieter Aertsen, the *sacer* subject matter and an extremely *profanus* wealth of visual images lead back and forth to each other (see Figure 39). We stare through a kitchen out into a courtyard set off so distinctly by its brightness that the light that suffuses it suggests a supernatural source. The latter source would, of course, be the Son, who holds forth (as reported in Luke 10:38–42) in a courtyard conceived within a classical architectural framework, thus suggesting *antiquity.* In looking into the depths of the painting we are looking into the past. Christ admonishes Martha that in complaining about Mary she is "fretting and fussing about so many things, but . . . the part that Mary has chosen [devotion to God] is best; and it shall not be taken away from her [as opposed to the worldly things upon which you are so focused]."

FIGURE 39 *Pieter Aertsen:* Christ in the House of Mary and Martha, *tempera on canvas. 1552*

It is those worldly pursuits that shape the foreground and middle ground of the painting. The "kitchen" is overrun with an overabundance of foodstuffs—implying gluttony—arrayed in a pyramidal configuration that leads toward the figures and the central arch in the background scene. The eye is doubly led by the food toward that scene through the luminous chain of elements—turnips, stuffed chicken, linens—that terminates with the figure of Mary, whose gesture and attention then carry our eye to Christ himself. The display of food is flanked by a scene, on the left, of a man in contemporary sixteenth-century garb attempting to seduce a young girl. One of the interesting features of this section is that the seducer, looking over his shoulder as if stopped by the sound of someone approaching, is looking back at the image of Christ and his circle, offering a second dissolution between present and past. On the right an eating and drinking scene in a contemporary setting but with figures in "biblical" dress more emphatically dissolves past and present into each other.

Is it mere coincidence that the number of figures in foreground and middle ground is eight—associated with the rebirth into eternal life? Certainly no viewer can miss the gigantic vase dominated by lilies that moves from bottom to top of the painting, literally connecting the kitchen to the courtyard while separating the seducer from Christ's admonishment to Martha. What is both a tour de force of the artist's ability to render still life and human figures is also a work that invites the viewer to consider the implications of the *sacer* filtered through a *profanus* lens. Aertsen's works were disseminated fairly widely in the form of prints that inspired many seventeenth-century Dutch artists. When we turn to familiar works of that century we shall consider the *sacer* agenda that may be recognized in them and with it an ongoing symbolic language, even if particular terms within that language are transformed.

CHAPTER 4

JEWISH AND MUSLIM SYMBOLS IN SACRED AND PROFANE CONTEXTS

Early Jewish Imagery

Judaism as we would recognize it—with its Bible, its prayer book, its life and festival cycle, its rituals—is a diasporatic phenomenon that resulted from the destruction of the temple and the Bar Kokhba Revolt (132–135 CE) some two millennia after the time of Abraham. Jews and Christians were initially ethnic and religious coheirs of the Hebrew-Israelite-Judaean tradition and heritage, but with increasingly divergent interpretations of it, which is reflected in the visual self-expression of the two religions.[1]

The foundation of Judaism is fourfold: God, the people of Israel, the covenant that binds the two together, and the land where the further details of that covenant were once worked out. The covenant is embodied most essentially in the Torah, the ethical core of which is the Decalogue. The temple was the location where the other three elements could be brought most effectively together, where God and the people could meet through the intermediation of the covenant articulated in the Tablets of the Decalogue, kept in the holy of holies, and through the priestly service and the sacrifices offered as an ongoing symbol of the relationship between the people and God.

But when the temple was destroyed, it became necessary for the people to find another means of maintaining that relationship and of centering the other elements of that fourfold foundation. The concept of the synagogue developed during and after the first exile. It flourished side by side with the second temple in Jerusalem, offering a temporary sacred center, a substitute until one might have the opportunity to make the pilgrimage to Jerusalem and participate in the ceremonies within the temple. It offered a *sacer* space away from that ultimate *sacer* space connecting the parts of the Judaean community throughout the world. After the destruction of the second temple, the synagogue was more emphatically perceived as a kind of temporary temple-in-exile, to serve until the awaited messianic time of return. The synagogue remained conceptually connected to the temple, focused on it, tied to it both in orientation and decoration.

The earliest examples of synagogue remains, predating the destruction, are those at Gamla and Massada, both oriented toward Jerusalem and the temple. With the proliferation of synagogues after the second destruction, the details of architectural structure and decorative vocabulary become more clearly defined. In Judaea and the Galilee—*Palestina* as the Romans renamed the province after the Bar Kokhba Revolt—we can follow this development with some clarity until the eighth century. The early types were built according to the Talmudic injunction that a synagogue be placed at the highest point in the community to facilitate its role of intermediation between the *profanus* below and the *sacer* above, and they were often situated on a platform for further elevation.

Platform elevation was typical of contemporary Roman temples; it was a feature that the Romans absorbed from the Etruscans. But the notion of symbolic elevation toward the divinely inhabited heavens *(sacer)* can be carried back as far as the Mesopotamian ziggurat. Talmudic injunction also dictated that synagogues be built near a body of water in order to facilitate acts of ceremonial purification. That this was in place quite early seems corroborated by the words of the New Testament in Acts 16:13, where Paul, proselytizing among his fellow Judaeans, goes on the Sabbath "out of the city gate, *by the river side,* where he thought there would be a place of prayer."

We see this double feature, and others, in the synagogue remains at Capernaum (Kfar Nahum) dating from the second through the fourth centuries, and rising by the northwestern shore of the Sea of Galilee.

The 360-square-meter structure was elevated on a platform, its interior divided by a colonnade in basilical style—but with a back row of columns perpendicular to the other two. More emphatically than at Massada we are offered a three-sided rectilinear configuration, open on the entrance facade. In turn, the front façade presents a threefold entryway. This configuration offered a symbolic echo of the three courtyards into the temple, which permitted gentiles, Israelite-Judaean women, and Israelite-Judaean men, respectively, to define the limits of access to the triple-divided temple, as well as the three divisions within the temple itself. For diasporatic Judaism, this also symbolizes the threefold configuration of the Jewish community for ceremonial purposes (most particularly that of reading from the Torah): those descended from the high priesthood of Aaron (the Kohanim, who served in the temple), corresponding to the central door, flanked, right and left, by the doorways that symbolized those descended from the broader priestly tribe of Levi, and those forming the remainder of Israel. It also suggests the rabbinic statement that "the world stands on three things: Torah, service, and righteous deeds." We recognize in this configuration the sibling of the later-developed threefold Trinity-symbolizing church doorway.

Further north, at Katzrin, a similar configuration of doorways prevails, as within, the remains of a similar configuration of columns is still to be observed, together with the surrounding benches and bouleterion-type interior. Other Galilean synagogues of the period also exhibit this configuration. The pair of pilasters that visually support the gable above the central entrance at Kfar Bar'Am may be understood to echo the pair of columns before the temple. Over the doorway, an arched gable, known as a Syrian gable, would have allowed air and light into the interior.[2] At Khorazim we find an apparently new aspect of the principle of orientation: a permanent Torah niche. This was an indentation in the wall facing Jerusalem (in the case of Khorazim, east by southeast), its temple and the temple's holy of holies. In the Torah niche, the scrolls inscribed with the expanded expression of principles engraved on the tablets once kept in the holy of holies in the temple would reside, either permanently or during prayer services.

The most dominating visual object from the temple in Jerusalem was its seven-branched menorah. The Romans depicted this candelabrum in bold relief on the Arch of Titus, being carried by captive Judaeans into Rome following the suppression of the Judaean revolt and the destruction of the temple (see Figure 18). We have observed how the decor of the temple menorah itself demonstrates the principle of eclecticism so prevalent in the Hellenistic-Roman world, adorned with a Persian frond motif and resting on a base marked by a Greek lozenge motif filled with the symbols of the zodiac recast as symbols of the twelve tribes of Israel (see Chapter 2).

Both the principle of syncretism and the symbol of the temple menorah prevail in the decorative schemata of early synagogues. But the menorah, in its sevenness, offers a reminder not merely of the temple candelabrum but of the seventh day commanded by God as a Sabbath—a commandment central to the covenant offered from Sinai at the moment of redemption from Egyptian slavery and return to the Land of Promise. Thus, its sevenness makes it a symbol of hope with all that that connotes with regard to covenantal promise and responsibility. The seven-branched menorah appears frequently both within and beyond the early synagogue. It will become the most ubiquitous symbol of Jewish self-expression over the centuries.

Other imagery also abounds. At Khorazim, a Greco-Roman vine motif repeats itself around the upper interior cornices of the synagogue, together with clusters of grapes and floral motifs. Derived from the Roman imagery of lush swags, as on Augustus' *Ara Pacis*, such motifs play the same sort of role, but differently oriented: they suggest, in their abundance, the fecund reality made possible by the all-giving God, not the all-giving emperor. Moreover, the grape-clusters suggest the ritual Sabbath and festival wine that symbolizes joy and also recalls the blood sacrifices at the temple, which help articulate the covenantal connection between the people and God. Thus, these motifs allude to the twin messages of the covenant: promise of redemption and responsibility for living up to the covenantal commandments. The *Mishnah,* in its treatise dealing with non-Jewish worship practices (*Avodah Zarah* IV:2), mentions wreaths made from vine branches and ears of corn—generic visual concomitants of fertility—but in early synagogue decor, such wreath-imagery also serves as a more specific reminder of the first fruits once brought to the temple at the time of the Israelite-Judaean autumn harvest festival (the Feast of Booths—*Sukkot*). By extension, such imagery also commemorates the passage in the wilderness from slavery to freedom during which forty-year period the Israelites dwelled in booths.

So, too, synagogue lintels at Khorazim and Katzrin are decorated with an egg-and-dart motif, a ubiquitous element throughout the Greco-

Roman world. For the Jews who prayed in such synagogues, this motif may have been merely part of an accepted decorative vocabulary, but in the pagan world of an earlier age, it was originally part of the artistic arsenal of addressing the *sacer* with the hope of its aid in fertility. (See Chapter 1.) That this sensibility is also part of the Jewish decorative thought of that time cannot be simply ruled out. So, too, prosperity is symbolized by the motif of the fish, as so many Galilean fishermen would associate that creature with survival. The fish would come to symbolize the fruitful goodness of the Sabbath and specifically the Sabbath afternoon meal (the *Se'udah Shleesheet*), just as for the early church it would recall the miracles of the draft of fishes and the loaves and fishes recounted in Mark 6:38–44.

An interesting instance of cross-connection from this period is a detail from a third-century synagogue or church mosaic floor at Tabgha in the Galilee. Some have interpreted the image of bread in a basket flanked by a pair of fish as Sabbath loaves and fish, which eventually became the main dish of the third meal of the Jewish Sabbath. But that idea may not have been in place until the medieval period in Europe. Thus others have seen the juxtaposition of bread in a basket and fish as suggesting the miracle of the loaves and fishes. The image underscores how blurred the line is between early "Jewish" and "Christian" places of worship and their visual symbols.

Then, too, the imagery at Capernaum also includes another ubiquitous symbol, the six-pointed star (see Figure 40). But this is *not* yet a Jewish motif. It is a frequent pagan symbol that ties the *sacer* to the *profanus* in offering two triangles opposed to, and intertwined with, each other: identical geometric forms that, in being opposed are *not* identical to each other even as they precisely mirror each other. Moreover, the triangle facing downward, as we have seen, is a symbol of the female pubis that first appears in the Neolithic period; here it is interwoven with the upward-thrusting triangle as a stylized male phallic symbol: *sacer-profanus* opposition/identity is expressed with reference to fertility.[3] The early synagogues include not only six-pointed stars but also five-pointed and seven-pointed stars reflecting the rich and varied vocabulary of the Hellenistic-Roman era. Each of these star configurations was in broad use and can ultimately be traced to important symbolic issues that reflect the *sacer-profanus* relationship. Thus, the five-pointed star refers to the connection between the four elements of *profanus* reality and the fifth—the

FIGURE 40   *Synagogue lintel, Capernaum (detail, with six-pointed and five-pointed stars). Third century* CE

*quint*essence, which from the pre-Socratic philosopher Anaximander to the Romans was understood to undergird reality.[4] The seven-pointed star relates to the seven *planetes* that, from Sumer to Rome, were understood to soar predictably and periodically across the heavens against the sphere of fixed stars and to be governed by the gods associated with them—gods who govern so much of what transpires in the *profanus*.

⸺⸙⸺

While most of the early-period synagogue remains are found in Palestine, a substantial structure has also been uncovered at the site of the ancient port city of Ostia—where the Tiber River pours out into the Tyrrhenian Sea after having flowed through the imperial capital, Rome. *Ostia Antiqua* served the Romans as playground and commercial center, as gateway to the western Mediterranean, and as defense against would-be attackers of the upriver metropolis. There, a synagogue flourished, the lower foundations of which go back at least to the first century CE, but which were rebuilt perhaps three times through the late fourth century. Away from Ostia's center, its placement conformed to the Talmudic injunction to be built near a water source, since the ancient course of the Tiber brought the river virtually curving around the corner of the synagogue building.

Architectural and decorative elements remain visible from the fourth-century structure, which is entered, not unexpectedly, through a triple doorway. Within, a pulpit at one end suggests the location from which the *sacer* text of the Torah was read and expounded upon, while at the other, what is identified as the Torah niche oriented worshippers toward Jerusalem. Such a double-focused internal structure for a synagogue—pulpit at one end, Torah niche at the other—will eventually emerge as the salient architectural feature of the medieval synagogue.

The carved relief decoration presents not only the ever-present temple menorah motif but also appropriate accompanying images: for example, the *shofar*—the ram's horn blown originally in the temple and then throughout Israel-Judah to announce festivals, and blown, still now, throughout the Diaspora to begin and end the ten-day new year celebration. The image of the ram's horn is an allusion to the critical moment near the inception of what would become the Israelite-Judaean-Jewish religion when, instead of allowing Abraham to slaughter his son Isaac, God provided and accepted a ram, caught in the branches of a thicket by its *horns*. The redemption of Isaac and the hope for redemption from exile for the Jewish people came forth with the sound and symbol of the *shofar.*[5] Other elements decorating Ostia's synagogue include the *lulav* (palm branch) and *etrog* (citrus fruit)—key ritual elements of the harvest festival of *Sukkot,* at which time of year the fertility of the land and its fruits is prayed for in distant corners of the Diaspora.[6]

There is an apparent second format for early diasporatic synagogue development. Frescoes and mosaics became increasingly dominant as media of decoration, and the use of relief sculpture diminished. The most extraordinary instance of this is found at the opposite end of the Roman world from Ostia, by the banks of the Euphrates River. There, at the edge of a Roman garrison town founded to guard the eastern fringe of the empire from the resurgent Mesopotamo-Persian power of the Sassanians, is a synagogue. The garrison town was called Dura Europus, and its last synagogue, with frescoes dating from the middle of the third century, offers a panoply of redemptive and historical symbols.

By this time, the eastern flank of the empire was weakening. To strengthen the most exposed wall of the city, in 256 CE the Romans tore the roofs from the buildings in the streets behind it and constructed a great rampart by filling buildings and streets alike with dirt. It didn't help. The Sassanians still overran the city, and Dura eventually disappeared: no more would be heard of it until the twentieth century. But as a consequence of being buried, the buildings and their decorations survived the centuries. The synagogue was one of these buildings; its decor a testimony to the fact that Jews have in many places and times not been inhibited about producing visual art, even of a highly figurative sort.[7]

Dura exhibits a fixed Torah niche, centered on the western wall, facing Jerusalem (see Figure 41). As the holy of holies was the most distant point from the entrance into the temple in Jerusalem, here its spiritual descendant was placed at the most distant point from the synagogue door. The niche offers a pair of columns—not actual columns but images painted on the wall in *trompe-l'oeil* Roman style to simulate marble columns—recalling the pair of columns said, in Kings and Chronicles, to have graced the entryway into Solomon's temple. The allusion to Solomon's God-guided temple construction project carries messianic implications. It is not merely the recollection of the temple but the hope for its future restoration—a restoration in a perfect Davidic-Solomonic kingship in a world that recognizes them as the ultimate kings and the Israelite God as the only true God. The décor of that niche identifies it as

FIGURE 41   *Western wall paintings of synagogue with torah niche, Dura Europus on the Euphrates. ca. 250* CE

a physical centering point for the present community and the meeting point between idealized past and redemptive future.

The area above the niche is adorned with symbols of the temple and of redemption. That most prominent of temple objects, the seven-branched menorah, dominates. Near it are the *lulav* and *etrog,* as at Ostia, as well as a schematized image of the temple itself. Finally, balancing the menorah is a representation of the moment of transmission of the *personal* covenant from one generation to the next to which the *national* covenant of Israel with God traces its origin: Isaac's redemption from intended sacrifice. The forms of Abraham, Isaac, ram, tree, altar are very rudimentary, as the very hand of God comes forth from a cloud to deliver Abraham's son. As Isaac was, so will his descendants be redeemed.

Other nearby images repeat the allusions to the temple, to hope for its restoration and with it, reclamation of the land and redemption of the people. The temple actually appears in two separate registers along the western wall fresco cycle, once with its gates thrown open, so that one sees within to the holy of holies, with a purple curtain—a *parokhet*—across it, as mentioned both in 2 Chronicles 3:14 and in Josephus, its royal color Davidic and therefore messianic. In lieu of three courtyards leading from the outermost area (accessible to all, pagans and Judaeans alike) to the women's courtyard (accessible to all Judaeans), to the innermost (accessible only to adult Judaean males), three doorways occupy the temple courtyard wall: a solution to the difficulty of representing three-dimensional space in a two-dimensional format. It is the number of doorways that develops in synagogue architecture.

Within the open temple courtyard, Aaron, ancestor of the Kohaynic priesthood—the high priesthood of the temple—is shown, accompanied by attendants, by animals for sacrifice, and by the objects of temple ritual. A second representation of the temple balances the first, this time with its doors closed. What one notices immediately in both scenes is that while they contain what we may call Jewish content—specific symbols of the temple—stylistic details synthesize Hellenistic Greco-Roman elements with Sassanian-Persian ones. Both temple representations are Greco-Roman in style. In the open temple image, the sacrificial animal on the left wears a wreath in the style of Greco-Roman animal offerings. Aaron is accompanied by attendants whose belted tunics are vaguely Hellenistic, but whose pantaloons are distinctly Persian in style. Aaron himself, his name written in Greek (the language, perhaps, another convention from the non-Jewish world around), is clothed in a wine-colored priestly robe with gold border and clasp, and a peculiar hood; these conform to the description of the garb of Zoroastrian priests in the Persian religious texts, the *Avestas*.

Along with scenes pertaining to the temple, a plethora of redemptive scenes from Israelite-Judaean history covers the Dura synagogue walls. Moses appears again and again. He leads the Children of Israel out of Egypt and through the Red Sea. Within the same register, a chronological sequence moves from the Israelite passage to the Egyptians drowning in the waves to the Israelites on dry land. This accords with the style of late ancient and medieval art: we are in the realm of the nonlinear *sacer*. Three chronologically ordered aspects of a story can appear in one register, and significance perspective renders the most important figures, not the nearest, as the largest ones. Thus David, larger than his brothers and garbed in royal purple, is shown in the act of being anointed by Samuel.

The message of redemption, shared with Christian art but couched in different conceptual terms (its emphases more within the post-messianic *profanus* than in the *sacer*), is nowhere more clear than in the rendering of the vision of bones refleshed and resurrected, based on Ezekiel 37. Another distinction from Christian visual self-expression is also evident here, for the struggle to portray figures as ethereal representations of what we shall become is accompanied by the struggle to represent an imageless, invisible, intangible God (rather than the tangible anthropomorphic God of Christianity) engaged in redemptive actions. The solution has been to depict disembodied hands—the metaphorical "hand of God" visualized literally—to symbolize the unportrayable deity, drawing the resurrected righteous ones up out of the grave.

Figures are generally schematized so as to deprive them of naturalism: is the artist's skill that limited, or is this a deliberate attempt, as with early Christian and Byzantine art, to deemphasize the purely physical in order to emphasize the spiritual? It is in fact not the majesty or power of the particular individual and that individual's character that is of consequence, but the authority of the abstract idea—divine will—of which the individual is the manifestation. Thus, while disembodied hands may be a means of concretizing the abstract God, denaturalized figures offer a means of deconcretizing the conveyors of abstract divine message. Flat, frontal, schematized representation of body is accompanied by large heads and eyes as windows into the soul. On the other hand, the square, black halo of mortality (the four corners connoting the four elements, and four sides the four directions of earthbound reality; the color connoting death) appears first in the Dura synagogue, in the image of Moses in historical earthly moments, and later at sites of early Christian art.[8] Here, too, the expanded use of the fixed Torah niche, orienting worshippers toward Jerusalem and decorated with reminders of God's redemptive covenantal relationship with Israel, is the ancestor of the early church apse, orienting worshippers toward Jerusalem and decorated with reminders of the *sacer* presence within the Christian *profanus*.

By the late period of early synagogue development—the fifth through eighth centuries—Christianity had established itself firmly as the only *religio* within the Roman Empire. Synagogues were reduced; the structures were apparently flimsy, reflecting the diminishment of communities both in Palestine and throughout most of the Diaspora. Thus, the synagogues of this era seem to have turned to the floor as a primary location for adornment—or at least that is the only part that has survived. A panoply of mosaics, easily disappearing underground, has survived in different parts of the Mediterranean world. The most famous and complete mosaic floor surviving from the early sixth century is in the Galilee, at Bet Alpha (see Figure 42). Its visual program divides the nave floor into three parts, a symbolic echo of that division for the temple: an entry area, a main area, a holy of holies. So, too, the entrance is marked by three doorways. One passes from the triple entryway to the synagogue foyer, where, in a rough-hewn figurative style, the binding of Isaac is depicted. Whereas the inscriptions identifying the artist at the main doorway are bilingual—in Greek and Aramaic—here the identifications are all in Hebrew. They include names and narrative details.

FIGURE 42 *Schema of mosaic nave floor from synagogue at Bet Alpha. ca. 525 CE*

The figures are extremely rudimentary, either because artistic skill has further diminished since Dura Europus, or because Bet Alpha is a provincial backwater in the sixth century, or because of the greater technical difficulties of the mosaic medium than that of the painted, or because of that ongoing struggle to represent yet not to represent figures connected to the *sacer*. The paradox of God's disembodied guiding hand emanates from a sunburst.

The main body of the Bet Alpha floor is an extensive circle within a squared area. The four areas formed outside the circle represent the four seasons—as the Hebrew inscriptions indicate.[9] The circle itself is a vast wheel-like formation; between the spokes the twelve zodiacal constellations are identified. This recalls the zodiac motifs on the base of the temple menorah depicted on the Arch of Titus. As there, we may here understand the adoption and adaptation of a common Hellenistic motif. The twelve symbols of the zodiac have become symbols of the twelve tribes of Israel—and thus the main area that united the community of Bet Alpha and tied it to other Jewish communities in prayer is decorated with a reminder of that paradoxic unity: separate tribes, separate communities, yet one people. Moreover, as a calendrical device, it is likely that this vision is a practical expression of that which binds the *profanus* of Israel together wherever it is dispersed throughout the world. The calendar with its festival cycle ties Israel together and ties Israel to God.

The center of the zodiac is occupied by another adaptation of pagan artistic representation. The figure of the sun god is drawn in his chariot by four horses, crowned by a burst of light—a "halo." This image may simply be a symptom of borrowing without concern for the potentially troublesome meaning of the motif. On the other hand, the era when the Bet Alpha floor mosaics were being devised coincides with the early period of Jewish mysticism called *Merkavah*—"throne"/"chariot"—mysticism. The take-off point of *Merkavah* thought is the mystical bridge between ourselves and God symbolized in the first chapter of Ezekiel by the chariot or throne—a *merkavah*—which he construed as the *merkavah* of God itself revealed to him, soaring and hovering in the heavens. One can't see an invisible God, but Ezekiel approaches that impossibility with his vision of the *merkavah* of God. The center of the whirling wheel at Bet Alpha perhaps offers the sun chariot become the *merkavah*—the vision of a vision of approach to the invisible Presence, the belief in which is the center of and binding force among the twelve Israelite tribes and the far-flung community of Judaism.

As one reaches the innermost area of the Bet Alpha floor, approaching the Torah niche oriented south toward Jerusalem, the *parokhet* has been represented as pushed aside to reveal the brass doors of the temple and the holy of holies. Thus, the temple and its holy of holies lead to—are symbolically part of—the synagogue Torah niche. Rather than representing protective winged lion cherubs, the mosaic separates the cherubim into pairs of roaring lions below and bird forms above. Accompanying these are diverse objects associated with the temple. Most prominent among them is the menorah. But that symbol is presented twice, a doubling that is observed hereafter with growing frequency. While on the one hand this serves the aesthetic requirements of symmetry, on the other hand—particularly since the two menorot are not identical—they may also be symbolic reminders of the First and Second Temples, each with its seven-branched menorah. Or perhaps the one (with flames extinguished) represents the temple in the past, the other (with flames kindled) the temple of the messianic future. As a symbol of redemptive promise, the double image also corresponds to the double articulation of the Ten Commandments in the Torah, once in Exodus and once in Deuteronomy.

We observe the need to overwhelmingly fill in the visual space with objects and geometric and other abstract forms, lest negative forces from the *sacer* enter the *profanus* through the work of art, which is the gateway to the *sacer*. This *horror vacui* reminds us of the distinction between what Judaism teaches and what Jews have actually believed. There should be no fear of negative forces entering the *profanus* from the *sacer* as Judaism understands the latter: singular, all-powerful, all-good. But Jews have believed, through the centuries, in demons and evil spirits. Is this what accounts for *horror vacui* at Bet Alpha, or was the artist merely following a convention?

Synagogue and Symbol from Medieval to Baroque

The symbols found in early synagogues abound in other aspects of Jewish life and death. The seven-branched menorah and temple motifs are found on everyday objects made of metal, pottery, glass, and wood from the earliest diasporatic period onward. Everyday oil lamps from the second through fourth centuries—bronze and clay, from Syria, Palestine, and Tunisia—are often decorated with the menorah, together with the ram's horn and the *lulav* and *etrog*. So, too, are gold leaf-decorated glass bottoms in the Jewish catacombs of Rome from the fifth century. But there is a rather abrupt interruption in the physical evidence of Jewish visual self-expression between the eighth and eleventh or twelfth centuries. It appears that Jews, as an increasingly outer-edge minority, turned away from objects that could not as easily be carried from one place to the next. Another possibility is that such objects, including synagogues themselves, have simply not survived.

The earliest surviving medieval synagogues are in Worms, Germany; Prague, Bohemia (the Czech lands); and Toledo, Spain. There is a continuity of symbolic language that connects them to what we have noted in antiquity. Architectural form and decorative style varies in feel, depending in part upon whether the synagogue was contrived in the Christian or the Muslim world. In all cases, the décor is limited to the interior, and any desire to build a structure that towers above the community has been thwarted by the reality of Christian and Muslim regulations limiting the height of synagogues and by a desire not to be conspicuous.

The earliest synagogue of which we possess continuous records into our own time, in Worms, nestles among the edifices of the narrow alley that once served as a Jewish quarter. It was first built in 1034; it was destroyed and rebuilt in 1175, and then destroyed and rebuilt a number of times in the thirteenth century and the sixteenth and seventeenth centuries, and most recently destroyed in 1938 by the Nazis. The current edifice was rebuilt long after World War II, more as a museum than as a functioning house of worship, since there is virtually no Jewish community left to use it. Its décor reflects the eleventh and twelfth and, to a lesser extent, the thirteenth through seventeenth centuries. The exterior is humble and unassuming. The tripartite doorway is gone and so, at first glance, is the tripartite interior characteristic of ancient synagogues. Absent, too, is any hint of basilical structure or even the cruciform presented by the nave-transept-apse configuration typical of Christian ecclesiastical edifices. In structure, the synagogue and its successors elsewhere resemble medieval town halls more than any other building type.[10]

The most common type in the eleventh through fourteenth centuries offered a "double-nave chamber." This structure helped solve the interior space problem posed by the double focus of the synagogue—the Torah niche, now evolved as the *aron hakodesh* and the *bimah,* both inherited from the ancient synagogue interior. The *aron* was placed at one end of the chamber, and the *bimah* was positioned in the center of the room, flanked by the two support columns that created the "double nave."[11] This sort of construction defines the interior of the Worms synagogue and the Alt-Neu Shul in Prague, said to date from the late thirteenth to early fourteenth centuries—its foundation stones, according to legend, coming from the destroyed temple in Jerusalem.[12] It is in any case the oldest European synagogue in continuous use. The double nave offers a kind of "anti-symbol" in being consciously non-church-like. The same is true of the stylistic details in the Alt-Neu Shul. The architect introduced into the standard Gothic style of the ceiling bays a fifth, purely decorative rib to eliminate the suggestion of cruciform that the standard repertoire of structural rib crossings presents.

Viewed from the side, the "double nave" *has* maintained the tripartite division of the ancient synagogue interior: the back area is dominated by the seats for the congregants; the middle area (which, around the periphery, may also include seats) is dominated by the *bimah*; the front area is dominated by the *aron hakodesh*. The division is simply not as obvious as it appeared on ancient mosaic floors. Moreover, by raising the level of the *bimah*, a symbolic elevated "synagogue" within the synagogue has been engendered: a raised central focus connects the community to God through prayer and the reading and expounding of God's word, and offers a sacerdotal space within the sacerdotal sanctuary space.

The fourteenth-century synagogue in Krakow, Poland, places the *bimah* in the center of the space, where an island is naturally created by the flanking columns that separate it from the areas before it and behind it (see Figure 43). The elevation and *sacer* separation of the *bimah* are even more pronounced here than in Worms or Prague. And a symbolic issue has been

FIGURE 43 *Synagogue, Krakow, Poland, interior detail with* bimah. *Fourteenth century*

emphasized. The Talmudic injunction to "build a fence around the Torah" has most often been interpreted with regard to fulfilling the Torah's prescriptions.[13] Here, that metaphorical phrase has been turned in a literal visual direction: the *bimah,* where the Torah is taken to be read, is ensconced within a wrought-iron fence.

The Torah is the ultimate sacerdotal intermediary between the people *(profanus)* and God *(sacer)* and thus is simultaneously separated from the community and intimately ensconced within it. This is expressed on several symbolic levels, from the fact that it is carried among the congregation and its outer coverings touched with reverence, to the fact that any adult male, and not a special priesthood, reads it, but using a special pointer, rather than touching its parchment with bare, *profanus* fingers. It is also expressed by the evolution of the Torah niche as the *aron hakodesh,* the holy ark. Like the *bimah,* the *aron* is also typically elevated. As with the Torah niche, the *aron* directs the faithful toward Jerusalem, but unlike that ancestor, its act of orientation eventually became more symbolic than actual. Thus the *aron* was inevitably placed in the eastern wall of the medieval synagogue, for "eastward" was treated as the direction toward Jerusalem and thus toward God, even when the *sacer* city was actually not due east.[14] The concept is reflected in the acronym offered by the Hebrew word for "east." The consonants of the word *mizrah* stand for *Mitsad Zeh Ruah haHayyim*—"from This Side [comes] the Spirit of Life." *Mizrah* is to Jewish verbal symbolism what *ichthus* is for Christian verbal symbolism, each indicating to its constituents the source of salvation.

There is more to this, for the ultimate focal point of orientation for the Torah niche and the holy ark was not merely Jerusalem nor even the temple in Jerusalem, but the holy of holies within the temple. In the temple, the entrance to the holy of holies was occupied by a decorated curtain: a *parokhet.* The orienting Torah niche in the early synagogue may have possessed a curtain. In the medieval synagogue a *parokhet* was hung before the *aron hakodesh,* further underscoring the role of the synagogue as a temporary temple-away-from-the-temple-until-such-time-as-the-temple-be-rebuilt, the primary focus of which, the *aron hakodesh,* in possessing such a *parokhet,* functioned as a temporary holy-of-holies-until-such-time-as-the-holy-of-holies-be-restored. The symbolic role of the *parokhet* continues into the modern era.

Contemporary with these architectural developments in central and eastern Europe were those in Europe's southwest corner. Sephardic Jewry derives its designation from the Hebrew word for Spain— *Sepharad*—and there, at the medieval crossroads of Christianity and Islam, a distinct Jewish culture evolved in the tenth through fourteenth centuries. The geographic heart of that culture was Toledo—and here in particular the beginnings of a variant on solving the problem of double focus on *aron* and *bimah—hechal and tevah,* as Spanish Jews referred to them—developed. In Toledo's Abulafia Synagogue, we know, from fourteenth-century miniatures, the *tevah* (the *bimah*) was placed not in the center but against the western wall. Thus its *hekhal* and *tevah* were at opposite ends of the spatial axis.

FIGURE 44 *Abulafia Synagogue, Toledo, Spain (detail of wall decoration).* 1356

The interior synagogue decor clearly absorbed the influence of Islamic style. In Toledo's late-twelfth-century Joseph Ibn Shushan Synagogue, the interior, subdivided by four arcades, is reminiscent of the great mosque in Cordoba. Thick octagonal columns (their eight-sidedness a reminder that on the eighth day after birth a Jewish male formally joins the community through the circumcision ceremony) are connected by distinctive Moorish-style horseshoe arches, and their gilded capitals are richly carved in the floral and geometric abstractions characteristic of Islamic adornment. In the Abulafia synagogue (1356), the interplay of decorative elements emulates the Islamic manner of connoting the interplay between God and ourselves: God is singular, eternal, and immutable, where we are multifarious, short-lived, and ever-changing. The decorative patterns are simultaneously infinitizing and finitizing: frames made of infinite patterns close off sections of infinitizing pattern.[15] Abstract and intricate, endless repeating, complex, attenuated details are the visual ground in which verses appear— divinely-inspired words from the Psalms—underscoring God's presence among us in this meeting point between *sacer* and *profanus*. Floral and vine motifs intertwine with inscriptions: double columns in a blind colonnade with poly-lobed arches, geometric configurations of endless variety, curving in contrast to rectilinear Hebrew print. Words inspired by and addressed to God interweave with the mathematical devisements of human mind (see Figure 44).

Although the demise of Spanish Jewry during the century that culminated with the Inquisition and the expulsion of Jews from Spain by 1492 aborted further developments in Iberian synagogue devisement, the bipolar solution to the problem of double-focus was carried into exile from Spain, appearing in the Sephardic synagogues of northwest Africa and southern France and carried to decorative perfection in northern Italy. In sixteenth-century Italy the flowering of the Sephardic bipolar configuration is wedded to an opulence of detail and exuberance of pattern consonant with the Christian Renaissance and baroque periods.

The placement of the *tevah* against the western wall was generally accompanied in Italy by its elevation, as in the Ashkenazi world. But ascent

to the *tevah* was then emphasized by a pair of staircases reflecting a chain of stylistic influence emanating from Michelangelo's design for the Senate building in the Campidoglio in Rome. In the 1648 Padua synagogue, such a staircase leads to a *tevah* that typifies the principle of an elevated *sacer* space within the *sacer* space, enclosed in elegant columns and crowned by an opulent top that alternates rectilinear with curved scroll forms. Moreover, the axis of *tevah* and *hekhal* is emphasized by the barrel-vaulted ceiling, coffered in baroque mode, which connects the two focal points from above (see Figure 45). This offers the additional virtue of permitting the placement of a window, reminiscent in form of the ancient synagogue's Syrian gable, that

FIGURE 45   Tevah *from synagogue in Padua, Italy. Sixteenth century*

allows light to pour in across the *tevah-hekhal* axis. Since light symbolizes God's presence, the Padua configuration allows God's presence to
sweep toward the *hekhal*. The configuration is also unusual in that the
tevah and the *hekhal* are placed along the long walls of the sanctuary—
the opposite arrangement from what we have ordinarily observed. This
feature combines the ideal of east-west orientation, placing the ark toward Jerusalem, with the practical: the limited space yielded to the Jewish community required that the synagogue be longer north-south than
east-west.

The entrance is on the ground floor of an unassuming structure; one
must ascend a flight of stairs to get to the synagogue sanctuary. Even
that detail symbolically addresses the desire to elevate the *sacer* space
in accordance with rabbinic injunction. Such a formulation, wedding
the conceptual to the practical, may have originated in Venice, where
frequent flooding from the canals would render it necessary for important rooms in any edifice to be above ground level. In Venice a series
of five synagogues originating in the sixteenth and seventeenth centuries clustered within the ghetto area.[16] There a vibrant Jewish community developed, made up of groups from different parts of the
Euro-Mediterranean world. The Scuola Levantina—the Eastern Synagogue—was built to serve Jews who came mostly from Greece, Turkey,
and Cyprus. The synagogue structure dates from 1535 to 1540, although it succumbed to serious renovations in the late baroque period,
sometime after 1650.

From the lower level, one ascends to an opulent sanctuary. The
hekhal commands one end, with a classicizing triangular pediment and
Corinthian-capped columns that suggest echoes of the temple in
Jerusalem. At the opposite end of the sanctuary, one ascends to the
tevah along curved steps identical to those in Padua. The *tevah* columns
are twisted: by way of the influence of Gianlorenzo Bernini, they evoke
the columns of the temple. So significant was Bernini's baldachin in St.
Peter's as a world-scale monument that its image captured the imagination of artists throughout Europe. The recurrent representation of
Yachin and Boaz as twisted columns on Jewish objects, from the late
seventeenth century until today, reflects the influence, directly or indirectly, of Bernini's baldachin.[17]

Many Sephardim, leaving the Iberian peninsula, took refuge in
southern France. In Provence, they built synagogues in Carpentras and
Cavaillon. The Cavaillon synagogue, just south of Avignon, has walls

that are said to date from 1494. But the structure was entirely rebuilt between 1772 and 1774. The sanctuary, elevated to the second floor of the structure, as in Italian synagogues, is nearly as high as it is long, and higher than it is wide: one feels as if one were in the interior of a large jewelry box. More obviously, it resembles the salons and private chapels of the late Louis XV period, with the curvilinear, floral, wood-carving in gold leaf, decorating its pure white walls with the irregular, nature-like forms of rococo adornment. That decor extends to the upper reaches of the *tevah*, raised as a balcony with a canopied center: the ultimately elevated platform from which to expound on the sacred scrolls. Along the opposite wall, near the *hekhal*, is a small, lushly decorated chair ensconced in an elevated niche. The Chair of Elijah is brought down to ground level for use every time an eight-day-old male child is joined to the community through the ceremony of circumcision,[18] over which Elijah is said to preside as a kind of patron. The influence of their neighbors' devotion to saints has made its way into the Jewish community, which accords an analogous status to the prophet who is also traditionally held to be the harbinger of the messiah. He who is associated with the beginning of a new era comes to be associated with the beginning of a new covenantal life.

Jews from the Sephardic world also converged on Amsterdam. In the seventeenth century, Holland was religiously tolerant and a hotbed of intellectual and artistic output and commercial well-being. The Sephardic Jews had established their congregation in Amsterdam by the sixteenth century, and by the seventeenth century were dedicating the edifice that still stands as the Spanish-Portuguese Synagogue. This structure brings us back into the Ashkenazi world of north central Europe. It is perhaps the fusion of Sephardic and Ashkenazi thinking that yielded, in 1675, a vast hall-type synagogue with its *tevah* toward the center.

The sanctuary is lit by 613 candles (symbolizing the 613 commandments of the Torah)—in a style not dissimilar from Amsterdam churches of the seventeenth century. The *hekhal* is a massive, tripartite neoclassical structure, with the women's section elevated as a balcony, encircling the sanctuary on three sides. The colonnade upon which this neoclassical gallery rests thus recalls the three-sided colonnades of the synagogues in Palestine in late antiquity. As general European ecclesiastical architecture of the period looks back, in part, to the Greco-Roman beginnings of Western style, synagogue style also looks back to that period when the synagogue edifice was in early formulation.

Imagery Within and
Beyond the Synagogue

The basis for Jewish ceremonial art, and in particular for adorning the Torah, is an interpretation of the words in Exodus sung by the Israelites after their redemptive passage through the Red Sea: "This is my God and I shall glorify him." *Anvehu* translates both as "I shall glorify him" and as "I shall beautify/adorn him." The invisible God itself cannot, by definition, be visually adorned, but the objects that are part of the ceremonies of addressing God, and the Torah as the mediating word of God, *can* be: to glorify God's word is to adorn and glorify God.

Torah texts are simple black on white: no imagery is permitted. But the Torah scrolls are covered, in the Ashkenazi tradition, in decorated and inscribed textile material. In parts of the Sephardic world the Torah casing—called a *tik*—is made of hard substances: woods inlaid with ivory, metals, and stones. The Torah scrolls are crowned, sometimes with two *rimmonim*: two small crowns, one to rest on each of the two spindles around which the double scroll of the Torah is wound. *Rimmonim* are often shaped like town towers, complete with bells, recalling those bells as a source of warning. The bells in the Torah *rimmonim* sound its passage through the congregation, so that all can both give way and draw near to God's word as it passes by. The high priest in the temple wore a garment fringed with bells that also warned people of his approach as he moved through the outer temple precincts, and the Torah is a symbolic stand-in for him until the messianic era.

The bells on the high priest's garment were pomegranate-shaped and so sometimes are the Torah *rimmonim*. In fact the meaning of the Hebrew word *rimmon* is "pomegranate." The pomegranate is a symbol of richness and plenty, with its numberless seeds—but one thread of tradition counts those seeds as precisely 613, the number of commandments in the Torah, and so the pomegranate symbolizes the Torah, with its endless richness of issues and ideas. Yet another tradition likens the neat rows of pomegranate seeds to rows of little boys studying the Torah day in and day out as they grow toward full adult enfranchisement in the *sacer profanus* that is the covenantal people.

Often, one *keter*—crown—covers both Torah spindles. Such a crown emphasizes that the Torah is also a symbolic stand-in for a once and future divinely anointed Davidic king. Torah crowns might be embellished with familiar Jewish symbols such as the seven-branched menorah. Their décor might reflect shared symbolic traditions. Thus deer (such as we have seen in the Christian visual tradition) that suggest the swift eagerness with which one embraces the study of God's word, or birds, ever a symbol of the soul and its desire to fly swiftly to God, underscore the Torah as a ladder of ascent to God's presence.[19]

The idea that the Torah occupies the place of both a Davidic king and of the high priest is further emphasized by the special pure white mantles that are substituted on the festivals in lieu of the red, blue, or purple mantles of "ordinary" hue: royal colors during most of the year; white at times recalling those when the high priest in the temple donned special attire for the festivals. As the high priest also wore on his chest a shield, decorated with twelve gems to symbolize the twelve tribes of Israel, so the Torah came by the sixteenth century to be further adorned, at least in the northern European world, with a silver *tas*—a shield—contrived according to the same patterns of décor that characterize other Jewish ceremonial objects. The style reflected location and period, and symbols reaffirmed the spirit of the temple within the synagogue: the seven-branched menorot, representations of the two Tablets of the Law (themselves a synecdoche for the Torah in its entirety), and pairs of vine-swathed columns—sometimes twisted—with crowns and cherub figures.

Given the dual symbolic "role" of the Torah, we should not be surprised to find layered allusions on other decorated elements associated with it. A *parokhet* before the ark might offer a crown that simultaneously symbolizes the Torah itself and both Davidic royalty and the temple priesthood. Pairs of columns don't merely allude to the temple but, interwoven with vines, refer to the prophet Hosea's words comparing the people of Israel to a "luxuriant vine" and the talmudic comparison of the Torah itself to the vine and its grapes. On the other hand, the image of Jerusalem—as the image of Jerusalem captured in Christian art from the medieval to the baroque periods—is often dominated by a temple whose form emulates the Muslim Dome of the Rock.

Such visual influence and counterinfluence can be layered. This is nowhere more apparent than in a seventeenth-century *parokhet* from Cairo. The entire visual structure of the *parokhet* emulates a Muslim prayer rug, with its presentation of the niched *mihrab* form to the devotee, framed by the seven borders of God's seven heavens and laden with the flora of Islamic decoration (see below). At the same time, its niche is hung with nine mosque lamps—reminiscent of the *hanukkiyah*—encompassed by a goblet motif, and graced with a Hebrew inscription from the Psalms: "This is the gate of the Lord; the righteous shall enter here." The weaver himself may well have been a Muslim, since the spacing of the Hebrew letters is incorrect, although the spellings are correct. Perhaps the words were correctly given in some cartoon form to the weaver by a Jew who knew the text so well that he did not think about spacing letters clearly in his model (see Figure 46). While both the Muslim *mihrab* and the Christian church apse are based on the orienting Torah niche of the early synagogue, here we are confronted with the

FIGURE 46   *Ottoman-style* parokhet, *Cairo. Seventeenth century*

image of a *mihrab* covering the entrance to the *aron hakodesh,* lineal descendant of the Torah niche. Displaying stylized twisting, Bernini-inspired columns, the Cairene prayer-rug *parokhet* interweaves two concentric circles of influence.

Like the early Christians, the Jews of Rome were interred in catacombs, but many Jews from throughout the diasporic Near East sought to be transported for burial to the Holy Land. An important catacomb was established in Palestine at a location that, from the second century, was also a center of Jewish scholarship. It was appropriately called *Bet She'arim*—House of Gates. Here, sarcophagi, initially containing the *profanus* remains of those whose souls are promised eternal life, are adorned with images—from the menorah to the egg and dart motif with its fertility-related statement of hope for rebirth. Geometric motifs are found along with heraldic animals: powerful protective eagles, fertile bulls, fierce snarling lions. The complex of catacombs is, as a whole, treated in a manner analogous to that of the early synagogue. A *trompe-l'oeil* threefold entryway carved out of the stone to simulate bronze appears twice at *Bet She'arim*: the visual relationship between temple and tomb is as present here as it is in the pagan and Christian worlds.

That conceptual relationship will continue from era to era as the burial nexus shifts from catacomb to cemetery. Grave stones in medieval Jewish cemeteries, such as those in Worms, Prague, and Venice, are often decorated with arched forms, with the names of the deceased inscribed within the arch: they symbolically pass through it into the *sacer*. The arches are stylistically drawn from the architectural vernacular of time and place. More particularized symbols may also be found, such as upstretched hands configured to offer the high priestly blessing—the fingers of each hand forming the Hebrew letter *shin*, with its three vertical elements (see figure 47). That letter is the first letter in *shaddai*, God's power-protective name. So the efficacy of the intended blessing is reinforced symbolically through the visual evocation of a power-protective God. The *shin*, which typically appears on the object attached to the doorposts of one's house—the *mezuzzah*—to protect it, here appears to protect the entryway into the next world.[20] Contrived of the hands of priestly blessing, such an image usually also refers to the name of the one buried—that his name was Cohen (or a derivative of Cohen), and thus his family traced its name to the high priestly division of Israel.

FIGURE 47   *Grave stone from Prague cemetery with upraised Kohaynic hands. Fourteenth century*

The ewer of ritual purification appears as a symbol of the broader priestly Levite tribe, and on tombstones signifies families with names, such as Levy, who trace themselves to this second division of Israel. Other images signify family or personal names (such as a wolf—Wolfenssohn; or a fish—Fisch—"little fish" having emerged as a good-luck first name by the medieval period) and professions (such a bunch of grapes to denote a vintner or a tavern-keeper).

The Star of David is evident as well. In the cemetery of Prague in particular, the six-pointed star is beginning its gradual shift toward being a specifically Jewish symbol. The hexagram and its sibling, the six-pointed star, as well as the pentagram and five-pointed star, were all associated in the course of the medieval period in Europe with alchemy and magic—and all were referred to, variously, as the "Seal of Solomon" or "Shield of David" or "Star of Solomon" or "Star of David." Since Jews were often regarded as magicians, these symbols were associated with them by many non-Jews.[21] An alchemical text of 1724 first refers specifically to the six-pointed star as the *Magen David,* devised of two opposed triangles, symbols of the opposition between fire and water—and of the harmony, therefore, of opposed elements inherent in that form and essential to the assertions of alchemy.

In Jewish magical and mystical texts, the phrase *Magen David*—"Shield of David"—was used, but without specifying which of these four geometric forms is the intended reference. By the sixteenth and seventeenth centuries, Jewish communities such as those of Vienna and Prague had begun to use the six-pointed star as a general symbol to distinguish themselves from Christian communities symbolized by the cross. By the eighteenth century some Jewish circles began to associate the six-pointed star symbol with messianic redemption. By the early nineteenth century, more broadly referred to as the Star or Shield of David, it began to appear widely on Jewish ceremonial objects, first in central, then in western, and finally in eastern Europe. But it is not until the advent of Zionism in the last decades of the century that the six-pointed Star of David began to achieve its status as a universally recognized symbol of Judaism. It nonetheless also continues to be used in Christian contexts, as a reference to Jesus as a descendant of David, as well as in Islamic contexts where, among other things, it is usually part of an infinitizing geometric pattern that refers to the infinite God (see below).

Everyday Jewish life is garlanded by ceremonies and objects echoing the symbolic language of synagogue and cemetery. Indeed, as the synagogue is conceptually a kind of temple away from the temple, every Jewish *home* comes to be viewed as a kind of synagogue away from the synagogue. Its *profanus* space becomes sanctified—made *sacer*—in varied ways. The dining table can be the spiritual equivalent of the *bimah,* which is the spiritual equivalent of the altar in the temple. Thus, for instance, the blessing of the wine and bread on the Sabbath and festivals recalls the blood of the animal sacrifices and the shew-breads in the temple, but instead of a *kohayn* making offerings at the altar, the entire family consumes these substances, preceded by blessings that have their echo in the prayers we recite in the synagogue. But even the most everyday meal, eaten alone, is entered and exited with blessings recited before and after, transforming the most *profanus* of events into something *sacer.*

This sensibility is also underscored by setting aside an area, in a traditional Jewish home, in which thrice-daily prayers may be offered when attendance at the synagogue is not possible. As in the synagogue one faces eastward to pray (conceptually even if not always actually toward Jerusalem), so the eastern wall in the home will be the focal direction of such a *sacer* space. The object actually focusing the Jerusalem orientation is called a *mizrah*—an east—tablet.[22] *Mizrah* tablets are typically hangings of cloth or cut or painted paper and are most often decorated with symbols such as the menorah or a pair of columns, or guardian figures: renderings of cherubim, or of griffins, or simply Lions of Judah, alluding to the royal house of David and the promise of its messianic restoration. At times, a *mizrah* tablet explodes with a vision of paradise with gates into the Garden of Eden and the figures of Moses and Aaron facing out toward the viewer.

Given the intensity of interface between the Jewish and Muslim communities across North Africa for the past fourteen centuries, affecting everything from gastronomy to symbols in art, we should not be surprised to find a nineteenth-century Moroccan *mizrah* with a menorah, over which the four-lettered name of God is inscribed, flanked by two upraised, outstretched hands (see Figure 48). The hand is a protective device—an apotropaic symbol—in the visual language of Islam, which is called a *hamseh* (or sometimes "the hand of Fatima") (see Figure 2). That such a symbol should have spread to Jewish communities within the Muslim world is not surprising. The configuration lends itself particularly well to Jewish symbolic thinking. It would represent the protective power of the five books of the Torah, which as the bridge between humanity and God symbolizes the protection promised by that relationship.

But in this *mizrah* there are *two* hands, and so the *hamseh* plays a double role. The image of two outstretched hands implies the high priestly blessing—even if, here, the hands have been regularized so that the configuration of the fingers does not assume the usual *shin*-shaped disposition of that benediction. That the intention is nonetheless to offer that blessing is confirmed by the Hebrew inscription that forms the boundary between the interior imagery and the frame of purely abstract vegetal elements, for it is that very benediction that is inscribed.[23] So a universal idea adapted by Islamic thought has been adapted to Jewish visual thought.

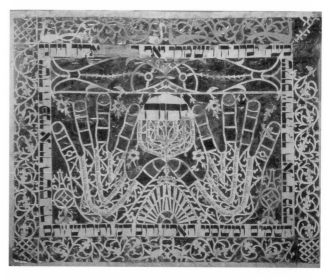

FIGURE 48   Mizrah *with double* hamseh *as priestly blessing, Morocco. Nineteenth century*

Jewish thought and Jewish art are in the end more about time than space: Jewish space is dispersed and temporary (although focused on the immutable temple); time, like God, is always and everywhere. In Jewish time the Sabbath is the *sacer* center of every Jewish week. The kindling of lights with which it begins symbolizes a weekly emulation of God's first act in ordering the universe, creating light. The blessing of wine alludes to the blood sacrifices offered in the temple as the special bread—*hallah*—alludes to the shewbreads at the temple. These symbolic elements have echoes in Christian ceremony and symbology. The Jewish Sabbath also ends with light and the blessing of wine in a ceremony called *Havdalah*—"separation." As ritual separates the time of the *sacer* Sabbath from the *profanus* of the week, so adornment of ritual objects helps concretize ritual. Eventually, wine goblets and candelabra specific to entering and exiting the Sabbath appear, but physical specimens have not survived from before the late medieval period.

The issue of longing to retain the sweetness of the Sabbath into the week from which it is separated achieves its most fascinating aesthetic expression in the forms accruing to the spice box: the *Hadas Liv'samim* that emerged in the medieval period as part of the *Havdalah* ceremony. Filled with fragrant herbs, the *hadas* is passed from person to person at the conclusion of *Havdalah* as a symbol of Sabbath fragrance extending into the week.[24] The earliest spice box that has survived to our own time dates from the sixteenth century, in "town tower" form. From Frankfurt, Germany, it is formed with fourfold turrets—like the four-lettered name of God.

The use of spices in the *Havdalah* ritual offers an echo of the use of incense and spices in the temple in Jerusalem. But spices, especially myrtle, were also universally deemed capable of warding off evil spirits. Bells, noise, and light were weapons against demons in a medieval world fraught with a sense of the ubiquity of the *sacer,* in which Jews feared the same demons feared by their neighbors.[25] Observing the Sabbath was regarded as a potent protection against the nefarious powers of the *sacer.* The *Havdalah* service, at that vulnerable border time of passage from the Sabbath back to the week, when the demons held in abeyance would be gathered for attack, is punctuated by light, by wine, which, poured out, gives the devil his due, and by spices, which extend the fragrance of Sabbath and also quench the odors of hellfire and keep demons at a distance. Keeping the spices in elaborate towers, fortifications against evil, decorated with bells and fierce animal faces and soldiers guarding against the negative powers of the *sacer,* makes symbolic sense.

The four turrets, to the four directions, the foot thrusting downward, and the spire pushing upward encompass the omnidirectional protective power of God who, in the allegory of the Song of Songs, is likened to a lover with cheeks as a bed of spices, as towers of perfumes. Moreover, in the outside European world, difficult-to-come-by and valuable spices were typically stored in the holds of fortified towers. Thus the "town tower" became the most popular shape for the *Hadas Liv'samim.* Town towers elevated on feet recall Christian monstrances, pixes, reliquaries, and incense stands, which no doubt inspired their general configuration. Motifs like the temple menorah are typically embedded in details that echo the ecclesiastical sensibilities of the non-Jewish architectural world.[26]

On the other hand, traditional Christian or shared motifs might be used as particularized Jewish symbols. Heraldic birds facing each other may allude to the bird as a symbol of the soul, but Jewish tradition asserts that in celebrating the Sabbath, a Jew carries an extra soul, which keeps evil at bay. Thus, on a *Havdalah* spice box, paired facing birds suggest those paired souls facing each other in farewell. More unusual, the unicorn, which in Christian art is a symbol of Christ and of virgin purity, is transformed in the complex foliage of a rococo-style, eighteenth-century *Hadas liv'samim* as part of Jewish legend. That legend states that Adam was frightened when he saw his first sunset—at the time of the first Sabbath eve. He was so relieved when it (and he) rose again the next morning that he sacrificed a one-horned creature to thank God.[27] Moreover, the same tradition asserts that the altar of the temple was built, millennia later, on the spot of Adam's offering.[28] The columns and arch that symbolize the temple frame the scene (see Figure 49).

The *Hadas* takes other forms as well. Pomegranate-shaped boxes, among other things, allude to the seven species of fruits in the Promised Land, which include the pomegranate.[29] The fish form reminds the *Havdalah* celebrants of the special Sabbath meal of fish just completed as a symbol of luck. However, in this particular context the source of that symbolic luck evokes an additional *sacer* connection, for the phrase (in Genesis 1), "and God blessed them," appears after the creation of fish, after the creation of man, and at the time of the Sabbath.

FIGURE 49 *Spice box* (Hadas liv'samim), *gold and silver, Poland. Seventeenth to eighteenth century*

While the Sabbath offers a weekly reminder of the covenant, the three festivals decreed in the Torah—Passover, *Shavuot*, and *Sukkot*—variously recall contextual aspects of the redemption from Egyptian servitude and the journey to restoration in the Holy Land. Passover in particular offers objects rich with visual and conceptual symbols. The re-experienced, retold story of Passover is set forth in the *Haggadah,* the Book of Telling, which has shaped and been shaped by the Jewish tradition of manuscript illumination and illustration. The most famous medieval *Haggadah* came to light in the late nineteenth century in Sarajevo, Yugoslavia—revolutionizing the art historical under-standing of the figurative limits of Jewish art, half a century before the discovery of the synagogue fresco cycle at Dura Europus would complete that revolution. The Sarajevo *Haggadah* is inundated with biblical and other scenes. These illustrations are Gothic in style with attenuated, boneless figures placed against flat, abstract back-grounds: skies that are the stylized skies of the spaceless *sacer*. Fig-ures are attired in the hooded gowns characteristic of Barcelona Jews at this time.[30]

The tradition of illumination also flourished in the Ashkenazi world of north-central European Jewry, but the visual results reflect a differ-ent sensibility. From fourteenth-century south Germany, the so-called "Bird's Head" *Haggadah* reflects a pronounced discomfort with creat-ing human images—and the solution to that discomfort: human figures with bird-heads, which are thus neither human nor animal. Unlike their Spanish counterparts, the artists of this and similar works preferred not to represent figures that directly reflect—and might be construed as sac-rilegiously competing with—God's work. But the forms made from parts of two realms, the human and the animal, analogically and sym-bolically link the two realms of the divine and human. On the other hand, the Erna Michael *Haggadah* from Germany of the following cen-tury, offers figures that reflect a complete loss of discomfort with fully human portrayals. But the seder celebrants it depicts wear horned hats. In a manner more obvious than in the hooded figures in the Sarajevo *Haggadah,* a Jew has portrayed Jews as they would be attired by de-cree, wearing hats that symbolize and emphasize the horns that non-Jews perceived Jews to have.[31]

The Jewish festival cycle, with its attendant rituals and the art of il-lumination as accompaniment to celebration, extends beyond what is mandated in the Torah. *Purim*, which celebrates the escape from de-struction in Persia half a millennium before Christ, is recounted in the Book of Esther.[32] The unique status of the *Megillah* (scroll) and the often wildly joyous nature of the *Purim* celebration have both con-tributed to a freedom and lightness of approach to it, which have caused its illuminations to rival *Haggadot* in splendor.[33] The festival of Hanukkah is not based at all on Hebrew scripture. The event it cele-brates—a successful rebellion against the insistence by the Seleucid monarch Antioch IV that Judaeans worship his image and images of his gods—is recounted in the Apocryphal books of Maccabees, which were never accepted for canonization into the Hebrew Bible. Yet Hanukkah has evolved and grown in the Diaspora as a popular holiday—due to its upbeat mood and its ability in dark December to offer light as a promise of the inevitable triumph of spring and, more recently, particularly to Jewish children, a balance to the light-filled Christmas celebration.

The *Hanukkiyah,* the Hanukkah candelabrum that bears this light, offers eight candles to symbolize the eight days of the festival recounted in First and Second Maccabees.[34] A nineteenth-century French neo-Gothic-styled work is typical, with threefold trefoil ogives associated with the symbolism of the three-entryway synagogue. Lions of Judah—with the crown of Davidic royalty—offer messianic hope fulfilled on the small scale by the Hanukkah story; they also represent a kind of word-play between the reference to "Judah as a lion's whelp" from Jacob's blessing of his sons at the end of Genesis (and its subsequent Davidic association) and the name of Judah Maccabee, redemptive hero of the Hanukkah story.

In the past century the heroine Judith—also from the Apocrypha, and thus, like her counterpart, Judah Maccabee, not part of the Jewish or Protestant biblical narrative—has come to be depicted sometimes on *Hanukkiyot,* holding the upraised sword with which she beheaded the Assyrian general, Holofernes. She who saved the people of Jerusalem from the Assyrians in one era is the analogue and symbol, through name association, of the one who saved Judaea from the Seleucids in another era. Among other typical symbols, the seven-branched menorah emphatically suggests the temple, since the culminating miracle of the Hanukkah narrative is directly focused on the temple and its menorah; not surprisingly, it is often framed by a pair of columns and an arch that symbolize the temple. In some cases, the columns are reconceived as palm trees, associated with the climate and topography of the Holy Land. This turn of image became particularly popular at the end of the nineteenth century with the advent of modern Zionism.

Monumental Muslim Symbolic Language

Arriving onto the stage of history five centuries after Judaism and Christianity had begun their mutual contention regarding the *sacer-profanus* relationship, Islam is built on the same four essential concepts: God (in Arabic: *Allah*)—absolutely invisible and intangible, as in Judaism, but not Christianity; peoplehood (all those—*Muslims—committed* to the

FIGURE 50   *Dome of the Rock (detail), Jerusalem. 691* CE

will of God); a text that connects the two—the Qur'an; and a place (three primary places) where the relationship between humanity and divinity is most directly and effectively focused.

We might expect and have already seen instances of visual overlap reflecting the conceptual overlap between Islamic art and its Abrahamic counterparts. We might wonder, as with Jewish art, how the contours of Islamic art express the nonimagable God and its concomitants. Islamic art should and does speak with a distinct abstract symbolic language. But it is not devoid of figurative aspects, just as Jewish art is not. Islamic art shares with its siblings the goal of conveying a sense of God as paradoxic—utterly opposite from us, yet, as our creator, somehow like us.

The first example of monumental Islamic architecture, Jerusalem's Dome of the Rock (see Figure 50), was inspired directly by the Haghia Sophia in Constantinople, and it marks a meeting point among religion, politics, and art. It was completed by the Umayyad caliph Abd'al-Malak around 691 CE in large part to intensify focus on Jerusalem—*al'Kuds* ("the Holy")—as a sacred center, due to its greater proximity to the Umayyad capital of Damascus than Macca and Madina. Proximity meant more effective stewardship not only of such a city and such a site but also of the evolving Muslim world.

The edifice rests on a rock with a threefold significance. It was the site where many Muslims believed that Ibrahim had offered up his son to God.[35] It was the site where, a millennium later, the Israelite King Suleiman devised the great temple to God. Most important, on his *isra'*—Muhammad's miraculous ride that carried him in one night on his steed Buraq ("lightning") from Macca to Jerusalem to heaven and back to earth and home to Macca—the precise point of departure and return to earth was that very rock. Thus the site was already, in the early Muslim tradition, acquiring a profound *sacer* significance for which Abd'al-Malak's structure offered visual confirmation.

Everything about the edifice and its décor bespeaks the simultaneously simple and complex relationship between God and ourselves. The dome itself, a microcosmic echo of the spherical dome of heaven, rests on an octagonal structure that, in turn, sits upon a squared base raised above ground level and approached by a sweep of staircases. The earth itself is symbolized by such a base, its four sides emblematic of the four directions, its stops and starts a reference to the stops and starts of human existence—in contrast to the circular dome without beginning or end, which emulates not only the heavens but also the realm of divinity.

The octagon intermediates, neither quite square nor quite a circle. Its geometry speaks of the *sacer-profanus* relationship in another way. Its form can be understood as two squares superimposed at 45-degree angles over each other. If the square connotes humanity (our four-directioned reality), and humanity is a reflection of the divinity that made us, then divinity can also be represented by a square—but clearly not the same square that represents humanity, which is its opposite. A square rotated 45 degrees over a second square (creating an octagon or an eight-pointed star) suggests a relationship of simultaneous identity and distinction.

The décor of the monument further underscores these issues, for the glistening dome is an undifferentiated expanse of color, expressing a monumentality that is consistent with the sense of God as undifferentiated and monumental, in comparison with ourselves, the *profanus,* as minute, endlessly differentiated beings. The *profanus* is symbolized by the minute details that overrun the upper half of the octagon and the lower part of the drum of the dome. On the other hand, those myriad details have an infinitizing quality to them; it is virtually impossible to locate their beginning and end points—so that they connote God's infinitude. The details simultaneously connote an aspect of God and an aspect of ourselves. Moreover, while infinitizing in aspect, those details are actually finitized—cut off—by the frames of the various blind arches that ring the upper half of the octagon and echo the form of the dome (and are, in turn, echoed by arcades that partially frame the base and mark the passage onto it from the approach staircases). The frames finitize the infinitizing patterns. Further, those patterns contrast with each other in being curvilinear or rectilinear, geometric or vegetal.

Thus, detail by detail, visual oppositions express the contrasts between God and ourselves and, in sometimes serving simultaneously opposite "purposes," suggest a greater complexity to that relationship than merely one of oppositional contrasts. The features articulating the visual vocabulary of the Dome of the Rock and marking it as a meeting point between realms are a combination, in brief, of architectural form and style of adornment. That adornment is one of both pattern and color contrasts: the blue of the sky and the green of the grass and trees are complemented by the gold of ultimate truth and the white of purity of purpose—in a natural environment, moreover, in which color is blanched by the sun to colorlessness throughout most of the year. Thus color offers a startling reminder of the relationship between heaven and earth. Finally, there is a textual bridge between *sacer* and *profanus*. The upper reaches of the octagon and the lower reaches of the dome, just before they yield to its monumental golden crown, are overrun with writing that flows around the structure: without beginning or end, though the astute reader of Arabic, his eye attuned to its calligraphy, might discern where these passages from the Qur'an start and where they conclude.

Monumental and minute, infinite and finite, coloristically and formally contrastive, yielding both abstract imagery and the even greater abstraction of the letters that convey the Word—all of these are features repeated again and again across the geography and history of Islamic art to convey the relationship between God and ourselves. They are features that are found most obviously but not exclusively as part of the structures that function as endemic border crossings between *sacer* and *profanus*. The domed form, resting on a cube—or on an octagon or a hexagon that in turn rests on a cube or a square—derived from Byzantine art will become the most fundamental aspect of Islamic public architecture and significantly visible in mosques and tombs throughout the *dar al'Islam*.

It is appropriate, given the fact that Constantinople and its Haghia Sophia inspired the turn to the dome in Islamic architecture, that the most extensive concentration of domes and of experimentation with dome-on-rectilinear structure should be found in that city within a century of the Islamic conquest of 1453 and the renaming of the city as Istanbul. To begin with, as the Haghia Sophia itself shifted from being a church to being a mosque, the most obvious external change was the introduction of minarets, towers from which the *muezzin* calls the faithful to prayer five times daily. In the case of the Haghia Sophia, four minarets punctuate the cardinal points that articulate the periphery of the mosque complex. Aside from a practical purpose—that a *muezzin* can call the faithful to prayer simultaneously in each of the four directions—the symbolic logic of this configuration is clear. The addition of the minarets at cardinal corners underscores the contrastive visual relationship between the squared, earthbound periphery of the squared understructure of the building itself and the circular form of its domed superstructure.

This last issue is explored from a slightly different angle in the mosque of Selim (Selim Çami), built in nearby Edirne by the preeminent Ottoman architect, Sinan, around 1575. It is the only mosque in the world with six minarets, extending the frontal area of the complex forward and suggesting the sixfold directionality of the *profanus*—east, west, north, south, up, and down—in contrast with the unifying dome of the *sacer.* Moreover, the introduction of the minaret reshapes a structure like the Haghia Sophia or the Selim Çami as a monumental exemplum of the egg-and-dart motif and the fundamental principle it engages. As decorative element has been transformed into architectural element, phallic arrow has become tower and swollen belly egg has become dome.[36]

The exteriors of Ottoman structures rarely rely on color to articulate the principle of contrastive décor. Instead, particularly with the work of Sinan and his pupil, Muhammad Aga, there is a concentration on the dome shape itself to suggest minute versus monumental and finitizing versus infinitizing symbolism. Thus in both the Selim Çami at Edirne and even more so the Sultanahmet Çami (the mosque of Sultan Ahmed I, 1609–1616), designed by Muhammad Aga, there is an apparent cascading down from, or mountainous aggregation up to, the dome by means of half-domes, quarter-domes, and blind arches as well as arched windows of various sizes, all echoing in their various scales and configurations the main dome, but connecting its unified monumentality to the earth below by means of an organic breakdown (buildup) of profuse, simple detail.

Moreover, the Sultanahmet mosque is popularly known as the "Blue Mosque" because its interior is so richly adorned with blue tiles that the very light that flows through the myriad windows seems to glow with a bluish haze. It is in the interior that Ottoman mosques carry on the eye-stopping tile tradition evident on the exterior of mosques elsewhere in the *dar al'Islam,* and here one can observe another aspect of the symbolic language of Islamic art: the use of negative space. In staring up at the décor of the Blue Mosque cupola, one notes a kind of "pillar" motif, filled by an infinitizing, minutely detailed abstract blue and white pattern; the "pillars" all meet below and above, creating a "ground" line between the dome and the inscription (and below it, the windows and below them the four squinches that support the dome) and between the main body of the dome and its cap (see Figure 51). The space that is left is a repeating bottle-form of bluish-white hue. But that negative space, if one adjusts one's eyes, pops out, making it a positive, not a negative, element and transforming the "pillar" motif into a background (therefore negative) space. Such a dynamic once again addresses God and ourselves: the "absent" or "empty" element, when it manifests itself by popping out at us is symbolic of a God that is invisible and therefore "absent" at first glance, but whose interventionist action makes its presence palpable to those attuned to that presence.

These various symbolic elements are not reserved only for mosques. One may observe very clearly the principle of coloristic intermediation between heaven and earth, for example, in the twelfth-century mausoleum of the Mongol ruler, Uljaytu, in Sultaniyah, northwestern Iran. Color mediates between heaven and earth in the contrast between the earth-colored bricks and the sky-colored tiles, the remains of which make it clear that the upper reaches

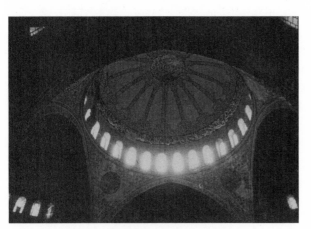

FIGURE 51   *Interior of Sultan Ahmed Mosque ("Blue Mosque"), Istanbul. 1609–1616*

FIGURE 52   *Taj Mahal, Agra, India. 1632–1648*

of the structure once scintillated with pigment. Its domed peak, 160 feet above the surrounding plain, can be seen from miles away. That monumental dome rests on an octagon, and its mass is broken into infinitizing, minutely detailed patterns. Similarly, the massive walls of the octagonal structure are relieved by a symphony of related arched forms that relate variously to each other and to the dome. The Tomb of Al'Ghazali (1225) offers a dome that has been rendered as a *gumbat* or *tuerbe*—it is conical, like the Seljuk tomb-towers that derive in form from the conical tents of Central Asia. The temporary dwelling places of the living have been transformed into a permanent dwelling place of the dead. The upper part of the structure has been submerged within an enormous cube: the principle of contrasting a circular with a squared shape remains intact, as does that of contrasting a monumental form with minute details that offer infinitizing and finitizing aspects.

The range of variation of these themes is further exemplified by the magnificent Taj Mahal, devised by Ustad Ahmad Lahori for the Moghul Emperor Jahan of India as a mausoleum for the emperor's beloved wife, between 1632 and 1648 (see Figure 52). It is a gleaming, white edifice, a dome surmounting a cube flanked by four minarets, the tops of which echo precisely the form of the small towers at the four corners of the main edifice. Aside from the graceful organic compartmentalization of the overall complex, its apparent massive continuity is infinitely broken up by the minute details of the brickwork as well as by the vegetal elements that offer further inlaid décor.

An additional feature underscores this temple-tomb complex as a symbolic doorway between earth and heaven. The combination of the long reflecting pool that leads from the entrance into the compound toward the structure itself—in which pool the mirror image of that structure shimmers and above which the structure seems to float—and the concealing of the stairway that leads from ground level up to the platform upon which the structure rests, offers to the eye a substantial yet incredibly weightless entity, hovering between earth and heaven. Given the Qur'anic inscription at the entrance to the compound—*sura* 89, *al'Fajr* (The Break of Day)—one cannot avoid the sense of the mausoleum as a pale sun rising above the horizon, and with it the hope of rebirth into eternal life in the paradise toward which both the shah and his spouse hope and expect to go when they cross the boundary into the *sacer.*

Pools are also used extensively in the complex popularly known as the Alhambra built in Granada in the fourteenth century by the Nasrid rulers, Yusuf I and Muhammad V.[37] There the solid structures that make up the maze-like configuration of the palace chambers are constantly echoed by water that, shimmering in evanescence as it does, offers another symbol of human/divine contrast. It is an obliquely layered symbolism: the edifices made by human hand in their solidity contrast with the watered reflections as the solid reality of Allah contrasts with the ephemerality of human contrivances. That the Nasrid princes recognized this is apparent in the repeated inscription carved into the stucco throughout the complex: *wa la ghaliba illa'Llah*—"and there is no conqueror but God." These words must have reverberated ironically for the last Muslim ruler who ceded the city to Fernando of Aragon in January 1492.

Within the mosque, the most obvious and important focal point is the *mihrab,* a niche in the wall known as the *qibla*—directional or orientation—wall facing Macca. Its purpose, like that of the church apse, is derived from the synagogue Torah niche: to orient the faithful toward the central point of contact between earth and heaven. For Muslims that point is the *ka'aba* in Macca. But the historical relationship between *mihrab* and Torah niche is demonstrated by the fact that Muhammad originally demanded of his followers that they pray toward Jerusalem, and only after 628 or so—by which time his relations with Jews had soured and he had conquered Macca—did he instruct them to face toward the city of his birth. There, rather than destroying the *ka'aba*—which would have meant destroying the most central shrine in the faith of his ancestors—he reoriented the understanding of the black stone that marks it. But rather than *worshipping* it as a manifestation of divinity, he taught his followers that it was thrust from heaven to earth as a tangible manifestation of contact between *sacer* and *profanus* offered by the intangible God who might be worshipped through *veneration* of the *ka'aba*.[38]

FIGURE 53   Mihrab *from Great Mosque, Cordoba, Spain. Tenth century*

The *mihrab* orients Muslims toward Macca and the *ka'aba,* and it is almost inevitably decorated in a manner that, like the Torah niche and the apse, underscores the redemptive presence of God in our world. In the *mihrab* of the Great Mosque in Cordoba, Spain, devised in the tenth century by the Umayyads, five features are particularly noticeable (see Figure 53). The first is the obvious manner in which the lower, more earthbound part of both the niche and its outer frame are separated and visually different from the upper, more heavenward part. The second is that the upper part is overrun with both infinitizing patterns that are finitized by frames, and that there is a contrastive range of such patterns. In the nineteen bands that immediately frame the niche (in turn shaped by a frame within a frame within a frame) positive and negative as well as vegetal, floral, and curvilinear geometric design is explored in ten different ways within the confines of red, black, and gold colors. Nineteen is a number associated with God through the numerology of *al-Wahad* ("the One") as well as with guardian angels, as mentioned in Qur'an *sura* 74:30.

The third noteworthy visual element is that the interior of the niche is faceted, contrived of five surfaces, corresponding to the number of pillars constituting the edifice of Islam. The fourth element that draws the eye is the pair of pilasters flanking the interior blind arches that echo the pair of double columns marking the entry into the niche. Visual and conceptual cross-fertilization are at work. Columns flanking a doorway of some central symbol (particularly a Torah niche) function, in Jewish (and Christian) art and architectural symbolism, to connote the temple in Jerusalem. The *mihrab* at Cordoba, as much as it orients the worshipper toward Macca, also reminds him of *al'Kuds*.

The fifth eye-drawing element of the Cordoba *mihrab* is the lengthy inscription from the Qur'an that marks the separation between the upper and lower parts of the *mihrab* frame. The word that intermediates between God and ourselves, God's word, spoken through the prophet to us, intermediates between the earthbound and heaven-directed parts of the structure. And the script in which the words are written is different from the script with which other words frame the outermost frame of the *mihrab*: words calligraphized as abstract imagery present another form of symbolically contrastive intermediation to the discerning eye.

If inside the mosque we are directed toward paradise by being directed in our prayers toward Macca, then it is not surprising that a precise sense of orientation defines aspects of the exterior as well. The *iwan* in Sassanian architecture, a vaulted half chamber with a pointed or barrel-vaulted ceiling, created the space in which the shah or his provincial governors received dignitaries and administered justice—analogous to the apse in Roman public buildings. As that apse combined with the purpose and décor of the synagogue Torah niche to yield the church apse and the mosque *mihrab,* so the *iwan,* with the arrival of Islam into Persia, also underwent transformation. In the center of each porticoed wall framing a mosque or *madrasa* courtyard an *iwan* was placed: a large aperture framed by a squared element (like the squared frame of the *mihrab* niche) and often pierced by multiple niches or arches or doorways. The principal *iwan* faces toward Macca and may even be flanked by a pair of minarets: the doorway through such an *iwan* leads into the mosque itself and is aligned, therefore, with the *mihrab* at the opposite side of the interior space of the mosque. In turn, the primary entrance from the outside world into the world of the courtyard may be shaped as an *iwan,* yielding a trajectory that follows from the outer *iwan* to the inner *iwan* to the *mihrab* to Macca and the *ka'aba*—to heaven.

But orienting one's prayers toward Macca raises a practical question. How does one go about one's everyday *profanus* existence having to stop five times a day to address one's self formally to the *sacer*? Both Muslims and Jews (three times daily) may pray alone wherever they can find a quiet spot. Islam remains more rigid than does Judaism regarding the timing and, in what for our purposes is more significant, regarding direction. Whereas Jews (and Christians) eventually became less concerned that they pray literally toward Jerusalem, Muslims make every effort to find the *qibla*— the direction toward Macca—wherever they are.[39] Concomitant with that effort is one of isolating a spot that is symbolically separate from the earth around. Jews merely bow the head in prayer;[40] Muslims fall to their knees and bring their foreheads to the ground, in a twice sevenfold pattern, in completely submitting to God. Thus an area distinct from the earth in which to accomplish this is a practical desideratum.

Figure 54 *Ottoman prayer rug. ca. 1550*

But the truer purpose is symbolic; in engaging the *sacer* in prayer, one kneels and touches one's forehead (which encases one's soul) in *sacer* territory, separate from the *profanus* of the everyday. This can be accomplished in the simplest way: a large piece of newspaper or paper towel can serve. But one of the most exquisite developments in Ottoman Turkish art is that of the prayer rug, offering an easily transportable *sacer* space on which and in which to pray, and typically presenting a framed *mihrab* as its basic design. In a prayer rug dating to around 1550 made for Suleiman the Magnificent, the devotee kneels within a *mihrab* embellished with at least five distinctive sorts of decorative elements, ranging from the red of the field to the three different forms of stylized vegetal and floral decoration in the spandrels, cartouches, and frames to the geometric motifs in the frames (see Figure 54).

The finitizing frame is made up of a limitless, infinitizing series of patterns. The central band is conceived as an endless garden, flanked by two bands marked by eight-pointed stars, the symbolism of which, like that of the octagon, is intended to suggest the paradoxic nature of the relationship between God and ourselves (as alike and yet utterly opposite to each other). But ultimately we count a total of seven components to the frame-configuration: we kneel surrounded by the seven heavens of God, by perfection and completion.

We kneel flanked by columns that allude to Suleiman's temple (and given the name of the sultan for whom this carpet was made, offers a pun on his name and his God-connected role) and to the rock at its site from which Muhammad ascended to and descended from heaven in a single night. We kneel and our head comes to rest precisely at the point marked by the stylized image of a lamp—the sort of lamp that hangs in a mosque within the *mihrab*. We recognize the sharing of the idea of such a lamp with Judaism and Eastern Christianity, the one with a lamp before the holy ark, the other with lamps before the iconostasis with the apse beyond it—in all three cases the lamp intended to suggest the presence of God who illuminates the world. But the lamp in the *mihrab* derives specifically from a passage in the Qur'an (*sura* 24:35) that refers to the world as a niche and Allah as a light shining within it.

God is a shining lamp in the niche of the world, and when praying toward the *mihrab* that directs us toward Macca, our way is illumined by the lamp hanging before or within the niche. A mosque lamp from the Ottoman Turkish mosque of Sokollu Mehmed Pasha and dating from the early sixteenth century presents such direction. The lower part is distinct from the upper part—the two parts separated by a decorative band—in three ways that convey the object's role as an intermediary between realms (see Figure 55). The décor of the neck clearly emphasizes blue against white; while on the body the blue is dominant enough to suggest white against blue—in short, a play with the issue of positive and negative space. The primary motif of the lower part is that of the *rumi* scroll, a stylized leaf-like element within a garden of paradise, whereas the upper part is dominated by the cloud motif that carries the viewer yet further into the realm of heaven (and is derived, by way of Persia, from China). Finally, each of the two parts contains a differently shaped series of lozenges with inscriptions, and each of the two groups of inscriptions is distinct in both calligraphic style and message. On the neck, in three parts, in *kufic,* we read, *ya emana ali, keennebi allah ali, kulullah ali.* "Oh trustworthy Ali; you, the prophet of God, Ali; the slave of God, Ali." The contrastive *suelues* inscriptions on the body, in three lobed rectangles, repeat the formulaic phrase, "Allah, Muhammad, Ali." The bottom of the lamp is also decorated; the primary motif there is an eight-pointed star. Among the other visual elements that overrun it is an endless series of miniscule triple dots, giving to the whole both an infinitizing emphasis and yielding a *horror vacui*-induced filling of every available area of open space.

Similar principles shape the entities that articulate the role of the Ottoman sultan as intermediator between *sacer* and *profanus.* An inlaid Qur'an box, designed to house multiple copies of the sacred text for Sultan Suleiman the Magnificent, offers a form—a

FIGURE 55   *Ottoman mosque lamp. ca. 1559*

dome resting upon a cube (which in turn is elevated by legs)—familiar on the architectural scale (see Figure 56). The upper band of the cube is marked by repeated inscription-filled lozenges (the particular script is *suelues;* the words are, appropriately, the Throne Verse from the Qur'an, among others). Below that band, dark and light colors alternate, creating a dialogue between negative and positive space, between hexagonal geometric motifs and floral as well as stylized cloud motifs. The overall feel of the cube is swirling and curvilinear, which contrasts with the primary decorative pattern of the dome, a series of never-ending alternating chevrons of the same dark and light hue as on the cube.

From Sacer *to* Profanus *Contexts*

Other decorative and numerological elements play symbolic roles in the *sacer-profanus* dialogue of architectural detail. They extend from the scalloped, honeycomb-like element, called a *muqarna,* that, endlessly multiplied, breaks up a monumental space into minute parts and, typically found where walls meet ceilings, obscures the boundary between horizontal and vertical planes—symbolic of that between earthbound and heavenly realms. On the other hand, a given detail of a floor pattern—such as that at Agra—might yield an eight-pointed star, but the center of the colored, sharp-edged, rectilinear star is a white, soft-edged, curvilinear eight-lobed floret, at the center of which is a single black circle. That center is perfect unity, without beginning or end; the floral element emanates from it; the star emanates from the floral element. Which is the negative and which is the positive visual element? And the configuration is part of a larger array of identical repeating elements alternating with pentagonal and five-star elements, carried toward an infinity that is not achieved only because a frame finitizes the pattern.

The five-pointed star motif is cognate with the *hamseh.* The word *means* "five" in Arabic and is used, among other ways, to refer to the outstretched hand as an apotropaic symbol. But in the vocabulary of Islamic art, this general condition is doubly reinforced by the fact that the five fingers of the hand symbolize the five pillars of Islam: thus we are protected by the principles that, as we live them, help us to be in a good relationship with God. Moreover, the configuration of the hand is such that four fingers—a symbol of our four-directional reality—are both disconnected from and connected to the thumb that, in its singularity, symbolizes God. Thus the divine-human relationship of simultaneous connection and separation serves as a protective device. *Hamseh*s abound in the liturgical and everyday *profanus* of Islamic art (see Figure 2).

And while the symbolic language of Islamic art is particularly rich in abstract vocabulary, it is

FIGURE 56   *Sultan's Qur'an box, Topkapi Palace, Istanbul. ca. 1550*

Figure 57   Sultan's yatagan *(detail). ca. 1550*

not exclusively nonfigurative. Floral and vegetal elements include among them foliage and flowers that are identifiable from and connected to the everyday world—such as roses, lilies, and above all, tulips. The tulip, carefully cultivated in Ottoman Turkey and used as an instrument of connection to the Christian infidel world—specifically by means of the franchise granted by the sultan to Dutch botanists in the sixteenth and seventeenth centuries—became a source of power and wealth for the empire in due time.

Conversely, the most *sacer* of flora and fauna may adorn the most *profanus* of implements. The jeweled and gold-inlaid *yatagan* made for Sultan Suleiman the Magnificent by Ahmed Tekelu,[41] as a weapon for the Defender of the Faithful, is embellished with reminders of his role as intermediator between *profanus* and *sacer* (see Figure 57). The monumental surfaces are infinitely broken up by minute details, and those details contrast in form and aspect with each other. Thus the hilt and pommel superimpose a gold *saz* (paradise or enchanted forest) scroll over ivory decorated with a black spiral vine. The myriad details all share the golden-white dominance of this material configuration and contrast with the black-highlighted-by-gold visual emphasis of the blade. The central portion of the latter presents, on one side, another variation on the *saz* motif, with *hatayi* (stylized lotus) blossoms and *rumi* leaf scrolls. On the other side large lion heads and smaller monkey, dragon, and bear heads punctuate the scroll.

The upper portion of the blade, closest to the handle, offers yet another version of the *saz,* in which a dragon and a *senmurv* (a fantastic bird similar to a phoenix) are engaged in combat. This is the eternal combat between supernatural antagonists, played out in the never-never-*saz* land of the *sacer.* Indeed flowers from the garden weave themselves around the scaly body of the dragon, as the tail of the *senmurv* evolves into forms indistinguishable from the branches from which the floral elements sprout. This is an appropriate visual symbol of the one who, wielding the sword in battle, preserves the *profanus* from its enemies, and who *is* the *senmurv* who represents the community of the faithful in their dealings with the *sacer*.

The image of the *senmurv*, symbolizing the sultan—singular and self-regenerating, as one sultan follows the next in a continuous rebirth of the sultanate[42]—is ultimately drawn, as is the image of an eternal combat between *senmurv* and dragon, from the manuscript tradition of Islam. In that tradition one finds any number of variously detailed images of the magnificent bird, as much stylized flame as feathers: a figurative representation of an entity that exists only in the realm of the *sacer*. There are other such creatures, not merely figurative, but humanly figurative, such as winged *genii*, in myriad Persian, Turkish, and Indian manuscripts. Like Christian angels, they reflect a visual history that begins with the winged victory figures of ancient Greek art and is carried forward by the Roman relief images carved into the spandrels of arches of victory.

One of the most important defining elements in the imagery not only of angels but also of saints and others who in one manner or another stand with one foot in the *profanus* and the other in the *sacer* is the halo. We have observed a continuation into Christian (and less so, Jewish) art, from the imagery of pagan antiquity in which a sunburst of some sort connotes a *sacer* connection to what in Christian art becomes stylized as a golden platter behind the head of the individual. We can follow the same visual idea into the Islamic manuscript representation of sacerdotal figures such as medical authorities, spiritual supermen, and political leaders. But not all figures whom we might expect to see haloed *are*. The Ottoman sultan, in spite of his role within the *sacer/profanus* matrix, is rarely depicted with a halo. On the other hand, one of the more unexpected instances of haloed figurative representation is Muhammad. One might assume that the prophet of the invisible God would never be visibly portrayed. This is partially so: the face of Muhammad is rarely seen, and in Orthodox representations his head is always shown covered. He leads Ali and Abu Bakr toward Macca in a 1594 court-style manuscript illumination, a detail from the *Siyar-i-Nabi*. What most draws our eye is the enormous flame emerging from behind and above the head of Muhammad; his halo is a heavenward-shooting golden outburst (see Figure 58).

The antithesis of such figural representation is offered by the various forms of calligraphy that abound in Islamic art. The emphasis on the Word shared by the Abrahamic faiths has meant, in visual terms, the illustration and illumination of myriad passages from the Hebrew Bible, New Testament, Qur'an, and other related works in all three traditions. But it has also led to the sense of letters themselves as aesthetic and symbolic instruments. This, not surprisingly, is particularly true of Judaism and Islam, whose traditional adherents assert, respectively, that the very language of God is Hebrew (for Jews, to whom God spoke the Torah through Moses) or Arabic (for Muslims, to whom God spoke the Qur'an through Muhammad).[43] The Word has letters as its most fundamental visual expression. In the art of Islam, this development has taken a particularly spectacular course, with the shaping of an extraordinary number of calligraphic forms.[44]

FIGURE 58   *Illuminated manuscript: Muhammad, Ali, and Abu Bakr traveling toward Macca; scene from the* Siyar-i-Nabi *(Life of the Prophets), Istanbul. 1594*

The symbolic intention of the calligraphic presence in a mosque becomes obvious when we consider highly stylized floriated *kufic* that is all but undecipherable. It offers the divine presence indirectly by being the Word of Allah, yet it is not intended to be *read* in the conventional, *profanus* sense of that verb. Surrounded by stylized, unreadable phrases from the Qur'an, the *hadith,* or merely referring to God's oneness, we are surrounded by God. Interestingly, where legibility is desired—in the writing and reading of Qur'ans (although committing its recited texts to memory is preferred to reading them)—*naskh* gradually tended to replace *kufic* as the standard hand in the course of the tenth century. In many contexts the use of contrastive forms plays a symbolic role analogous to that of contrastive geometric and vegetal forms, contrastive colors and the plays on finite and infinite patterns, positive and negative space, monumental and minute form. Particularly when the contrast is between passages from the Qur'an and from the *hadith* or some other source, the divine-human contrastive yet overlapping connection is firmly underscored.

No instance exemplifies this more apparently—while reminding us both that the contexts for such visual adventures are secular as well as sacred and that in the context of the sultan's ambit the line between those realms is in any case obscured—than some of the large ceramic plates from the sultan's kitchens in early sixteenth-century Ottoman Istanbul. In one of these, a deep double-blue and black central medallion offers complexly interweaving *rumi*s outlined in white around a complicated white-lined, eight-pointed star motif. In turn, a series of three concentric circles pushing out to the rim of the plate is decorated with *hatayi* floral elements—however the central ring is additionally enhanced by a *kufic* inscription. To the unlettered, another abstract element in white has been added to the layered visual dialogue between blue and white, black and white, black and blue. To the literate the letters speak words, but even without them the perpetual flow of which the forms are part echoes the rhythm and harmony of the universe itself around its invisible divine center.

In some cases, particular scripts have been interpreted to offer particular ideas. Thus the *thuluth* style was preferred in Mameluke Egypt of the late thirteenth through early sixteenth centuries, presumably because that society was a rigid hierarchical one governed by a military mentality. "The tightly disciplined parade of multiple vertical strokes immediately brings to mind massed ranks and state processions, particularly when done in white, the official colour of court dress throughout the summer months."[45] *Thuluth* and *naskh* are both styles of which Hafiz Osman (1642–1698), one of the greatest of the Ottoman calligraphers, was a master. He is credited with inventing the *hilyah*—a formal word-portrait of Muhammad. One of these includes a description of the Prophet ascribed to Ali, written in *naskh* and framed in a circle (without beginning or end, singular, complete, and perfect). Around it in cloud forms are the names of the four orthodox Sunni caliphs (Arabic: *khalifa*, meaning "successor" [to Muhammad]) and above it the *Basmallah* ("In the name of Allah the Compassionate, the Merciful . . . ") inscribed in *thuluth*. The *Basmallah* itself—*Bism Allah al-Rahman ar-Rahim*—used before *sura* openings throughout the Qur'an, assumes its own aesthetic life and is found inscribed in various calligraphic styles in varied media, from manuscripts to metalwork grills. There are instances where the *Basmallah* has been inscribed in a *thuluth* allowed to take the shape of a bird. In Islamic (as in Christian and Jewish) thought, the bird symbolizes the soul, rushing to wing its way to God; no animal form could be more appropriate to encompass such fundamental statements of God and our relationship to God.[46]

The zoomorphic *Basmallah* is really a subset of a much larger category of combinations of calligraphy with figurative and abstract imagery. In the Ottoman world, *gulzar* evolved: the technique of filling in the area within the outlines of large letters with various ornamentations, from floral designs and geometric patterns to portraits and hunting scenes.[47] Other zoomorphic patterns with diverse phrases evolved. Shi'ite prayers in the forms of falcons or horses in *thuluth* or *naskh* from nineteenth-century Persia are examples of this, and there is also a cleverly contrived lion of ornamental *tawqi'* script that reads *Ali ibn Ali Talib, radiya Llah Ta'ala'anhu wa-Karrama wajnhahu:* "Ali ibn Ali Talib, may God Almighty be pleased with him and honor him!" The symbolic significance of a lion to represent such aspirations is obvious and relates to a long history of that image in contexts of royalty or power. Mirror writing, where the two sides of an inscription reflect each other perfectly, usually offers a phrase referring to God and the perfect order of his work. The technique is called *muthanna* or *aynali* and is also known as *ma'kus* ("reflected").

Within the Ottoman vocabulary, the most distinctive subset of fancy decorative vocabulary is the *tughra*. This is the ornamentation of the name of the sultan to create an official monogram. Each sultan's calligrapher developed a distinctive *tughra* for his master. The *tughra* of Suleiman the Magnificent—a *gulzar* in which the illuminations that fill the spaces left by the letters of the sultan's name offer the various gold, blue and white, positive and negative-composed elements of a *saz* garden—is a logical extension of a floriated *kufic* reference to God or God's word: stylized to the point of indecipherability, intended not to be read but to convey the aura and the presence of God's *sacerdos,* his lieutenant on objects and documents that, in turn, connect us to God. The name as visual symbol expresses the relationship between *profanus* and *sacer,* intermediated by political personality and visual verbiage (see Figure 59).

The ebbing of the power of the Ottomans and their sultans—between the last siege of Vienna in 1683 and World War I—coincided with a

FIGURE 59   Tughra *(illuminated signature) of Sultan Suleiman the Great, Istanbul. ca. 1525*

succession of changes in Western Christendom. These extended from increasingly secular patterns of thought to political revolutions to technological and scientific innovations. One might suppose that the rich symbolic vocabulary of the previous millennia, diversely evidenced among the Abrahamic faiths, would diminish with diminishing spiritual imperatives. On the contrary, in the centuries that have followed, symbols of faith have continued to be marked by the two features so dominant in centuries past: continuity and transformation.

CHAPTER 5

—∞—

THE SURVIVAL OF SYMBOLS
IN A SECULARIZING
WESTERN WORLD

From Counter-Reformation to Emancipation

The religious and political "New Jerusalem" message broadcast to the world by the dome of St. Peter in Rome would, after its completion in 1564, be echoed in places that had fallen away from Rome. In England, for instance, between the time of Henry VIII and Oliver Cromwell, the English capital grew in stature. One important group among Cromwell's supporters believed that the final world empire and Promised Land would be England—led by a Cromwell who presaged the messiah. Thus London would be the New Jerusalem.[1] So when Christopher Wren began new designs for St. Paul's Cathedral in the summer of 1666, in the midst of this spiritually politicized fervor, the dome he planned, while architecturally derived most directly from Lemercier's Val-de-Grace in Paris, offered an underlying symbolic intention of declaring St. Paul's role as the New Temple.[2]

That sensibility jumped obliquely across the Atlantic in the next century with the building of the capital of the United States, placed on the hill called by the Founding Fathers the Capitoline, for part of the self-conception of the new American republic was to emulate the honest rusticity of the early Roman republic.[3] But the allusions to Rome were only part of its self-conception. That we are "one nation under God," who viewed the English King George as a pharaoh and George Washington as a Moses implies that the Founding Fathers saw their community as Israelite—whose capital, divinely ordained, would be Jerusalem.[4] The dome that would rise above the Capitol Building and dominate the city skyline, as it was first conceived in 1793 by William Thornton—although it would take seventy years, nine architects, and an expanded vision of it by Benjamin Latrobe to complete the whole project—echoes and emulates that of St. Paul's in London, that of St. Peter's in Rome, and ultimately that which had come to be associated with the temple in Jerusalem (the Dome of the Rock) and simultaneously, the Pantheon in Rome. This was to be a newly conceived capital that would both reflect democratic political principles and offer religious principles untrammeled by individuated creeds: Rome and Jerusalem in a new synthesis.[5]

In the nearly three centuries between Michelangelo's and Latrobe's domes, the Western world underwent significant political, technological, intellectual, and spiritual changes. The primary competitors for English commercial hegemony in the seventeenth century were the Dutch. In Holland a commercial middle class developed, which inspired middle-class genre paintings like Jan Steen's *The Life of Man* (1665). Steen offers an everyday interior with ordinary people strewn about it engaged in various everyday actions. Light pours in naturally through the windows toward the rear of the image; children play; adults sing, strum instruments, flirt, eat, and drink; a dog stops to stare at something deeper within the space carved out by the curtain and the open-ended diagonal sweep toward the vanishing point of the floor tiles; odds and ends lie about on that floor. The moral message is not obvious, but there is one. The casual scene is prepared for our benefit: after all, a thick curtain is raised to reveal it, and the stage has been set by a director who wishes us to see the drama in just *this* manner. A closer look at the primary food being consumed reveals that it is oysters—a conventional aphrodisiac and thus a sexual symbol.

Since there is an abundance of oysters in evidence we can understand the painting to include a disguised but unambiguous erotic meaning; it pertains to the human games that involve love, procreation, the continuation of the species, but under irresponsible conditions, the failure to maintain moral strictures due to erotic desires. Moreover, precisely at the point where the curtain rises to a peak toward the center of the work, a little boy is blowing bubbles, with a skull next to him. Viewers would readily recognize the *memento mori* import of the skull, but the boy and his game are more subtle symbols. They play on the classic adage referring to *homo bulla:* "man [as a] bubble," which refers to the empty insignificance of worldly matters—that is, the activities and objects strewn throughout the painting. All the details acquire a symbolic connection to the fleeting quality of those material aspects of life, all of which shrink before the eternal question of our soul. Here a clock has ticked (that's what catches the attention of the dog), there floral branches casually lie against the table on the floor, symbols of fleeting time and ethereality. The painting is a visual parable—a message spoken in indirect illustrative terms—like those offered verbally by Jesus.

It is a small jump from such works to Dutch still-life paintings packed with *memento mori* aspects. Myriad "Vase of Flowers" paintings are not merely exercises in the expression of beauty. The beauty of each blossom will fade, just as individual humans will die, but nature's ongoing cycle of leaf, blossom, and fruit, and even bare-tree branch continues. One subtype of early seventeenth-century Dutch still-life painting is the *ontbijtje*—"breakfast"—still life, with its subtle but insistent moral intention. These works depict food in the interrupted midst of being consumed—as if the diner had suddenly departed, leaving the meal unfinished—just as life's events can often unfold: a suddenly interrupted breakfast, the day seemingly barely begun, when the *sacer* pulls one from the table. If, as is often the case, an open and ticking watch is left on the table (as in William Claesz' 1629 *Breakfast Still-Life*), the unpredictable and fleeting nature of life is further underscored. Is the predilection for including fish, aside from its obviousness as a Dutch breakfast food, a subtle reminder, too, of Christ's charge to Peter, whom he transformed into a fisher of men—to say naught of the other instances where fish figure into Christ's miracles and parables?

Nor is it an extended leap to the array of *vanitas* paintings that overtly draw on symbolic vocabulary to point out the transitory nature of human existence. The skull is the most obvious element, which carries back to the earlier Crucifixion images—but in these still lifes the cross is replaced by the various concomitants of everyday life. Harmen Steenwijk's *Vanitas* (ca. 1640) offers a skull, books (history books, in fact), a candleholder and candle (the light still burns, but faintly), and an overturned container of water or wine (symbols, respectively, of life and joy). To this array he adds a seashell, a musical instrument, smoking pipes that have gone out, a sword and a gourd, together with a lush red swatch of fabric. The flute's music has been stilled; the sounds, however lovely, have faded into the air. The arm that wielded the sword is stilled. The candle sputters, the pipes have already gone cold, and the gourd will soon dry up. If the viewer is schooled enough to make an association with the story of Jonah, he or she will recall that most famous of gourds that shriveled in an afternoon, and perhaps even the more extended connection will be made: Jonah's journey into the belly of the fish can be seen as a symbol of life, death, and resurrection. Perhaps the juxtaposition of the gourd and the red fabric—the traditional color of Christ's sacrifice, but now also used to symbolize pride—further underscores the message of withering and fading, but alloyed with Christian hope.

All of this is part of a naturalistic style that reflects the everyday *(profanus)* world, but it also contains within it a sense of the importance of other realities—aspects of the *sacer*—that percolate beneath the carefully crafted surfaces of both the paintings and the world they represent. That world is found both in interiors and in the array of landscapes being visually explored. At the same time that rich displays of objects and splendid vistas reflect a Dutch sense of well-being and success at moving through the world, they also offer, through symbolic language, an awareness of God's presence as the source behind the vastness and wild beauty of nature, as an underpinning of worldly success (and of the ability to subdue nature, as in the huge project of reclaiming land from the sea), and as the eternal truth that awaits even the most powerful and accomplished of individuals, who all inexorably cross into the *sacer*. Even the intense focus on gem-like detail may be understood in part as a statement of the significance of examining every tiny aspect of God's work as well as of the artist's role in emulating that work.

Thus, while we can find in the seventeenth century the beginnings of an exit from the crisis of the Reformation/Counter-Reformation into secularist thinking, we also find a reinvigorated perspective that recognizes the hand of God ever-present in the world. Even overt religious subject matter moves in new directions during this period. There is a new genre of interior paintings that focuses a detailed lens on the insides of churches (and synagogues). Works by artists like Pieter Saenredam and Emanuel de Witte can be construed simultaneously as secularized, objective investigations of the stately spaces—the lines, and the light and shadow that shift through them—and as pious explorations. The very stateliness they offer suggests the underlying piety— along simple reformationist lines—that motivated the shaping of such spaces, an activated sense of how and in what physical context one might best address God.

There are also biblical works, as in Rembrandt's magnificent *The Wedding Banquet of Samson* (1638), but with a new perspective. Rembrandt's painting of this scene echoes the traditional composition of earlier works in which an array of saints move toward a Madonna and Child enthroned beneath a canopy, or in which Jesus addresses the apostles at the Last Supper. Is it accidental that there are twelve figures around Delilah? The groom is engaged in excited conversation with his Philistine guests, and we can begin to piece together how things are not quite right—how a sacrifice analogous in its way to that of Christ is taking shape, already anticipated by some of those at the celebration. Delilah's distant look, the appraising glance of the figures to her left, whose heads we see just above the head of Samson, and above all, the way in which Samson's Christ-like head is turned as he speaks (it is not he but Delilah who is in the center, surrounded by the numerically evocative dozen feasters), so that we can see the full glorious display of his hair, which is the secret of his strength and will become the source of his martyrdom. All of this is placed before us in dramatic dark and bright tones (see Figure 60).

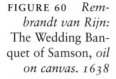

FIGURE 60 *Rembrandt van Rijn:* The Wedding Banquet of Samson, *oil on canvas. 1638*

The paintings of Rembrandt embody the dynamic tension between traditional symbolic terms and the ever-changing vocabulary that was shaping the world of Christian art in the wake of the evolving Counter-Reformation. Alongside the conceptual changes regarding the *sacer* that one can chart in writers from Descartes to Nietzsche, there were changes by the end of the seventeenth century at a more mundane level. Warfare did not abate, but its underlying purposes did. By the time the League of Augsburg pitted a handful of nation-states—including both Protestant England and Catholic Spain—against the France of Louis XIV in 1688–1689, the primary concerns were political and nationalistic, not religious.[6] Even with regard to the Ottomans, one can see a shift from previous wars between Europe and Muslim powers. The major such confrontation of the fin-de-siècle seventeenth century (the 1683 Ottoman siege of Vienna) was one of culture, not religion. The Turks were feared for their different sociocultural values and way of life, not for being Muslims.

⸙

We might suppose that the increasingly secular air of the following era would all but eliminate the *sacer* symbol-laden consciousness expressed throughout the many previous centuries. But Western Christian art continued to draw from a familiar visual well. On the other hand, changes in the Christian sense of the world affected not only Christians but also Jews, for with the late eighteenth-century Enlightenment thought that questioned the very existence of God and focused on the world from a strictly human perspective, the diminished religiosity of western and central Europe loosened the iron-clad antagonism between Jew and Christian. Jews found themselves increasingly able to step from the fringe of European culture to its center (see Note 12).

By the mid-nineteenth century, Jews were increasingly counted among the visual artists of a self-consciously modern era, and an expanded visibility for synagogues in western Europe emerged by late in the century. In Italy, for instance—in the Florence of Brunelleschi's dome—one of the first examples of bold, proud visual self-expression in synagogue architecture since antiquity was completed in 1882. The most striking feature of this synagogue is its soaring copper dome, which reflected how free Italian Jews had become to boldly announce their faith. But at issue is also an internal matter. The question, "How, now, shall we be Jews in this new emancipated environment?" led to the reshaping—the reforming—of Judaism. Among the ideological aspects of Reform Judaism taking shape in Germany by the 1810s (which later spread elsewhere) was that synagogues, traditionally understood as temporary substitutes for the temple in Jerusalem until it be rebuilt, ceased to be called "synagogues" and began to be called "temples." The use of the latter term was intended to connote the permanence of the structure for the community praying in it; the temple in *this* time and place is as valid as the temple in Jerusalem was in its time and place.[7]

FIGURE 61   *Tempio via Farini, Florence, Italy. 1882*

Thus the soaring dome of the Florentine *Tempio* is connected to the same conceptual principle (equation with the Jerusalem temple) underlying St. Peter's dome, albeit from a different perspective. The same notions underlie the symbolic logic of a second feature of the *Tempio,* its synthesis of Italian and Islamic decorative elements: on the one hand, an alternation of horizontal dark and light bands around the entire exterior, and on the other hand, an endless proliferation of geometric and vegetal forms, breaking up every monumental surface into infinitizing minute patterns, particularly on the interior (see Figure 61). The first element symbolizes the sense of being interwoven into the Italian architectural landscape that includes not only the cathedral in Florence but notable churches in cities like Pisa, Siena, and Orvieto.[8] The second suggests a connection to the indigenous decorative style of the Near East and therefore, by the same kind of indirect association that caused the Jerusalem temple to be thought of as domed in Christian and Jewish representations, reinforces the legitimacy of the *Tempio* by embellishing it as its designers imagined its Jerusalem sibling must have been nearly two millennia earlier.

In the latter part of the nineteenth century and the beginning of the twentieth, the idea of large domed synagogues spread, expressing the same principles symbolized by the Florentine structure, each with its own details. The *Gran Tempio* in Rome, for instance, built between 1896 and 1904, offers a soaring dome as it rises along the Tiber River across from St Peter's. But the details of this structure draw (albeit vaguely) from the visual vocabulary of ancient Babylonia, Persia, and Egypt. In Essen, Germany (the country where Reform Judaism originated), an enormous and prepossessing synagogue was built on the eve of World War I, with a dome that rises from the structure like a mountain. Crowned with the representation of the two tablets of the Decalogue, the symbolic intention was to suggest Sinai itself. As if the symbolic references to Sinai and Jerusalem were not enough, its overall floor plan suggests the entire city of David (perhaps due to an archaeological focus on Jerusalem that emerged during that era). The bulging area over which the dome rises represents the Jerusalem temple, and the area behind it, where the synagogue school and offices were situated, the Solomonic palace complex.

Oddly enough, though, it is the rural context of eastern Europe that offers the most distinctive form of synagogue flourishing between the seventeenth and late nineteenth centuries. These wooden structures were most often created not only where Jews had lived for centuries but where the local Jewish population was equal to or even greater than the Christian population. These communities achieved an intellectual golden age in the late sixteenth century and first half of the seventeenth century, as well as a spiritual revival through Hasidism in the mid-eighteenth through nineteenth centuries. In this region, an unwavering sense of identity and the right to express it within the non-Jewish world predated that of Western Jewry by two hundred years. Many timber synagogues offer impressive exteriors.

The dominating hipped roofs, usually flanked, left and right, by smaller gables, are related, on the one hand, to wooden structures found in Scandinavia and, on the other, to the manor houses of the Russian country nobility, with a main house flanked by adjoining guest houses. The towering roofs present a mountainous ambience, as if to offer not only a new adaptation of complying with the *sacer*-addressing need to elevate the synagogue above the community but also a microcosm of the mountain from which Moses brought down the Torah (see Figure 62). It is as if the concept of the Sumerian zig-

FIGURE 62
*Timber syna-
gogue, Wolpa,
Poland.
Eighteenth
century*

gurat has been translated into new spiritual and visual terms miles and millennia away.

On the interior, folk art motifs merged with a baroque sensibility that mixed wood carvings and the color sensibilities of Jewish painters like Eliezer Katz and David Friedlander—for by the nineteenth century, Jewish artists were beginning to gain name recognition. Soaring above the lushly adorned, centrally placed *bimah,* the cupola hovers—simple wooden geometries at Wolpa, rainbows at the oldest known 1651 timber synagogue at Chodorov, painted in 1772 by Israel Ben Mordecai Lisnitzki of Jaryszow. There is frequent but not absolute avoidance of human figures and the occasional appearance of zodiac motifs, suggesting some continuity with ancient synagogue décor and, ultimately, the base of the temple menorah in the Roman period.

By the late nineteenth century, new archaeological discoveries were revealing the classical structures of ancient synagogues in Judaea-Palestine. It is thus no coincidence that, aside from a dome emphasis, a general Greco-Roman synagogue style begins to appear in the West, carrying into the United States. The synagogue built in the 1890s for the oldest Sephardic congregation in New York City and perhaps the continent—the so-called Spanish-Portuguese Synagogue of congregation *Shearith Yisrael* ("Remnant of Israel")—has a visual vocabulary that is distinctly Roman. The symbolic intention of that style is to suggest a connection with antiquity in Judaea-Palestine in the era before Jews were forced to focus architecturally and decoratively inward.

These various aspects of external self-expression—dominant domes and Greco-Roman, Near Eastern, and Arabo-Islamic elements—continue into the twentieth century, particularly in the United States. No instance among the many variants offers a more distinct symbolic visual statement than does the synagogue of congregation *Tiferet Israel* ("Beauty of Israel") in Cleveland, Ohio. That structure, simply referred to as "The Temple"—emphatically affirming the Reform ideological viewpoint—was completed in 1924.[9] The viewer is confronted with an enormous edifice surmounted by a dome echoed by arches, smaller domes, and partial domes, with details that combine Islamic and Byzantine elements.

One recalls the echoing of domes in the Haghia Sophia and the use of mosaic and gold leaf in general in early Christian art, for mosaic in particular abounds in this structure. One also recognizes elements revived from antiquity, as one does in all of the western European and American synagogues just mentioned, such as the threefold doorway and steps leading up to the entrance that suggest its placement on a platform to elevate it above the community. Not surprisingly, nineteenth- and twentieth-century churches also offer traits such as the threefold doorway, but for them this represents a *continuum* since antiquity, not a return to a form abandoned for many centuries.[10]

From Emancipation to Postimpressionism: Toward an Old-New Vocabulary

With the secular mood that carried western Europe into the eighteenth century and that, in some arenas, all but overwhelmed it by the end of that century and the beginning of the next, there was a further proliferation of secularly motivated art. Landscapes devoid of an underlying connection to a divine artificer offered a perspective distinctly different from those of the seventeenth century, as did the expanded repertoire of genre and portrait painting that reflected a growing socioeconomic class below the old nobility but with cultural and social ambitions to match its economic success. Nonetheless, straightforward religious works were still common, and there remained a continuing interest in mythological subjects. Within these works one can recognize a continuum of symbolism flowing out of the previous fifteen centuries, in addition to further symbolic transformations and syntheses.

In France, Antoine Watteau's signature *Embarkation for Cythera* (1717) focuses on the paradoxically *sacer* double nature of love—pleasure and pain, the joy of fulfillment and the sadness of cessation—rather than on the *sacer* as depicted up to this point. There is symbolism in his very aesthetics, to be sure: the colors of this splendid landscape are tinted toward the fall, rather than spring or summer, the time when nature is beginning its long swoon toward winter's death, too early for the hope of spring and its inevitable rebirth to reach our consciousness.

The title defining the painting's subject is laden: Cythera is the island near where, in one thread of the Greco-Roman mythological tapestry, Aphrodite is said to have been born from the sea, a place deemed sacred to the Goddess of Love and Beauty in pagan antiquity. So there is irony here: the gathering of quiet, well-dressed celebrants prepares to leave, in couples, for the island of love, but they are surrounded by colors that hint at love's eventual, season-like dissolution. The skies beyond suggest sunset rather than sunrise, much less full day. In a different era we might suppose that we are being confronted with a *memento mori,* but in this time and place, few viewers would think beyond the sweet sadness of love's brevity toward that of life itself.

Even fewer would have made a political association between a work such as this and the transition from the glorious but tumultuous age of Louis XIV to the quieter age of his successor. During the reign of Louis XV, Watteau's successor, François Boucher, was a favorite who stripped the melancholic patina from his predecessor's visual investigations into love, leaving a feast of pleasure before the viewer's eyes. After Boucher, Jean-Honoré Fragonard continued that direction but also turned late-eighteenth-century French painting back (and thus forward) toward another, more serious direction. On the one hand, works like *The Pursuit* (ca. 1771–1773) and *The Swing* (ca. 1766) offer variations on the theme of love as an innocent and delightful game. On the other hand, Fragonard's *Coroesus Sacrificing Himself to Save Callirrhoë* (1765) turns the viewer toward a classical setting framed by the remnants of enormous columns as well as toward a much weightier aspect of love. Love that yields self-sacrifice under difficult conditions; love that leads the lover toward willing death on behalf of the beloved—this is love understood in spiritual and moral, not physical and amoral, terms.[11]

Such a work leads directly to Jacques-Louis David. David's paintings, such as *The Oath of the Horatii* (1785), are pristine in their return to the classical style and sweep back to the classical past as a source of moral

FIGURE 63   *Jacques-Louis David:* Death of Marat, *oil on canvas. 1793*

nourishment. Drawing from Roman mytho-historiography on the founding of the republic, his paintings engendered patriotic sensibilities—which would spill over into revolutionary action in the following decade. David's *Marat* (1793) turns a slain hero of that most secular of political revolutions into a *profanus pieta*. The figure is bathed in light that flows in from beyond the image, as if from a supernatural source about to envelop this *sacer*-connected being. The head-wrapping is reminiscent of a halo, the lolling head beatified by a soft smile, the knife wound in his chest reminiscent of Christ's fifth wound, and Marat's drooping right arm, feather pen still clutched in his fingers, reminiscent of the drooping arm of any number of images of the dead Christ—the whole offers a figure who died for us. The political revolution looks to the spiritual revolution of eighteen centuries earlier for part of its visual inspiration. Without a single overt Christian symbol, the image draws from the visual history of Christian art to shape its homage (see Figure 63).

Jacques-Louis David would become the preeminent visual articulator of the political revolution that *followed* the French Revolution, when an imperial "monarchy" was restored to France through Napoleon's seizure of power in late 1799. David was the first among an array of portrayers of Napoleon as Caesar and even as a god. Others, both painters and sculptors, echoed the exalted neoclassical style and its symbols in their representations of other members of the Napoleonic upper crust. Thus, for example, the Italian Antonio Canova sculpted a dazzling portrait of Napoleon's sister, *Pauline Borghese* as Venus Victrix, in 1805 in Rome. The luxuriantly half-nude figure is laid out on a chaise lounge (an invention of the *Empire* style), so skillfully rendered that one imagines the marble as a plush textile into which one could press one's fingers. Pauline looks over her shoulder toward the viewer, with a facial profile that derives from classical Greek images. In her hand, lightly held, is a small apple—presumably the fruit presented to her by Paris/Alexandros, the Trojan shepherd-prince on Mount Ida who judged her the victor in the famous beauty contest that resulted in the Trojan War.

It is difficult to imagine that Canova's viewers would not have seen a visual pun before them when their eyes finally came to rest on that small fruit being dandled in Pauline's hand. They would have considered that other famous female—human, not divine—whose relationship with an apple has come to be associated with the bringing of disaster on a scale grand enough to encompass all wars, including that at Troy. That Venus is the goddess of love and beauty and that Eve's newly acquired knowledge (after eating that fruit that she then shared with Adam) included sexual knowledge—so that the original sin of disobeying God long ago came to be associated in Christian thought with sexual activity—would surely not be lost on the viewers of this sculpture. The symbol of disaster and destruction is doubled. The Empire touting chasteness could apparently use a salacious instrument in promoting chasteness.

Among other consequences of the political revolutions that defined the late eighteenth century was the birth of the United States of America, newly separated from the empire of which it had been a colonial appendage for a century. In religion, the revolution of deism, first articulated in the early seventeenth century and culminating in the writings of Viscount Bolingbroke (1678–1751) in the mid-eighteenth, was achieving unprecedented popular success by the last third of the century. The principle that the pursuit of a pious and a virtuous life is the most desirable form of religious devotion (any particular liturgical bent or particularized sense of what God is or how one must address God is functionally irrelevant) attracted, among others, the Founding Fathers of the new United States, who separated religious conviction from political life.[12]

So, too, the Industrial Revolution, starting in England about 1760, set in motion a sweeping series of advances in technology, which offered a confirmation that humans are capable of virtually anything. A corollary, for some, was that God is either nonexistent or more limited than theretofore assumed, or at least self-willed into the background of human enterprise. The factories of technological revolution appear again and again in the visual media of the era, like the temples of earlier eras: meeting points between *sacer* and *profanus* and statements of the human ability to be *super natura*—where human inventiveness and productivity shape two sides of our ability to act *in imitatione dei* as creators. Thus, in the watercolor by Peter le Cave of the *Goscote Iron Foundry* (ca. 1800), for example, the foundry—bathed in light from beyond the image—looks, at first glance, like a church, or a church that has been converted into a factory. The enormous opening from which a window appears to have been removed, dominating the pitch-roofed main structure, the smoke-spewing chimneys reminiscent of bell towers, their heavenward thrust, evoke a spiritual impression in the unconscious or even conscious mind of the viewer.

The principle of the human mastery of nature, working not so much with the gods but in their place, would extend from the temples of production to architectural monuments yielded by that productivity, such as railroad tracks, trains, and bridges. All three seem to meet in the colored aquatint *View of a Stone Bridge at Risca* (ca. 1805) by Thomas Cartwright (based on a work by Edward Pugh). The long arcaded stone bridge is reminiscent of a Roman aqueduct and accomplishes visually and conceptually the same end: cutting through, over and under, the irregular forms of the natural landscape to which it offers such a strong contrast with the repeated, perfectly ordered rhythms of its arches and the ruler-like precision of its horizontal sweep.

The Roman capacity to order space, to bring water over long, irregular distances, to function both *super natura* and *in imitatione deorum* is echoed in Cartwright's image of an innovation that conveys human passengers over long distances while denying the difficulties of the lay of the land. Whereas the Romans believed that their ability to accomplish these feats was largely a result of their being the darlings of the gods they emulated, the early-nineteenth-century understanding of this human ability was that it rested on *transcending or ignoring* whatever might have prevailed as divine mandate to accomplish their own ends. What at first appears to be a railroad train on its tracks sweeping at right angles to the bridge is not: it is merely a well-ordered row of buildings that bisects the irregular landscape with a dark power that is the light-and-shadow antipode of the bridge.

The fascination with magisterial sweeps of extension bridges and tunnels as statements of human cosmogonic ability is observable before mid-century. One goes over, the other under earth or water, but both re-order the natural landscape to make human passage through it simpler. Among the more impressive images that record the underground passage is the 1846 wash drawing by John Cooke Bourne of *Box Tunnel*. In it we follow the train tracks and the powerful, puffing locomotive as they carry us by way of an obliquely Albertian sweep of orthogonals deep into the mountain. That is, we are led by the sacerdotal child of our own genius into the *sacer* whose dark depths have no identifiable shape or extent: we know out of the faith derived from having found the way back to the *profanus* in cutting the tunnel and laying the track that the spaceless dark space does not go on forever. Here, as in similar images, the fear of and hope invested in the *sacer* expressed in the imagery of earlier eras and its symbols has been transmuted into the awe in what we of the *profanus* can accomplish so that our reality is less at the mercy of the *sacer*.

That England is the context of most of these images is to be expected, since that is where the Industrial Revolution first blossomed. But English painters—William Hogarth, for example—also continued to produce the kind of "moral" imagery that grew out of Netherlandish painting of the seventeenth century, though rarely with such detailed use of symbolic elements. Hogarth's genre scenes—paintings of social life, which he himself called "modern moral subjects"—have an overtly instructive agenda. His concern for the social ills in the world around him—not only in broad terms but also with regard to specific groups, such as women prisoners at Bridewell or the mentally ill in Bedlam—led him to a varied series of works intended as visual protests and instruments to shock his viewers.[13] At a time when his world was surging toward increasing self-confidence regarding the human capacity for cosmogony, Hogarth was taking our species to task for failing to live up to the responsibility of moral and ethical cosmogony, particularly when we have declared God irrelevant or nonexistent.

On the other hand, Sir Joshua Reynolds, in the following generation, offered a different sort of lesson with dramatic scenes such as *The Death of Dido* (1781), in which the swooning Carthaginian queen, having been abandoned by Aeneas, perishes by her own hand. Her glistening white flesh is largely enveloped by a dark background, and her woe-struck sister, Anna, throws her arms up in the kind of gesture of despair recognizable from an earlier era and a different, Christian, context—as, for example in that of John peering down toward the dead Christ in Giotto's *Lamentation* in the Arena Chapel in Padua, or looking up at the crucified Christ in Piero della Francesca's *Misericordia* altarpiece in Sansepulcro. This is not to say that the intention is to invoke religious subject matter in a specific manner (Dido as a Christ-figure); rather, the artist intends for an association to be made by the viewer between such scenes and this one in order to reinforce the sense of the humanistic pathos of the moment. A pagan queen betrayed by a pagan hero is as worthy of our tears as the God-man betrayed by Judas. Powerful grief is simply powerful.

A different sense of the world—of the here and now, not the exotic other—melts under the brush of Joseph Mallord William Turner. In his painting, earlier symbols have disappeared, together with the edges of objects, which we naturally expect to be visually sharp. It is as if the artist has set out to express in static visual terms the Heraclitian-Platonic notion that, in our reality, there is no stasis. The flow of light and shadow, ever changing as those elements move over and around and across objects, constantly recontour object edges. If, in addition to the sky and earth as sources of visual transformation, we add water—canals and the Adriatic Sea around Venice, or the Thames River slipping through London—then the reflective feature of that ever-restless commodity offers an even more emphatic nonsolidity to the objects we stare at. If the fog born between the sky and water further envelops them, then the entire image becomes a gauzed passage between permanence and ephemerality.

Turner's works can be seen as experiments in the dissolution of line under the pressure of these natural elements. But they can also be viewed as symbolic statements regarding the inadvisability of human certainty regarding the accomplishments touted in the art and thought of the previous few generations, particularly when so many of the subjects Turner painted were man-made. An obvious instance is his *Houses of Parliament on Fire*. In this work he uses another of the elements that hovers between concretion and abstraction (one cannot grasp fire as a solid element but can be burned by its very tangible heat), depicting it in the act of consuming one of the ultimate symbols of solid human accomplishment (in both architectural and administrative terms).

By the time of Turner's death in 1851, the path that he carved through the visual landscape was barely a generation away from being widened by the French impressionists. Monet, in particular, but also Renoir, Pissarro, Sisley, and their followers, focused on the role of light in shaping the way in which we see objects. Claude Monet was obsessed with light: his work evolved away from the manner in which objects are shaped by the passing and shifting of light across their surfaces toward the way light itself changes as it passes over the objects in its path. He pondered what Pissarro wrote about after reading the scientific literature: how light is actually a compendium of colors—and therefore colors are by definition aspects of light. Every color is also affected by the colors around it, and we thus perceive the same color differently depending upon its pigmental environment. Both light and shadow are colored by that environment, rather than being simply white or black.

One recognizes this readily if one considers the groups of paintings done by Monet as he moved into his mature period, of haystacks, for example, or of the façade of the Rouen Cathedral, where the same subject is repeatedly portrayed under changing conditions of daylight, weather, and season. With the Rouen Cathedral there is a particular sort of irony from the perspective of traditional symbols of faith, for the religious significance of the structure—its threefold doorway, its ogive arches and soaring towers, its sculptures, columns, pilasters, and crockets—is not at issue. For the purposes of the artist's explorations, it is no different from the haystacks which he treats in the same way. Nor even, for that matter, is the edifice itself the subject, as a solid entity contrived by human labor, its geometries contrived by human intelligence. The exploration of any one of these paintings—with blurry outlines and dramatic contrasts of strongly lit and harshly shadowed areas, its colors subsumed into a scintillating, silvery patina—suggests that the true object of the artist's interest is not the object affected by light but light itself, as its constituent coloristic elements are altered by passing over the object. When an entire series is seen together, the changing conditions under which the light makes its transit become obvious elements within the exploratory process.

There is more: such a painting isn't finished until the viewer determines the distance from which to view it most effectively. If one views the painting from a very short distance, not only will the entirety blur toward abstraction, not only will the eye clearly perceive the painter's brushstrokes, but the viewer will even discern strands of hair from the brush still embedded in the paint. The work requires an effort from the viewer, whose viewing process completes it. Just as the Rouen Cathedral does not appear the same at any two moments in time because the light that washes over it is never the same, so even the paintings that necessarily encapsulate a series of those moments are never identical from one viewer to the next or even, perhaps, for the same viewer at different times. The Heraclitian-Platonic issue of nonstasis and the inclusion of the viewer in the work have both been engaged at a new symbolic level.

The painter to whom Monet looked as his master, who embarked on a course away from moral issues toward purely aesthetic issues in painting, was Edouard Manet. It has often been said that Manet painted his famous *Déjeuner sur l'herbe* (1863), which shocked Paris by its juxtaposition of naked (female) and clothed (male) figures—the latter in contemporary dress, thus leaving little room for the viewer to maneuver the image into some other, exotic reality than his own—to make the point that the only responsibility of an artist is to paint, not to offer moral commentary on this world (or the next). The fact that the central figures are derived directly from the Italian tradition of Gorgione and Marcantonio Raimondi and connect to the visual world of Watteau, Boucher, and Fragonard is part of the statement that Manet's symbolic language is intended to be *anti*-symbolic.[14]

The same may be true of Manet's *A Bar at the Folies Bergère* (1882): it is simply an exquisite example of the artist's desire to present painting for the sake of painting. But it strikes me that we undersell Manet if we ignore another perspective of the viewer's role. We see a beautiful, unsmiling barmaid leaning on the bar, across which an array of bottles, together with a bowl of fruit and a small vase of flowers, are all displayed. More precisely, they are disposed left and right, and she occupies the center; she is, moreover, sandwiched between these objects and a further array of bottles on the surface behind her. Behind *that* is a mirror, and angled off to the right we see her back—and the dandified man who, facing her, stands where we do, on the near side of the bar (see Figure 64).

The ingenuity of completing the circle of involvement by implying the presence of the viewer of the painting is an aesthetic tour de force: she stares at us who stare at her as does the customer we glimpse. On the other hand, given the place, its occupants, and the disposition of objects before us, she, this stunning centerpiece who is as silent and unemotional as any of those objects, is one of *them*. From her double bottle-like curves (hips to waist and upper torso to neck and head) to the dark-light contrast of her lower to upper parts echoing that of the champagne bottles, she is less a human being than an object designed

FIGURE 64   *Edouard Manet:* A Bar at the Folies Bergère, *oil on canvas. 1881–1882*

for our visual consumption and, if we are like the gentleman who contemplates her with us, perhaps for more than visual consumption. She is a symbol of a particular version of male-female relations typical of that time, place, and quadrant of society, and the ongoing subject and object of visual exploration in the Western tradition, from Praxiteles' *Knidian Aphrodite* to Fragonard's *The Swing*.

—ᴏꙎ—

Manet was pushed by Monet into accepting a role as mentor to the impressionists. The figure among them who was most conscious of the issues of how we see and the relationship between art and the world—who was reading the new scientific literature on optics and was writing about these matters to his son, Lucien—was Camille Pissarro.[15] Although there are many other issues to consider regarding Pissarro's work, for the purposes of this narrative, it is important to recognize that he was a Jew, for two reasons. First, this reminds us that we have arrived at the point where the distinction between Jewish and Christian has become moot—at least as far as the visual, non-narrative issues raised by impressionism are concerned. Second, there is nonetheless a course specific to Jewish artists that brings them to Pissarro's non-symbol-laden concerns.

Jewish genre painting emerged during the nineteenth-century expansion of general genre painting occasioned by increasing patronage from a growing merchant middle and upper class seeking its own image (and not that of the old nobility or the Church) in art. Interestingly, many Jewish genre scenes look back nostalgically to aspects of earlier Jewish life or record their ongoing presence in spite of Emancipation. Others suggest the struggle to bridge the traditional world of the past with the evolving world of the present. Thus, in Poland, for example, Mauritzy Gottlieb swept through the firmament of both genre and portraiture in the 1870s with the brief brightness of a meteor. Gottlieb was a tragic figure—dead by 1879, at the age of twenty-three, of cancer of the larynx. In his *Yom Kippur in the Synagogue,* painted when the artist was twenty-two,

FIGURE 65   *Mauritzy Gottlieb:* Yom Kippur in the Synagogue, *oil on canvas. 1879*

Gottlieb portrayed himself, contemplative, in the midst of a light stratum that illuminates the setting and the moment and that divides men below from women above—female faces are particular hot spots of luminescence—as a symbol of ordering a new year: as God divided waters below from those above, in ordering the universe. Heaven is separated from earth yet connected by the lightning flash of God's final decisions at the end of the final service of the Day of Atonement, when the world, as the year, is begun anew (see Figure 65).

Most intriguing of the painting's symbolic details is the cruciform created by the architectural arrangement that dominates the scene: the pensive artist is a Jew in a world that is Christian, even if in some of its parts Jews have been emancipated from the restrictions of the previous fifteen centuries. The interior of the synagogue at the height of the Jewish ritual year is dominated by the symbol that cannot be avoided by the population wrestling with its God at this season. On the other hand, the Torah, held by the rabbi in the procession, is placed so that the central pillar in the composition seems to grow from it. The answer, if there is one, to the implied question of how to be a Jew in an increasingly tolerant Christian/secular world is the Torah, as tree of life and pillar supporting the Jewish world within the non-Jewish cosmos.

Still more famous at the time was Moritz Daniel Oppenheim of Germany, whose commissions rose with the growing number of Jewish lawyers, businessmen, and civic leaders by mid-century. His genre scene, *Sabbath Afternoon*, painted about 1850, offers a visual summary of issues confronting mid-nineteenth-century middle-class central and western European Jews. The artist has divided his canvas by creating an arch of dark color that encompasses the young people, while the old grandfather leans away from that semicircle and is dressed in contrastive white (Oppenheim did at least two versions of this subject; in one the grandfather is attired in a dark garment). The separation of the grandfather from the other figures is further emphasized by the stream of light that, pouring in from the window, bathes the old man as, eyes closed, he is also bathed, perhaps, in afternoon dreams of the past. While he may be listening to a recitation by his grandson—perhaps it is the latter's Bar Mitzvah speech that he is trying out on his grandfather—he is compositionally disconnected from everyone else. Although the child faces out toward his grandfather, he is, ultimately, part of the future, not the past. Formally, he is encompassed by the arch of the "modern" generation (see Figure 66).

FIGURE 66 *Moritz Oppenheim:* Sabbath Afternoon, *oil on canvas. ca. 1850*

All of the figures sit around the post-Sabbath-meal table, at which a young man (the son of the old man, perhaps, and the father of the little boy) engages in a traditional Sabbath afternoon activity: expounding a page of Torah. But this is the modern world; the setting is not the male-dominated house of study but the female-dominated dining room. And the audience is not fellow scholars nor even fellow males but, in this new reality, women! Rather than having retired to the kitchen and their own gossip, they are an eager part of the encompassing arch of study. It is a new world, rising above the foundations of tradition. Both subject and stylistic details offer a symbolic vision: a moment from Jewish life of the time, reflecting the quiet tension between the ghetto-bound medieval world and the problematic modernity toward which so many Jews were aspiring.

Other Jewish painters made names for themselves in the late nineteenth and early twentieth centuries, according to their particular stylistic proclivities. Josef Israels in Holland, Lesser Ury and Max Liebermann in Germany, and Ernst Josephson in Sweden offered works that reflected on the world of the past and its symbols as that world was slipping away, but more often turned toward the sort of landscape concerns that impressionists like Pissarro embraced—all four of these painters were drawn to the impressionist style—on a track not so much parallel to as contiguous with that of their Christian colleagues. In some cases, the degree to which a state of comfort with Christianity had been achieved was reflected from the opposite side of the mirror, taking on Christian imagery either as part of an aesthetic or national (as opposed to religious) vocabulary, or deliberately as a symbol of benignity rather than antagonism.

Perhaps the most accomplished of the second-generation of *peredvizhniki*—artists who abandoned the St. Petersburg Academy and its constraints to go out and paint in the multiethnic world of the Russian empire—was the Jew Isaac Ilyitch Levitan. Levitan's inspiration is romantic realism, and his Jewishness is only subtly accessible. His works are imbued with a brooding melancholy that some see as a reflection of the topography of his Russian homeland and others see as rooted in the experience of his Jewish heritage. Both sources seem to coexist, with an emphasis in his landscapes on grandeur and understated emotion, and his inward sensibility perhaps sharpened by his experience as a Jew in all-Russian Moscow when he attended the arts school there, where the threat of expulsion from the city always hovered. Levitan developed an awareness of and perhaps identification with the Zionist movement growing among Russian Jews by the late nineteenth century, as his *Pilgrims to Zion* exemplifies. Dark forms lead the eye up the canvas to a blinding sunrise-like light—the sacred city—suggesting the artist's growing conviction that the path to a brighter world for his people led to *Eretz Yisrael*. But at the same time, many of his most successful and popular paintings focus on the churches and monasteries that are the man-made equivalent of the birch forests and broad steppes of the Russian world. His *Quiet Monastery* (1890) offers onion-domed ecclesiastical structures, at a distance, as connectors between the tree-filled earth that surrounds them and the sky above them. They do so twice, for they are reflected in the river that separates and connects the viewer by way of the foreground and a footbridge across that watery boundary toward another, *sacer,* realm, which shapes the image's background. The monastery is depicted both as a bridge between *profanus* and *sacer* and as part of the *sacer* so distant from us—perfectly consonant with what we might imagine to be the feelings of an artist whose sense of self is both Jewish and Russian.

More radical are the works of Levitan's countryman, sculptor Marc Antokolski, and those of American sculptor Moses Jacob Ezekiel. Antokolski was born in Lithuania in 1843. A child of the era when even in eastern Europe the winds of secular learning had begun to blow across the landscape of traditional Jewish education, he was carried by his art to the St. Petersburg Academy. There, nationalist romantic realism chafed against the bonds of academic form; the desire to depict the people and their yearnings competed against the obligation to portray the upper crust nobility in idealized guise. Rustic and untrained, Antokolski swiftly distinguished himself among his fellow pupils, as their later reminiscences attest. The sculptor's earliest works not only included Jewish genre figures, such as *A Jewish Tailor Threading a Needle*, but also a remarkable figure of a *Bound Christ Before the People,* not crowned by thorns, not hovering in crucifixion or lying in beatific death, but simply bound. When questioned about his choice of subject, the artist responded, "I appreciate his teachings no less than Christians do, for he was a Jew who preached love for humanity." Thus he asserted the universalist contours of his commitment to his art and his perception of Christ as a symbol of universalist love, not particularist hostility, as much as he did his position as a leader in the revolt against academic formalism.

Moses Jacob Ezekiel was the first American-born Jewish artist to achieve international recognition. In 1869, he traveled to Berlin to study sculpture, where he met and became friends with Antokolski. Ezekiel's memoirs describe the impression made on him by Antokolski's *Bound Christ,* and that work probably inspired the American to also depict the Nazarene. After his stay in Berlin, Ezekiel settled in Rome, thanks, initially, to his winning the Michel Beer *Prix de Rome,* awarded by the Berlin Academy of Fine Arts in 1873. He won the *Rome* Prize for a bas-relief sculpture titled *Israel:* "I cut the name 'Israel' in the lower edge of the frame," he wrote, "although Ahasuer would have been just as appropriate . . . Ahasuer is the traditional name of the Wandering Jew." Elsewhere, he commented: "Ahasuer's agony is the type of *all* human woe . . . [it] is the hope of redemption that throbs in *every* human heart; it is an allegory founded upon the history of Israel."[16]

His heroic Israel, rendered complete with nails in his hands as a heroic Jesus, a massive allegory of Jerusalem and her fallen kings, together place a traditional Christian theme, the Crucifixion—ordinarily flanked by the Virgin and John the Evangelist, or by allegorical figures of the defeated synagogue and the triumphant church—at the service of a different sensibility. Even in despair, the figure of Israel surges up and out toward the viewer, his outstretched right hand pushing out and with it, thrusting the nail head toward the viewer. The suffering Christ shares symbolic visual territory with suffering Jews.

The subject of Jesus would occupy Ezekiel a number of times. *The Martyr* of 1876—a bust of Christ "born and bred a Jew," as Ezekiel wrote—is one instance, and it is another example of Ezekiel's imposing a Jewish sense of Jesus on a traditional Christian vision of him. The Son of Mary becomes a symbol of suffering Jews rather than of redeemed Christians. *Christ in the Tomb* of 1889, is a third example, sculpted because "I wanted to make the greatest Jew and the greatest reformer of millions of people." These works by Ezekiel—and those of Antokolski—were the artistic consequence of Emancipation and assimilation. Both artists appropriated and re-explored the most Christian of Western, Christian art historical themes, re-presenting it as universal and transforming it from a symbol, in Jewish thinking, of the victimizers to a symbol of the victim and the victim's intrinsic nobility.

The image of Christ construed differently from centuries of Christian representation leads back to the impressionists and specifically to Paul Gauguin. Following his mentor Pissarro, Gauguin understood a key purpose of color to be the expression of emotion—a reference not to external objective reality but to the internal subjective feelings of the artist. Gauguin transformed Pissarro's teachings regarding the use of color to the dictum: "If you feel that the tree is blue, then paint it blue!"[17] Gauguin's *Yellow Christ* (1889) exemplifies this, as it explores the meaning of faith by transforming a gray, stone roadside shrine into the crucified Savior through the piety of the Breton peasant women who have paused to venerate the image on their way home from a long day of laboring in the fields.

This focus on unwavering faith by means of startling visual innovation is even more apparent in Gauguin's *Vision after the Sermon* (1888). Here the tradition-bound Breton women have been so inspired by the sermon they have just heard that upon leaving the church they actually see the wrestling match between Jacob and the angel described in the sermon (Genesis 32), as if it were taking place on the lawn before them. We see them seeing the vision; we look over their shoulders to see what they see; we see enough of the faces of two of them to note that their eyes are closed and understand that they are seeing with an inner vision—a vision that we have been allowed to share. Thus the entire painting plays on the complex notion of how we see, internally and externally, subjectively and objectively, alone and as part of a group—a family, a community, a species. The grass in this vision within the canvas frame is bright red, bursting with emotion and passion: not as the symbol of blood sacrifice but of faith-bound, spiritual, love-focused emotion (see Figure 67). The

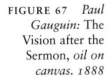

FIGURE 67 *Paul Gauguin:* The Vision after the Sermon, *oil on canvas. 1888*

external reality of the God-bound *sacer* and the internal reality of the imagination-bound *sacer* meet; between them the *profanus,* of which we, the viewers, are part, is squeezed so powerfully by the inner and outer *sacer* that the rendering of our world on the canvas has been transformed into a flattened, brightly hued vision.

Gauguin was a disciple of Pissarro's impressionism, but he would go on to become, along with Emile Bernard, the center of a group of painters at Pont-Aven and Le Pould. Among those in the circle at Pont-Aven was Paul Sérusier who, returning to Paris, together with Maurice Denis and others, formed a new group that they called the Nabis. The name derives form the Hebrew word for "prophet" *(navi).* In the work of the Nabi painters, brilliant postimpressionist color (reflecting the *sacer* power of the imagination and its passions) dominates, as symbols and allusions to the faith of those depicted are rampant. Gauguin's Pont-Aven group and the Nabis spawned yet another postimpressionist group, the symbolists. Inspired by such poets as Baudelaire, Mallarmé, Rimbaud, and Verlaine, the symbolist movement developed in France at the end of the nineteenth century and gave rise to the decadents in England and related movements in Belgium, Austria, and Germany.[18]

The principles of the symbolists and decadents presented a logical paradox on at least two levels. First, their visual vocabulary was drawn from within the mind or imagination of the artist in self-conscious opposition to the materialism that was an outgrowth of the success of the Industrial Revolution, and that vocabulary lived in the realm of the Other—be that Other a medievalist past, a distant land, or a dream-vision. Yet as much as they opposed the urbanized material outgrowth of that revolution, their movement was not a return to nature, for that, too, as part of the *profanus,* was rejected in its objective state by the inner *sacer* sensibilities of the symbolists and decadents. Therefore, the overall sensibility is one of enervation and malaise. Second, in an age seeing itself as increasingly secular, the symbolists, decadents, and their cognates possessed an intense—specifically Christian—religious streak, even as they also transferred the sense of the *sacer* from its place within the realm of religion to other realms.

An obvious alternative realm is that of dreams. This is not accidental, since the field of psychoanalysis, in evolution at the end of the nineteenth century, reached a crescendo with the publication, in 1900, of Sigmund Freud's *The Interpretation of Dreams.* That signal work drew from and pointed toward the dream realm as one in which the elements of the *profanus* are transmuted into expressions of hope and fear, blessing and curse, sweetness and nightmare. It is not surprising that in the attenuated atmosphere of major European cities—Vienna, Paris, London, Berlin, Prague, Brussels, and Budapest—there would be artists drawn toward the visual exploration of the dream aspect of the *sacer*. That such explorations were laden with symbols (whether or not the artist was specifically called a symbolist) and that there were those for whom that language pointed most directly toward dissolution and death (whether or not the artist was specifically called a decadent) is also not surprising.[19]

One thinks, among the artists associated with another forerunner of these groups, the pre-Raphaelites, of Dante Gabriel Rossetti in England. His painting *Beata Beatrix* (1863) offers multiple bridges between aspects of the *sacer* and *profanus* realms (see Figure 68). The exquisite foreground figure who dominates the work is a pun: the "blessed blessed one" is Beatrice, who guided Rossetti's namesake, the early fourteenth-century Florentine poet Dante Alighieri, into paradise in the third part of his *Divine Comedy,* but in Rossetti's painting she is the painter's own beloved wife, Lizzie Siddal, who died shortly before the painting was begun.[20] Lizzie has crossed into that other realm, where she may be hoped and expected to await her artist husband and lead him into heaven when the time comes. The background underscores the connection between poet and painter and between the amanuensis of the one and the amanuensis of the other: hovering in the light that envelops Lizzie-Beatrice's head like a halo is a bridge that is recognizable as part of Florence's architectural landscape. Emerging from the shadows to the right and left are two indistinct figures, the one gesturing toward the other to follow; the second turned toward the first

FIGURE 68   *Dante Gabriel Rossetti:* Beata Beatrix, *oil on canvas. 1863*

in questioning. These must be Beatrice and Dante themselves, in that spaceless space beyond Florence and every other earthly realm.

The spaceless space of the background and the more naturalistic space of the foreground are mediated by the suggestion of a wall, on the edge of which rests a sundial, measuring timeless time—since the light and shadows that suffuse it come from no logical directional source. Lizzie/Beatrice leans forward and throws her head back; her eyes are closed in silent ecstasy—the *ek-stasis* of being outside one's living self in the sense of both death and *la petite mort* experienced by saints such as St. Teresa. Her forearms and hands offer opposing diagonals echoed in reverse by the wings of a dove alighting toward them (and echoed, again, by the diagonal of the sundial above them). The dove—red, the color of passion (in both religious and secular senses of that word) and love—is adorned with a small, delicate halo and bears in its beak both a sprig of green and a ring. This is an annunciatory bird, bearing the tidings of eternal marriage consummated in the *sacer*—the eternal life of death and the eternal fertility of the artist's imagination.

Beata Beatrix shares ground with works by Rossetti's fellow pre-Raphaelite painters, especially Edward Burne-Jones and William Morris. One of the constants among these artists—and others of their direct or indirect circle—was their infatuation with women. It was an often self-contradictory infatuation: women as exquisite, exotic, infinitely desirable and idealized creatures who are also infinitely dangerous (especially if they fail to remain planted on the idealizing plinth where the artist would have them remain). King Arthur's Queen Guinevere is both virginal and seductive; her spiritual siblings include not only Beatrice but also Salome (calling for the head of Saint John) and Eve, leading all of mankind (not *human*kind, but *man*kind) into perdition.

In this, part of the prelude to English decadent art, we find a path back to France and to the work of Gustave Moreau and Odilon Redon. Both of these symbolist painters swoon with the bad dreams of dangerous, sensuous, long-haired women who entangle men in their serpentine tresses. Redon was friends with Mallarmé and with Joris Karl Huysmans, in whose 1884 novel, *A Rebours*, the hero, the decadent Duc Jean Floressas des Esseintes, is described as owning a large number of works by Redon—and of viewing certain women, such as Helen (whose beauty sent a thousand ships to Troy and destroyed two cultures), the Sphinx (part woman, part feline, destroyer of men at the crossroads who cannot give her the answer she wants from them), and especially

Salome, as embodiments of destructive femaleness. "She [Salome] was no longer just a dancing girl who extorts a cry of lust and lechery from an old man by lascivious movements of her loins . . . she had become, as it were, the symbolic incarnation of undying Lust."[21]

Redon's drawings and paintings repeatedly speak the language of nightmare: balloons become enormous eyes, and hairy spiders arrive over the horizon (or push out from the cleft between two sides of a landscape in imagery that would make Freud blush with its transparency). Moreau's 1876 watercolor, *The Apparition*, offers an exotically attired female, the curves of her body pressing against her long, flowing, bejewelled garments. She appears to have been brought suddenly to a halt by a vision toward which she gestures in simultaneous contempt and terror. We understand that it is Salome, and that the vision is of the head of John the Baptist, sad-faced, encircled by a jewel-like halo in an explosion of light—and dripping blood from its neck. Thus a Christian symbol has been broadened in scope: Salome functions as a symbol of all females who plot the destruction of males.

This is the *femme fatale* (the very phrase is a coinage of that era) who is the nightmare vision of Woman and who breathes the enervated fin-de-siècle air of Edvard Munch. One among many examples is Munch's 1895 lithograph *Vampire*, which depicts an apparently unclothed female with a clothed male embracing her, his head against her breast, her face buried in the nape of his neck. It is at once a terrifying reprise of Manet's *Déjeuner sur l'herbe* with its clothed males and unclothed females, but one in which the *déjeuner* has become the feast of the female upon the male—a kiss and dance of love and death—and a symbol of the reunion of male and female, but with nefarious, not glorious, results.

The *femme fatale* is the repeating imagery, swathed in Byzantine patterning and gold, offered by Gustave Klimt in his paintings of fin-de-siècle Viennese women—the very sort of women whom Freud was analyzing in his consultation room. Dreams and hysteria are part of an understated vision in Klimt's imagery.[22] In *The Kiss* (1907–1908) his figures are positioned in an awkward, angular embrace, as if one will devour the other. Klimt's *Judith I* (1901) portrays the devourer not as the heroine who saved Jerusalem by making drunk and beheading the Assyrian general, Holofernes, but as a licentious, bare-breasted woman, her head lushly framed in thick hair and rich gold, who holds the head of her victim as it slips off the canvas, below waist level, while she stares out at us with eyes half-closed and lips half-opened in silent ecstasy.

Such symbolic visual statements of a fin-de-siècle sensibility would yield further visual echoes a generation later—by which time the Great War was turning dire visions into prophecies—in works like Egon Schiele's *Death and the Maiden* (1915). This is not a new theme, by any means; it is just articulated with a new vehemence, shaped by impressionism and expressionism and reshaped by symbolism, decadence, cloisonisme, fauvism, and early cubism. In the dark, swirling vision in which Schiele's two figures wrap themselves around each other, ensconced in a sea of black, blood-red, white, and an outermost carapace of earth-brown, we find the ultimate angular, curved, and sharped-edged statement of the paradox of what we are as a species. The embrace is love and love is life (for love prompts the procreative embrace that begets life). But the embrace is with *death,* which means that the embrace *is* death—which means that life is death. Love equals death; love equals life; death equals life.

The period between about 1880 and the end of World War I is reflected from yet another angle in Auguste Rodin's *Gates of Hell,* which presents a sweeping symbol of human descent. The towering double gate is ensconced in a massive frame that squirms with figures, its lintel dominated by the contemplative, questioning seated figure of *The Thinker* and surmounted by three male figures joined in a manner that recalls earlier representations of the Three Graces. That trinity of figures, along with the entire contrivance, cannot help but evoke comparison with doorways such as that by Ghiberti on the baptistery in Florence. But where Ghiberti's work and those of his contemporaries are emblematic of an age still largely wrapped around faith and are overrun with symbols of it, Rodin's doorway is a pessimist's response to faith: no hope here, only a vision of humankind "adrift in an empire of night; separated from, rather than being the victim of, its deity; born with a fatal duality of desire and an incapability to fulfill it; damned on both sides of the tomb to an internal Hell of passions."[23]

We are the engenderers of all the hell imaginable here in the *profanus,* regardless of what the *sacer* may offer in some other realm. The realm that Rodin explores is the imagination and the unconscious, those reservoirs of the *sacer* within the human being. The twisting figures on and around his gates, turning and separating from each other, are ourselves; vision and viewer are one and the same. The world depicted is the world over which, some say, we were granted dominion by an all-powerful God. Others contend that such dominion has evolved through a lengthy process that began with the explosion of a hydrogen molecule. In either case, our dominion has been an egotistical and an increasingly destructive one.

Between the time of Gauguin's death in 1903 and Ezekiel's death in 1921, the world at large and, within it, the world of art survived the first phase of a century that dwarfs all previous ones in the volume and intensity of not only scientific and artistic creativity but also human-devised destruction. In such a context we might expect art to respond in two different ways: it might take refuge in aesthetic principles that ignore the world outside the work of art, or it might take on the world, reflect upon it, respond to it—perhaps even try to repair it within the microcosm of the canvas, sheet of paper, slab of stone, or block of wood. One might expect either a further distancing from the symbols of faith of previous millennia or the embrace of those past symbols and their transformation into new ones. As it turns out, all of this has transpired.

CHAPTER 6
⚬⚬

SYMBOLS OF FAITH

IN TWENTIETH-CENTURY

VISUAL ART

Re-vision in a World in Crisis

Art—particularly painting—crossed the threshold into the twentieth century engaged in the expanded aesthetic concerns of the impressionists and their followers. From Monet to Cézanne we can chart a path of increasing interest not only in the product on the canvas but in the process of creating it; the viewer is emphatically aware of that act of aesthetic re-vision of reality and even participates in its completion. At the opposite end of the spectrum, works depicting traditional biblical and religious subject matter continued to be produced, perhaps with less frequency than in previous eras, and ritual objects continued to be produced throughout the Abrahamic world, using traditional symbols and reconceiving them in a more "modernist" mode.[1]

But contrary to what one might suppose if one were directed only to the aesthetic concerns of the work that followed Paul Cézanne, many artists of the twentieth century, while concerned with aesthetic issues, also addressed the issues and problems of the world beyond the canvas using a vocabulary of symbols both familiar and new. Given the horrors that define the twentieth century, from the Great War through the rise of Stalin and Hitler to the Holocaust and Hiroshima, and beyond that through an ongoing parade of genocides and ethnic cleansings, it is difficult to imagine that artists would not use their medium as a vehicle of commentary and response to the world, or even for charting out prescriptions for improving it.

There are other issues to explore in the drawing, painting, sculpture, architecture, and other media of the ultimate century of technological success and human distress. New forms of confrontation between Christendom and the *dar al'Islam* in the new geopolitics of the Near East, for example, might be expected, sooner or later, to yield visual reflection. Where does the work of Muslim artists fit into the shaping of twentieth-century Western art? The events of the twentieth century, including the Holocaust and the establishment of the State of Israel, might be expected to provoke visual commentary from Jewish artists. If the previous sixteen centuries of Western art were primarily sixteen centuries of Christian art, then how do Jewish artists fit into twentieth-century Western art?

The new relationship between *sacer* and *profanus,* wherein the first refers to the interior space of the mind and the latter to the outside physical world, is the major transmutation of the *sacer-profanus* duality that has governed human thought for so long, and the visual expression of that transmutation is a significant aspect of the shaping and reshaping of visual art and its symbols in the twentieth century. If, in traditional terms, the *sacer* is understood by the long history of religion to have created the *profanus,* then a corollary of that proposition in modernist terms suggests the re-creation of the *profanus* by the *sacer* of the human mind harnessed to the eye and hand, which combine to yield re-visions of reality on the microcosm of the canvas.

⊷∞⊶

Cass Gilbert's Woolworth Building opened a new era as it rose to a precedent-setting height in 1913. The gothic style of that soaring tower cannot have failed to resonate for the viewer a modernist expansion of the heaven-scraping spires of medieval cathedrals. This is a spire without a church, one might think at first. But then one realizes that the skyscraping spired structure *is* a church, just not in the traditional sense. By the eve of World War I, the religion of secularized New York was already becoming commerce, and this was one of its temples. Critics of the city who saw it moving in the wrong moral direction would have interpreted such sky-scraping edifices as Towers of Babel.[2] In the epoch in which the gothic style was born, such an edifice would have taken generations of contributions from an entire society to build; now it could be erected in a matter of years or even months, and the construction could be funded by a small group of financiers.

On the other side of the Great War, the intense expressionism of Berlin painter Max Beckman follows directly from Rodin's *Gates of Hell*, which served as a bridge between the centuries. Beckman's vision encompasses a sinister *profanus* of dark cities of impersonal Woolworth-like buildings, war-turned ideologies, and tense interweaves of love and death. His *[In] the Night* (1918–1919) harnesses the careful order dictated by compositional aesthetics to the chaotic horror of war's aftermath and its connotations (see Figure 69). A family is being tortured. The male figure upstage left, facing us with his legs akimbo—his head angled, kerchief knotted around the throat as if the figure behind him is hoisting him up by the throat to strangle him—offers a *symmetria* opposition to the female figure downstage right, facing away from us with her legs akimbo, her hands seemingly tied together and to a stick that is also placed as if the square-jawed man beyond her is ramming the stick into her chest. The angle of that stick (it is actually part of the window frame that connects and separates the room from the dark night

FIGURE 69
Max Beckman:
[In] the Night,
oil on canvas.
1918–1919

beyond) is echoed by the left lower arm and right upraised hand of the right-hand-most figure (and in turn by the second arm of the square-jawed man). While some inflict cruelties, others watch impassively or helplessly. The darkness of this night is both physical and spiritual. One taper still glows while at a precarious angle, and another has already fallen over and is extinguished; the flotsam and jetsam of table, hats, and other garments echo the skewed and topsy-turvy limbs and twisted fingers of humans victimized by humans.[3]

Everything takes place in a flattened foreground. There is little depth, no Albertian space into which some of the ugliness might diminish into the distance. It is like the compressed space in a medieval image of the damned being punished in hell—except that these individuals suffer in a lawless hell on earth. Every aspect of stylistic invention reinforces the symbolic statement that the human/*profanus*-engendered night-ugliness of war has continued beyond the war. Part of the image's power is that the horrific behavior it depicts anticipates even deeper darknesses to come in the following generation and another war: as a work of symbolic significance, it mediates *sacer* and *profanus* by being prophetic as much as historiographic. It shapes past and future into one agonized present.

Beckman carves up his canvas into dark-hued quadrants, drawing, in their wedges and geometric sectionings, from the style of the cubists who, before the Great War, turned the elements of external reality inside out on the canvas, reducing them to their fundamental geometric properties. The irregularities of nature were stylized into regularized lines and planes. Three-dimensional entities were not only deliberately flattened into two-dimensionality—so that it is clear that what resides on the canvas is the function of the artist's reinterpretation of external reality, rather than of some goal of illusory imitation—but in some forms of cubist exploration and visual reformulation the viewer simultaneously looks at an entity's structure from different angles. The deliberate flattening of the image circles back to the medievalist sense—particularly the Byzantine sense—of the image as an instrument to convey the spiritual and the metaphysical, rather than the material and the physical.

Like Henri Matisse and the color-obsessed fauves, the cubists asserted the legitimacy of imposing a vision of reality on the canvas and calling it as real as what resides outside the canvas frame. If I perceive and represent the tree as blue then it *is* blue for me and can be accepted by the viewer as blue, if I am convincing at depicting it. Con-

FIGURE 70   *Pablo Picasso:* Guernica, *oil on canvas. 1937*

versely, the cubists deconstructed reality, reconstructed it, and asserted that reality's essence had been revealed. The face seen from two
simultaneous viewpoints reveals itself to us in a different manner, but
no less legitimate, than that which, outside the canvas, we can only
see from one angle at a time. The artist uses the *sacer* of his mind to
accomplish this feat—substituting a secularized sense of the *sacer* for
a traditional religious sense—and with his mind he has offered a solution to another problem endemic to the visual art of the previous
twenty-five millennia: how to convey in a static medium the nonstasis endemic to external reality. The double viewpoint both im-
proves on external reality, where we can see from only one angle at a
time, and also reflects external reality: the face I see is, to some degree, always in motion and thus can never really be seen from a single
viewpoint for more than a brief moment.

Pablo Picasso created one of the great post-cubist works of the twentieth century, continuing the Beckmanian nightmare of the horrors of
human-initiated destruction: *Guernica* (1937), painted in the context of
the Spanish Civil War—a prelude to World War II (see Figure 70). In
this work, which records and mourns the bombing of the small Basque
town of the painting's name (by German bombers serving the Spanish
fascists), the reduction of reality to geometric elements is accomplished
in part by reducing reality to shades of gray. In symbolic terms not only

has all of the glorious color of the natural world been drained out of this heroically sized microcosm of the human-made world, but the entirety reads like the shades of a newspaper page. (Areas of it look like oversized newsprint.) If a picture is worth a thousand words, all of the words of a news report have been concisely reduced to one powerful image.

Like Beckman's painting, *Guernica* is constructed along classical compositional lines and simultaneously deconstructed; order and chaos intermingle, as do sharp and soft edges, rectilinear and curvilinear forms, dark and light passages. The central section is constructed in the energized pyramidal form utilized by High Renaissance painters. The carefully strewn horizontal elements that extend a base from one end to the other of both pyramid and painting (a hand to the left, a foot to the right, in *symmetria*) offer a counterpoint to the verticals that, articulating a rhythm that echoes from center to sides, complete the anchoring of the composition. The traditional representation of glorious warriors in heroic action has been transformed: these are the civilian victims of an aggression undertaken from a safe distance. The fierce horses of knights churning in action, seen in works from the Alexander Mosaic of the Hellenistic/Roman period to Paolo Ucello's *Battle of San Romano* (ca. 1455), have been reduced to one terrified horse being torn apart—literally—by forces well beyond its comprehension. (Its body parts are traceable through the newsprint pattern that tattoos them.)

The ultimate symbol of Spain, the bull—with all of its connotations of fertility, virility, survival, and its connections beyond Spain in history and art history—is the one living creature that appears not to be bellowing. Although the bull appears to be a quiet observer (the bull, so often a god in antiquity and its art, remains just that: a *sacer, ethos*-bound observer, not *pathos*-connected to the chaotic action of the *profanus,* but above it, beyond it), it is not simply apart from the image. He, too, is truncated: a second look clarifies the fact that his body is all there, but twisted, and its dark and light parts are so extremely opposed in shade that at first glance we see nothing but the foreparts of the figure. His eyes are askew—wide open, observing calmly, but askew. If in the flattened presentation the bull can be construed as a *background* figure, then he is our mirror opposite, as we stand *before* the image. The symbolism of the painting as a sacerdotal mediator between *sacer* and *profanus* has been deliberately collapsed. The viewer's space and the space of the horrors in the image are as much one as are the space of the bull and that of all the other figures in the image. If we have made gods of ourselves by means of our technological development, we have used that technology to turn the *profanus* into the hellish side of the *sacer.*

This idea is addressed from another viewpoint by Marc Chagall, the quintessential purveyor of the *sacer:* creator of a unique visual universe engendered from within his memory and multiplied by his imagination. Chagall's work is generally overrun with the characters of his past—especially his family—transformed by his mind, and a memory that sees gray and brown as vivid greens, yellows, reds, and blues (thus furthering the emotive ideology passed on from Pissarro to Gauguin to Matisse and the fauves). His early efforts reflect the shock to his senses of his 1910 arrival to Paris from eastern Europe—a world of color and light, where surrealism, expressionism, fauvism, and cubism might be synthesized with the romanticized elements of his past. Chagall's universe is dominated by love and the affirmation of life, suffused with a *sacer* sense of unbounded time, space, and perspective. The nostalgia of Vitebsk constantly soaks in the grandeur of Paris.

Among the most powerful of Chagall's works is one that emerged a year after Picasso's *Guernica,* as war drums were sounding a steady beat in Europe, and Nazi rhythms drove Chagall into darker visions. His 1938 *White Crucifixion* picked up—from Antokolski and Moses Jacob Ezekiel in particular—the idea of Jewish artists addressing Christ as a symbol (see Figure 71). The painting was executed in the very year of *Kristallnacht,* the first instance of concerted and concentrated Nazi-sponsored violence against Jews throughout Germany.[4] It is bathed in a sea of bright light, yet enveloped by a narrative immersed in darkness. Anti-Jewish violence would have resonated with the artist from his own experience in revolutionary and postrevolutionary Russia. Among the timeless, spaceless elements of this *sacer* re-vision are allusions to that experience. A village, topsy-turvy and on fire, is beset by a mob of pogromists with red flags waving, suggesting the Bolshevik-Menshevik conflict during the Russian Revolution witnessed by the artist, in which Jews were often caught between the two factions. At the same time, the world of the present is suggested by a small boat that carries refugees to the already-doubtful refuge—because it is controlled by the British—of Palestine.

The central figure, Jesus, bathed in a diagonal of light, wears a loin-cloth that bears a strong resemblance to a *tallit*—a Jewish prayer

FIGURE 71   *Marc Chagall:* White Crucifixion, *oil on canvas. 1938*

shawl—suggesting that his subject is a Jew. This notion is reinforced by an array of other elements throughout the painting. Where angels would be hovering in horror in a traditional crucifixion scene, phylactery-wearing (and thus obviously Jewish) elders hover in horror; a synagogue burns, and someone runs toward it to rescue its Torah scrolls. Other figures flee off the picture plane, including an Elijah-like figure, pack on his back (which suggests that he is the Wandering Jew, and, by way of Chagall's native Yiddish, in which to "bear a pack on one's back" is to shoulder a world of troubles, a Jew by visual/linguistic pun). Another figure, moving in the opposite direction, wears a blank placard on his chest. X-rays of the painting have shown that the artist originally wrote "Jude" on it, German for "Jew," but for some reason subsequently deleted it, perhaps because the allusion was too specific to the Nazi German world of 1938 and thus too limiting.

The central image hovers over the symbol of Jewish hope—the seven-branched menorah. But a close look reveals that it bears only six candles; the seventh, Sabbath-and-paradise-and-future-redemption candle has been left out, so the symbol is devoid of its hope-filled essence. A

Torah scroll burns with white fire but is not consumed; the flames from it lick at the base of the ladder leading up against the cross of light. Such a ladder in traditional Christian imagery would most frequently be part not of a Crucifixion but of a Deposition—in which case, Nicodemus or Joseph of Arimathea would be upon it, climbing up to gently lift the body from its terrible location. But Chagall has left the ladder empty—it is surrounded by empty space, a space pregnant with silence. There *is* no redeemer for the Redeemer, no savior for the Savior of humankind; he is simply a suffering Jew. Ezekiel transformed the ultimate Christian symbol into one of universal humanistic significance. In a different time and place, Chagall offered a darker reflection on the question of where a Jewish painter might fit into Western Christian art with his own transformation of that image.

Catalan artist Salvador Dali carried the symbolic language of an interior *sacer* reality into new territory. Perhaps the most renowned of Dali's early surrealist paintings is his 1931 oil on canvas, *The Persistence of Memory (Soft Watches)*. The title suggests that memory transcends *profanus* time and space. The fact that the modernist symbol of time, the watch, has been multiplied and rendered as a flaccid, almost liquid series of entities in this painting also suggests the flexibility of memory: we remember not the objective chronology of events as they actually occurred but a selective collage of subjective experience. There is thus a visual pun in this work: the visual distortion is a symbol of the mental distortion endemic to memory. That quality also connects memory to that other, interior aspect of the *sacer,* so dear to the symbolists, the dream world. This is not surprising, for Dali was making specific references to Freud in his *Diary of a Genius* around this time, and he would become increasingly focused on Freud in the 1930s.[5]

If most of Dali's hallucinogenic visions offer secularized symbolic aspects of the *sacer,* he also—eventually, after World War II and the explosion of the atom bomb—applied the same sort of visual methodology to traditional Christian images, transforming them into something altogether new. Thus his *The Madonna of Port Lligat* (1950), his *Nuclear Cross* (1952), his *Corpus Hypercubus (Crucifixion)* of 1954, and his *The Sacrament of the Last Supper* (1955) all present Christian religious subject matter re-visioned. Moreover, they all reflect two simultaneous realities. The first is the millennia-old relationship between art and religion. The second is the notion that the past few centuries of Western art are an exception to that long history, that art has moved from the spiritual context of the church (and its equivalents in other faiths) into the secular context of the museum, and as such, is intended to present a predominantly *aesthetic* offering to the viewer, rather than a *religious* experience. Works like these are intended both to be displayed in a museum or gallery and to offer religious commentary and not merely visual concerns.

The Sacrament of the Last Supper re-visions a traditional scene along both familiar and new lines (see Figure 72). Jesus presides at the center of a table occupied by a loaf of bread broken in half and a glass of wine perilously near the inner edge of the table. The first unusual feature we might notice is the way in which the geometries of the table are echoed and reflected by a golden metallic construction—it offers the aspect of a multipartite window frame—that rises from it (or descends to it) toward (from) the top of the painting. The construction is pentagonally shaped—in traditional terms, an allusion to the five wounds of Christ's martyrdom—while framing four "windows." The latter are an allusion to the four-armed cross of that martyrdom, even as their translucence alludes to the issue of Christ as a window through which the redemptive light of God shines onto us. Indeed light is beginning to burst from behind the mountainous horizon and to surge toward the viewer. The foreground of the painting, closer to us, is darker; the background, further from us, beyond the figure of Christ, is brighter—and in fact the area of the table itself that leads to and from the figure of Christ is overrun with light, while the rest of it is immersed in shadow. That figure arises out of a preternatural sort of seascape, as if it is in part an ethereal contrivance of light—we can see the small boat floating on the water, which we might assume to be the Sea of Galilee, and the boat, that in which Peter, fisher of fish, came forth to become a fisher of men's souls as a disciple of Christ—even as he is solidly enough a body who presides over this table.

He who is both earth and heaven gestures with one hand pointing vertically and the other horizontally across his body; the one hand offers three fingers in an extended position, signifying the triune nature of God, while the other, with the thumb up and the index finger out, refers to the dual nature of Christ. Christ's duality is reinforced by his position in the middle ground, between table and floor, and sea and hills, as between disciples to left and right. Moreover, the man-made "window" construction that frames him contrasts with the God-made forms of the "natural" landscape that may be seen through it. The ir-

FIGURE 72 *Salvador Dali:* The Sacrament of the Last Supper, *oil on canvas. 1955*

regularities of the one and the carefully wrought regular lines of the other are another part of the symbolic vocabulary of coexistent antithetical elements that symbolize the figure they surround and, by analogy, refer to his dual nature.

The other figures in the painting are striking. The apostles are disposed to either side of Christ; two of them kneel on the outer side of the table. They all bow their heads toward the table, so that we can discern no face in this gathering except that of Christ, and we must guess that Judas is the one who wears a yellow cassock (on Christ's side of the table, to his left; he is *not* one of the two on our side of the table). Since in traditional Christian visual terms, by means of its association with Judas, yellow is most often a symbol of betrayal, it is appropriate that the figure who precisely balances this one, sitting on Christ's right, wears a blue cassock, for this is the color of the sky and thus of God's truth. Truth and betrayal are held in dynamic balance in this image, and given the necessity of Judas' betrayal for the narrative that will send forth Christ's truth into the world—and, moreover, the constantly blurring line between truth and betrayal in the human world of the twentieth century—is it any wonder that these two colors stand out? They are another pair of antipodes reflecting on the central figure.

Jesus—whose face bears the details of Dali's wife, Gala—is echoed by a figure that hovers above him with arms outspread—a headless torso, since, at the top of the image, the torso is terminated at the neck by the frame of the painting. The viewer might at first be inclined to read this as the crucified Christ to whose martyrdom the Last Supper is the prologue. However, the absence of wounds suggests that this is the Father, his arms thrown out in benedictory presiding over the scene that contains within it the Crucifixion, but also the redemption of those who participate in its sacrament. The painting leads from this figure down and out toward the viewer; our eyes are led from below, through Christ, to the vault of heaven and its divine kingdom. Dali's own words echo from the natural and supernatural elements that contrive his image: "the temple whose walls are built by special techniques will not stand without the perfect vault of heaven as its roof."[6]

<hr>

What of Jewish artists and *Jewish* symbols? In the era before World War I, when so many young artists were drawn to Paris, an explosion of Jews also arrived to become part of the "Paris School." The innovative Paris art scene was particularly attractive for them because for once they could be outsiders, not as Jews, but as artists romantically misunderstood by the world around them. They offered a panoply of styles, symbols, and subjects. Many, like Chagall, came from eastern Europe.

The Lithuanian Jew Jacques Lipchitz was among them. He was also probably the first major sculptor to translate the terms of cubism into a three-dimensional medium. One of his more interesting works, the quasi-cubist *Pierrot Escaping* (1927), suggests at least a partial answer to the question of where Jews fit into twentieth-century Western art. Pierrot is a stock character in the emergent *commedia del'arte* of several centuries earlier. He is the quintessential tragicomic figure: the clown who weeps inwardly while his outer antics entertain his laughing audience. Lipchitz has recast Pierrot in the abstract form of a six-pointed star: the Star of David, which by the time of this work was universally perceived as a Jewish symbol. Pierrot represents the Jew, in silent grief during centuries of oppression, offering an entertainment within the theater of tragicomic history.

Pierrot may escape from a room through a window, but he can never escape being Pierrot. In Lipchitz's vision, the iron bars of the window form a series of crosses—symbols of the Christian world of which he is inescapably part. The ladder of would-be escape is made of the same unbreakable material—as if to underscore the fact that it leads from nowhere to nowhere (since its upper and lower extremities terminate at the window frame): there is no real escape. This Pierrot-Jew remains trapped between imprisonment and the illusion of escape; he is eternally caught between the window behind and the ladder in front—between a world that, for all its pretense at secular spiritual openness, is Christian and the false ladder out of his identity. It is in attempting to abandon his identity that the Jew is reduced to a two-dimensional image, a flattened six-pointed star. By 1927, the nightmare was growing in Germany that would eventually turn this work into a prophetic vision. Even religious conversion would offer no refuge in Nazi-controlled Europe, where the gates of extermination camps would make a mockery of the conviction held tenaciously by some Jews that there was a fairly accessible window of identity-escape, called baptism.

Among Lipchitz' friends was Amadeo Modigliani, an assimilated Jew from the Italian town of Livorno. Modigliani had been nurtured in a home dominated by secularist free-thinking. He developed an early taste for symbolist poetry and embraced a self-image as a romantic outsider artist—an *artist maudit*—with which mind-set, he arrived in Paris in 1908. As we follow Modigliani's painting and sculpture through the next decade we recognize the inspiration he found in Cézanne and Brancusi, in the Italian Renaissance tradition—particularly Duccio, Botticelli, and Parmagianino—and in African art. There are other circumstances that one might assume influenced his work as well. He arrived in Paris just as the notorious Dreyfus Affair, with its anti-Semitic overtones, was winding down. He moved, in 1911, to the impoverished artists' *abbatoir*-turned-domicile, La Ruche, which was dominated by Jewish artists who had come from eastern Europe. Thus in Paris he developed a sense of his Jewish identity.

All of this feeds interestingly into one of his late works. After a brief sojourn at home in Italy before World War I, Modigliani returned to Paris, where, by 1917, he was largely identified as a portraitist with a distinctive style. By then, he was tubercular and over-immersed in alcohol and drugs. As he spent the late spring with an odd assortment of friends in southern France—the *Midi*—it should not surprise us that a landscape he painted at that time is so dismal. This *Paysage du Midi* is no sun-splashed southern view. Stylistically, the artist emulates Cézanne—permitting canvas to show through the brush strokes and structuring the canvas with foliage in the foreground, houses in the middle ground, and a mountain in the background—except that Modigliani has turned "foliage" into one lonely tree and has telescoped buildings and mountain into a dismal, towering house with a dark window.

Modigliani's acute depression is evident. The road past the house leads nowhere as it faces toward an Italy for which he reportedly longed (both his correspondence and the recollections of Soutine and Utrillo, his best friends, suggest this) but would never reach in the few years of life left to him.[7] In his heart and imagination, it remained an Italy of childhood recollection—which included, in its halcyon aura, an acknowledged Jewishness. Perhaps this motivated the particular configuration that appears on Modigliani's canvas: the tree that dominates the composition bifurcates into two three-branched arms. Together with the house peak or vertical window, it presents a seven-branched candelabrum—a menorah form, even to the two branches tipped by leaves that assume a candle-like glow. The ultimate historical Jewish visual symbol of hope rises in the midst of his desperation—a symbol derived from warm memory and from the same unconscious and dream-related *sacer* sources that Freud was then unraveling.

By the time of Modigliani's death (1920), post–World War I Palestine was in British hands. In Jerusalem, Boris Schatz, former court sculptor and painter to King Ferdinand of Bulgaria, was still shaping what had received the Zionist leadership's imprimatur back in 1906: the founding of an arts academy. Schatz intended to create a Jewish national art that would be essential for fulfilling Jewish national aspirations. Art that came out of the Bezalel School was fraught with religious and political symbolism, connecting back to and leading away from what is familiar from the Jewish visual past.[8] Biblical subjects and symbols like the menorah and the newly popular and recently ubiquitous Star of David would reconnect the Jewish people to its ancestral land. Less obvious symbols also appeared, such as the rising sun, symbol of the dawning of a new day in Jewish history.[9]

One of the more interesting images that synthesizes a number of these elements was created by Ephraim Lilien, one of the key figures associated, albeit briefly, with Bezalel. Lilien's portrayal of *Moses* (1908) offers a face that his audience would have immediately recognized as that of Theodore Herzl, father of modern Zionism. He is portrayed not only as a muscular, heroic figure, soaring above the clouds and displaying the tablets that he has hewn out of rock with his own hands, but wearing the kind of headgear used in ancient Assyrian art to adorn kings and gods. He is backed by a rising sun that functions as a gigantic halo. Since Moses is portrayed as Herzl, then the man who carved the Torah out of the rock to shape a people and guide them to the Promised Land and the man who penned *The Jewish State* to reshape the descendants of those people and guide them back once more to that land have coalesced as one.[10]

While the Bezalel School was developing and Europe was poised between two wars, America and its art were coming of age. But America was not devoid of ugly prejudice. In 1920 two Italian Americans, Nicola Sacco and Bartolomeo Vanzetti, a shoemaker and a fish-peddler, were accused of robbing and murdering two men. In court the presiding judge openly showed his contempt for these recent immigrants with anarchist political beliefs and willfully ignored testimony that might have exonerated them. He condemned them to death on July 14, 1921. After a six-year delay, amid protests from around the world, the two were executed on August 23, 1927.

"Ever since I could remember I'd wished that I'd been lucky enough to be alive at a great time—when something big was going on, like the Crucifixion. And suddenly I realized that I was! I was living through another crucifixion. Here was something to paint!" the Jewish artist Ben Shahn wrote.[11] The central image among the series he painted on this subject in 1932–1933 is *The Passion of Sacco and Vanzetti*—the very title of which alludes to the Christian narrative. Most obvious with regard to symbolizing hypocrisy is a pair of white lilies held in the hands of two of the Lowell Committee Blue Bloods who stand by the coffins. The white lily so often placed in the hands of the angel Gabriel in representations of the Annunciation is also the symbol of death and resurrection, and the blood-red that fringes those being held limply in the hands of these "mourners" underscores the bearers' guilt, as they stand, blank-looking, at the head of the two victims' coffins. Their job was to see justice carried out, but they did the opposite, at least in Shahn's opinion. A world away from Lilien's *Moses,* a religious symbol has been impressed into political statement.

In retrospect, the ugliness of the early twentieth century was merely a prologue. Man-dwarfing skyscrapers proliferated as a parallel to the reduction of fellow humans to ciphers and the shift in geopolitical borders that created vast hordes of stateless people in the course of the second and third decades of the century. The jump to factories of destruction through which millions of people and not just industrial material might be processed became part of *profanus* reality, rather than merely part of a *sacer* realm of imagination and nightmare, by the end of the fourth and beginning of the fifth decade.

The question for the artist in the aftermath of all of that was how to respond to it; for the role of art as a reflection of reality, filtered through the sacerdotal sensibilities of the artist, suggests an imperative of response. The dominating visual force of the postwar era was the abstract expressionism being created in New York City, which has frequently been understood as turning art away from that imperative. The vast canvasses of the abstract expressionists have more often than not been viewed as purely concerned with aesthetic matters, separated from the world and its events—in a manner opposite from work such as that of Ben Shahn and the social realists.[12]

It is certainly true that Jackson Pollock's canonical paintings may be appreciated in purely aesthetic terms. They turn the invisibility of energy into something visible. Color, blasting across the picture plane in well-scattered layers, recedes and proceeds from the depths of the canvas. The notion of perspectival depth has been turned on its ear by the artist's instinctively felt adherence to the laws of optics: that certain colors are "warm" and others "cold"; that some seem to pull away from and others seem to push outward toward the eye of the viewer. Standing before a large Pollock work one can feel oneself hurtling into those dynamically fashioned depths. One feels as if the canvas is exploding simultaneously inward away from us and outward to the unframed sides, as if the canvas can barely contain the power of the explosion. But such dynamism may also be understood to speak the language of symbolic statement. Pollock's paintings can be seen as microcosmic mirrors of a world that had exploded from Verdun to Auschwitz to Nagasaki by the time he was painting. Each work reflects the explosion inward and outward of the world that humans had been crafting for themselves since the early part of the century—or since the beginning of the Industrial Revolution (or since the beginning of "civilization"). Pollock is thus a successor to Beckman and Picasso in their tearing apart of the world, their reduction of it to fragmented parts. He has merely completed the process of fragmentation and raised the chaos quotient to a higher degree.

A second type of response to the horrors of post-Holocaust, post-Hiroshima reality would be to suggest in symbolic visual terms a means of putting that forcibly deconstructed reality back together. This is, in part, the process that the chromaticists were engaged in. In Mark Rothko's canonical large and unframed paintings, the canvas is subdivided vertically into three sections (like the Trinity), the viewer's eye is drawn toward the unifying center of the image, and the entirety is held together *as* a unity by the power of the light that seems to emanate from the canvas. That force with which God began the physical ordering of the universe in Genesis is utilized to replicate that process on the micro-ordered scale: reality on the canvas is reunified, recentered, restored. There is a heroic, messianic quality to such paintings, albeit in a purely secular sense, as if, spilling over their unframed edges, they seek the power to put back together what was so decisively torn apart by two generations of war.[13] To be surrounded by Rothko paintings is to be soaked in a light that engenders ordered reflection. In the most secular of terms such works offer contemplative calm, spiritual uplift of the sort that, in more traditional terms, prayer might offer.

Rothko is not alone in this endeavor. Adolph Gottlieb's *Burst* paintings unify chaotic and ordered elements with white light. But Barnett Newman was the one who articulated most continuously a spiritual agenda for the chromaticists. He was one of a group of artists who gathered in one another's studios to discuss and debate issues, including the question of how to define "Jewish" art and how, as Jewish artists, they might respond in visual terms to the horrors of the Holocaust and Hiroshima. Among the subjects of discussion was the sixteenth-century Jewish mystic from Safed, Isaac Luriya, and his doctrine of "repairing the world": *tikkun olam*. Many of Newman's titles—such as *Covenant* and *Onement*—offer explicit evidence of his beyond-mere-aesthetics agenda. His "zip" paintings—in which a central element emerges from behind the larger fields of color that flank it, which are being driven apart by it (as when, in the beginning of Genesis, the ordering process leads from the creation of light to the separation of the waters above from those below)—express the hope for the restoration of moral order. The central "zip" also draws the eye *toward* it, functioning as a symbol for putting together the world blown apart by the events of mid-century.

Newman's *The Name II* (1950) adds a double theological issue to the matter of unifying the canvas as a symbolic statement of repairing the world. The painting is all white, which is to say that it offers both the absence and the totality of color—since white light contains all the colors within it, albeit invisibly. The image is thus an image of nothing and everything in the coloristic terms that are endemic to traditional painting. The canvas is divided by a pair of barely visible vertical lines. As such, it may be construed as a triptych, that most traditional of Western—Christian—forms of visual self-expression throughout the centuries. In Christian art the center would be occupied by a crucified Christ, flanked either by the two crucified thieves, or by the Virgin and John the Evangelist—or the center might be occupied by a Virgin and Child flanked by saints. In short, images of God and its concomitants would be the visual subject matter offered to the viewer. But the Jewish view of God is that God is invisible and therefore cannot be portrayed. Thus the question of where a Jewish artist might fit into Western, Christian art connects to the question of how a Jew might visually represent God as religious art has done for millennia.

Newman seems both to have asked and to have answered that double question. He has appropriated a classic Christian form of visual self-expression but, in furthering a course pioneered by Chagall and others, transformed the substantive elements that fill out that form. His triptych is filled with the image of the imageless God, for he has offered both the absence of color and the totality of color; like the Jewish concept of God, the colors on the canvas are invisible and yet present. Symbolically speaking, God is simultaneously absent and present on the canvas. The name of the painting confirms this as part of the artist's intention. For in traditional Judaism one never uses the word "God" in contexts other than prayer; the circumlocution customarily used is *HaShem*—a Hebrew phrase that translates as "The Name." Newman has transmuted verbal circumlocution into visual circumlocution.

The painting also offers a response to the question raised by Jewish and Christian theologians regarding where God was during the Holocaust. How could an all-powerful, all-loving God have been present and yet silent in the midst of those horrors? The answer is paradoxical: God was both present and absent—as human action was both moral (those who helped would-be victims survive) and immoral (those who actively or passively helped victims to end up as victims). The question of how to be a Jewish artist in a world of essentially Christian art is wedded to the question of how Jews and Christians can understand the existence of God in such a horror-filled context.

That double question is asked by Samuel Bak from a more personalized perspective. Bak, born in Lithuania in 1933, was six years old when World War II began and not much older when it intruded into his world, carrying away with it the childhood left buried in the ashes of Vilnius. In Bak's paintings, the Decalogue and the number six are recurrent motifs. *Otiyot* ("Letters") offers the tablets disintegrating in mid-air, as they float in their stony weight. The letters themselves, symbols of the commandments, peel off the crumbling surfaces and float upward. We are reminded of the Hassidic story of the righteous illiterate who simply recited the letters of the alphabet, which, floating toward heaven, were gathered by God and formed into words of prayer. But we wonder if the Gatherer is still there—or if what is missing is our memory of how to adhere to the commandments. The sixth letter, *vav*, is the only one not fully visible. Its prominence is evident both in its absence and in its repeated replacement with the number six—which is the number of points on the Star of David, the number of Jewish millions killed in the conflagration that was well on its way by the time the artist was six years old, and the number of the disintegrating commandment "Thou shall not murder."

Responding to and Repairing the World

These issues exploded in the second half of the century. The symbolic language invented by the abstract expressionists continued the dialogue between *profanus* and *sacer* along lines nontraditional and nonfigurative as well as secular. Robert Rauschenberg's all-white paintings of 1950–1951 offer no subject but the shadowed reflection of the viewer; thus the viewer participates in the process of "completing" the work of art. In the painting *Crucifixion and Reflection,* the viewer sees his own shadow, and if he raises his arms (as the title might instinctively cause the viewer to do), it is he who is crucified. In the past several centuries, we have proudly arrogated power to ourselves, particularly over life and death, which, in traditional Christianity, is reserved for Christ as God. But in so doing, because we are not all-merciful, no matter how powerful we may imagine ourselves, we have sacrificed much of the world and ultimately ourselves. In Western, Christian artistic and theological history, Christ is a symbol of God become man, spirit become flesh to bleed. Rauschenberg's version of God—portrayed as absence of color, no-thing-ness, pure substanceless essence—merges with the shadow of any and all humans, God's created reflection, who bleeds in the post-Holocaust world of Europe, America, the Middle East, Biafra, Bangladesh, Cambodia, Rwanda. The Judaean become Christian God has become us; the suffering Jew has become humankind responsible for its own suffering in the second half of the twentieth century.

The eradication of the line between *sacer* and *profanus* has been paralleled by the blurring of the boundary between everyday objects and the secular sanctity of artworks, the development of museums without walls, the redrawing of the line between sacred and profane space. Pop art epitomizes this trend, and the high priest of pop art was Andy Warhol. He re-visioned—with the populist repetition of the silk screen, rather than the exclusivist singularity of the painting—sacerdotal figures of the American cultural consciousness. Marilyn Monroe and Jackie Kennedy Onassis were subjected to the sort of devotional representation that had previously been reserved for saints. The richness of the Catholic tradition surely was not lost on the Catholic-born and -raised artist, who applied that *sacer* sensibility to the *profanus* images he paradoxically elevated, even as his use of a repetitive motif pulled them down to the lower reaches of the museum wall. The paradox was enhanced when he expanded our vision of Campbell soup cans. There is something religious about the antireligious depiction of this object from the supermarket shelf, reduced to flatness, to color and form—to the attributes that are intended to cause the buyer, unconsciously, to turn to this can of soup instead of another—within the white spaceless space of a canvas that hangs in the same gallery in which an image of God and His Mother sitting in gold spaceless space might hang.

This sensibility circles around itself in the *Pop Icons* of Ruth Dunkell painted in the mid-1970s. Dunkell was struck "on a visit to the Jewish Museum . . . by the beauty of the Judaica, and decided that I must paint it."[14] She created dozens of *Pop Icons*—paintings of ritual objects in a deliberately flat representational style (see Figure 73). They are like Warhol's soup cans in that the object is enlarged and is presented in a simple, stylized design. Dunkell causes us to see in a fresh light the ritual objects that are so familiar that we forget their beauty and craftsmanship—analogous to yet different from Warhol's effort to get us to see the artistry we customarily ignore in the Campbell's label that draws our eye and our wallet. Moreover, the ritual objects have been taken not out of the synagogue but off the museum shelf, where they have been *reduced* to mere art objects. The synagogue for which they were intended is gone; the congregation that used them is dispersed or deceased. However, in refocusing our attention on them *as* art objects, she has, in an oblique way, returned them to life.

In the next generation, the questions multiply. Susan Schwalb's work continues where the triptych form of Barnett Newman's *The Name II* leaves off. Her *Creation* series is a group of triptychs of folding wooden arched forms, recalling the Syrian gables of early synagogues. Schwalb was also inspired by "the Sarajevo *Haggadah* [with its] images of arc and circle . . . I interpret the arc which encloses the

FIGURE 73   *Ruth Dunkell:* Pop Icon: Sabbath Lamp with Deer, *acrylic on canvas.* *1976*

picture, as a symbol of the universe."[15] *Creation XX* symbolizes the six days of creation by six circles textured with progressively agitated silverpoint, placed in six square silver "frames," the entirety, within a blood-wine red background across the lower part of the triptych, framed in gold. This gold-framed earth filling the lower part of the arched form extends to the wings of the work as does the sky-blue of the upper parts. Within the center of the blue upper part of the central panel, a larger silverpoint circle—the seventh day—beams like a Gothic oculus whose stained-glass forms have been replaced by textured light. The media of medieval and Renaissance Christian religious art shape a series of abstract geometries.

Many of Schwalb's works add to the arc-circle configuration a downward-pointing triangle with a vertical line from mid-base to apex. This is recognizable as a symbol of femaleness going back to Neolithic art. The role of artistic creatrix long suppressed for women is restored in the textures of the silverpoint surface she so frequently works. Thousands of fine lines engender an active energy—flesh-like, water-like, sky-like—within the static confines of the framing forms. The watery, wave-like webbing of the silverpoint surface within the tumescent frame recall the verbal images of *Ti'amat*, dragon-primordial-water-mother goddess of Mesopotamian religion, and her linguistic cognate, *T'hom*, watery depths over which the spirit of God swoops in Genesis. It suggests the amniotic fluid of the womb, which connects the birth of humans to the birth of the universe. But the emphasis on female elements and the matter of reenfranchisement is also connected to the artist's Judaism and the question of where women fit in the ritual life of traditional Judaism.

This last triple question—of Jews within Christian art, women within Western art, and women within traditional Judaism—has been raised with increasing intensity by artists from Judy Chicago to Carole Hamoy and Helene Aylon. This concern is not limited to Jewish women artists, however. Geoff Laurence's 1999 triptych, *T'fillah*—meaning "Prayer"— breaks the body of a woman into three discontinuous parts, around each of which is wrapped the leather thong of the phylactery, which a pious Jewish male wraps around his arm and forehead for the daily morning prayer, literally fulfilling the Torah injunction to "bind it for a sign upon thy hand and place it as a frontlet between thine eyes." Those prayers include words thanking God "that He did not make me a woman." A Christian tradition of viewing Jews as "feminine"— because of their centuries-long association with indoor activities and not with the manly (killing) arts of hunting, fishing, warring—has been turned twice around, by way of the triptych form that is composed vertically, forty-five degrees from its normal axis. This gives the whole a cross shape, since the middle panel is wider than the upper and lower panels, and has the effect of wrapping the Jewish-Christian question around the question of traditional Judaism's constraints on women. The generalized issue of women as commodities (bodies made of parts without souls within them) and the specific issue of excluding women from important Jewish rituals (such as reading from the Torah or wearing phylacteries) interweave the question of contemporary sexual mores (a nipple ring depicted on the middle panel causes the leather thong that "binds" to pun on the issue of sexual bondage). Which are the ties that bind and who are those who are bound?

The question of what binds us *together*—of who and what we are— is addressed by Sy Gresser's carved steatite *Tribal Faces (Menorah)*

(1996). In a not-quite-complete circle, faces extend from the stylized form of a seven-branched candelabrum. The faces represent different races and ethnic types, held together by the most consistent symbol in two millennia of Jewish art. The faces—one eye open, the other closed—have both outer and inner vision. The unfinished circle suggests an unfinished world that needs fixing. A paradigm of how the world might be fixed is offered by Gresser's 1994 Texas limestone relief, *Last Supper*. The sculpture reminds us that Jesus' last meal was a Passover seder. It includes among the assembled faces an African (a dark face, but it is *not* Judas), a Canaanite (modeled on the artist's grandfather, and thus connecting personal memory with tribal memory), and an Egyptian (the traditional villains in the Passover story). In this work Gresser visualizes the fulfillment of the opening inclusive statement of the Passover meal—"*all* who are hungry, enter and eat." Gresser reflects on this only from a historical and cultural, not a religious, viewpoint: God is not part of the scene that he shapes. Yet Passover is part of that larger pattern of memory that begins as a divine commandment not to forget the experience in and coming out of Egypt and God's role in that experience.

A hemisphere away from all of this, in a Soviet Egypt where the only acceptable art by 1934 had become Soviet socialist realist art, a parallel world of artists working in secret grew up. Within that world, Jewish artists struggled both with the issue of placement in the limited "official" art world and with the matter of whether their Jewishness could fit into either the "official" or the "unofficial" art world. Occasionally, a Christian artist like Natalya Nesterova has reflected on this question by using Jewish "subjects"—readers of Hebrew-language books on New York City park benches, for instance—as symbols of all the victims of the Soviet system and its machinations.[16]

More often the reflection operates in the opposite direction, with Jewish artists using "Christian" subjects. The Jewish artist Vitaly Dlugy's most consistent image is that of a pomegranate, a Jewish symbol for him, but not one that he uses in a traditional Jewish manner. On the contrary, thirteen pomegranates arranged along a table define *Last Supper* (1989). Three rectangles that may be read as windows (as in Leonardo's *Last Supper*) mark the background. One pomegranate, the largest, placed off-center but as the center and apart from the others, situated against the central window, glows with light. One, split open so that its seeds are visible, is also placed apart from the others, beyond the "table" on the right-hand "windowsill": it is Judas who has broken open and hovers on the edge of departure. Traditional Christian imagery has been re-visioned—as humans have been re-visioned as this fruit peculiarly related to us. It bears the blood of Adam's misuse of the gift of free will, which results in his acquisition of the ultimate fruit, knowledge.[17] Therefore, the pomegranate can be construed as a key source of human knowledge (and in Jewish terms, a symbol of that most important source of knowledge, the Torah, which is the tree of life). It bears in its red seeds the blood that humans began to spill from the moment we gained knowledge (the blood of birth, for after the knowledge that they gained from eating of the pomegranate, Adam *knew* Eve; the blood of death, for the first son of that union, Cain, slew the second son, Abel; the blood of endless wars and genocides that have characterized human existence up to our own era). That the knowledge is at least part sexual is further signified by the distended, phallic stems of the fruits that populate the table of this *Last Supper*.

Michael Iofin managed to emigrate from the Soviet Union to the United States by the time images of Lenin and Marx were being dismantled and the name of his native city was becoming Petersburg.[18] Iofin's work is overrun with symbols. His etching *Christmas Day* (1984) parodies Stalin's mandate of Soviet socialist realism by focusing with a hyper-realist style on the unhappy realm of Hitler, and not an idealized "happy" Soviet world.[19] Within a cattle car, a small crowd of people assembles—identifiable by their striped garments, gaunt faces, and shaven heads as concentration camp inmates, presumably Jews. There are twelve of these, like the number of zodiacal quadrants in the heavens, the number of Israelite tribes, and the number of Christ's apostles assembled for the Last Supper. The artist has divided them into two groups of six. Behind each group gathered in the darkness of the boxcar, a doorway allows light to enter.

Between the groups, lying in the center of the car on the floor (in a sparseness that makes the traditional image of the manger seem comfortable by comparison) is a young woman, her arms extended horizontally as if visually to connect the two groups. We see her from the top of her head down in a tour de force of perspective that reverses the position of Andrea Mantegna's renowned late fifteenth-century *Dead Christ*. The curves and diagonals of the boxcar's struts offer a dynamic contrast to the diagonals and irregular forms of the figures surrounding

her in reverential poses, including one figure on his
knees in an attitude of prayer.
But in yet more dynamic contrast with all of this is the
soaring cross of light the vertical arm of which emanates
from the lower body and partially opened legs of the young
woman. Where the vertical
meets the horizontal sweep of
light a small baby hovers, its
arms spread in a cruciform
position. That this is to be understood as the Christ Child
soaring above the scene is
clear from its position: this is
the moment of Christ's birth.
Chagall's re-visioned Christ as
suffering Jew has been reborn
in a cattle car.

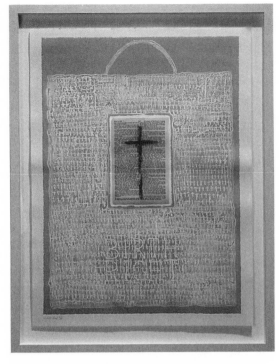

FIGURE 74   *Willie Little:* Birthright, *etching
and chine colle.* 2000

Layers of birth, identity, and suffering are shaped by Willie Little, in
his *Birthright* (2000) (see Figure 74). The North Carolina-born and
bred, African American artist offers a page from Malachi, last of the
prophetic books in the Hebrew Bible, hovering over and in the center
of the image of a shopping bag etched with scores of tiny crosses. A
larger cross has also been drawn over—looking as if it has been burned
into—the page of biblical text. The words of Malachi are taken from
chapters two and three, in which the prophet asks, "Have we not all
one father? Hath not one God created us?" He goes on to criticize the
abuses of priests in the temple and the faithless "abomination[s]
. . . committed . . . in Jerusalem" and then affirms God's blessing upon
the keepers of the covenant and asserts, "I [the Lord] send my messenger, and he shall clear the way before me." This last idea is reiterated
somewhat differently in the final passage of Malachi (3:24), where the
prophet promises, "I [the Lord] will send you Elijah the prophet before
the coming of the great and terrible day of the Lord."

Pressed between a dark cross and the pale, white image of a shopping bag covered with numberless crosses, the import of the text condemning an abusive religious leadership, the interpretation of the last part of which separated Judaism and Christianity two millennia ago, encompasses the conviction of possessing the true understanding of the prophetic words. The sense of the large cross upon the text as a *burnt* cross evokes both the suffering of Christ and the burning of crosses by the Ku Klux Klan in the name of a God reserved in all its universal loving mercy for Caucasian Christians alone. Nor is it accidental that the primary background image is a shopping bag. This is an implement for carrying home our material gains from a day in the marketplace. In the America of the late twentieth century, fancy shops provide their customers with fancy shopping bags, embellished with colorful images and beautiful writing. They become works of art in their own right—and symbols of status. It *is* about possession—*birthright*—such as Esau sold easily enough to Jacob (the Jewish tradition midrashically treats Esau as the "ancestor" of Christianity; Christianity views the descendants of Jacob-Israel, who became Jews, as having lost the birthright—the covenant—which was passed on in a new mode to Christians).

It is about the birthright of Truth that members of each Abrahamic faith believe is theirs. It is about the birthright that many Americans feel to the economic success that, in turn, allows them to exercise prejudice, bigotry, and hatred toward those less successful, or those whose religion or race is different from theirs, or those in the wide world that is not America. The symbol of the shop whence the bag and the baggage within it came is called a "logo." How many of those who wear the logo of the cross think either about the layered significance of that geometric configuration or of the fact that "logo" derives from Greek *logos* and what that word, meaning "word" in New Testament Greek, *means* in the context of the new covenant? Is the Cross or the page from Malachi the logo on this bag? And who reads that text, and who, reading it, considers that there might be different interpretations of it—and that humans have been killing each other for nearly two millennia over those different interpretations?

There are other angles and issues of engaging symbols pertaining to the *sacer* on the part of Christian artists in the last decades of the twentieth century. One of the most obvious of these is the photographic work *Piss Christ* (1987), by Andres Serrano. A pale white version of the crucified Christ is flooded with golden light: in traditional Christian color symbolism, purity is enveloped with the preciousness of ultimate truth. That the stunning luminosity was effected through bathing the object in urine led, not surprisingly, to the controversy that emerged with the work. Those who were scandalized missed the fact that this was one of a series of works in which the artist shot objects of religious significance through various body fluids, bathing them in an ethereal, variously hued light. Blood yields a reddish pigment; milk yields white. The fact that these are body fluids is consistent with the centuries-long tradition of visual representation and verbal reference to the blood of Christ and the milk of the Christ-and-humanity-nurturing Virgin. The red that symbolizes the blood of Christ's sacrifice has been turned back to its source: blood yields red that yields blood that refers to sacrifice.

But in the modernist twist applied to this visual tradition by Serrano, urine might be said to depart from the tradition of liquid symbolism and its sometime accompanying color-symbolism. But perhaps that is the point: it carries the notion of Christ as the synthesis of the *sacer* and the *profanus* to a new place. The most sacred of images is bathed in the most profane of liquids. Moreover, perhaps the glowing color—is it gold or is it yellow or is it both?—is intended to suggest a re-vision of the confluence of gold and yellow in traditional Christian symbolism. The first connects to Christ by way of the spaceless, timeless value of his *sacer* Truth; the second connects to Judas, Christ's betrayer—without whose betrayal the salvational sacrifice could not have taken place. Thus, in the last part of the twentieth century—when Christian and Jewish artists were looking over the past century and millennium and recognized that the association of yellow with Judas' alleged spiritual descendants, Jews, led to intense suffering (analogous to that of Christ on the cross) that culminated with the Holocaust and the yellow stars imposed upon Jews by their Nazi tormentors—the enveloping of the most sacred of images with the most profane of substances might also be understood as a Chagall-like commentary on the administering and enduring of suffering.

Tom Xenakis draws on visual specifics of his Greek Orthodox Christian heritage to shape a vision that wraps religion around politics by way of commentary on the *sacer*-and-*profanus*-shaped world in which we live and the ironies of its shape. Xenakis' multimedia *Christ the*

FIGURE 75 *Tom Xenakis:*
Christ the Merciful in the
Balkans, *mixed media. 1992*

Merciful in the Balkans (1992) raises the question of why humans who
worship the God of love and mercy have managed so consistently to
shed each other's blood, even in God's name, without a thought of love
or mercy (see Figure 75). Xenakis—who has roots in the Balkans
where ethnic cleansing erupted just a few decades after the Holocaust
concluded with the sentiment "never again"—has created a Christ
who is consonant with traditional icons: stylized, severe, frontal, wide-
eyed, gesturing with one hand while clutching the Book of his Truth in
the other. He is placed against a gold-leaf background with a cruciform
halo around his head.

But Xenakis literalizes the tradition of interpreting icons as windows
into the *sacer* by placing the wooden framing of a hexapartite window
before his image: we are looking *through* a window at the icon/image.
Similarly, he hangs an oil lamp from it, as there might be before an icon

in a church—a symbol of the eternal light of God that shines before the faithful at all times. On the other hand, the window aspect of the work is reinforced unconventionally, by the shutters that push out into the viewer's space. Like the windowpane, they are broken, and they are burned as well—as if this window has been damaged by the ferocity of a natural disaster or of war. War is the context in which the God of Love is submerged in hate and strife: the small black and white images attached to the icon are martial images, of individuals being harmed or martyred. Xenakis' art is a political commentary that focuses on the wars fought in the name of God—politics using religion as its hand-maiden—for whom art is traditionally the visual handmaiden of ad-dress. And maybe *Christ the Merciful in the Balkans* is a visual prayer to that God to help us heal ourselves, for whom he sacrificed himself so long ago.

The influence of icons in the painting of Simonida Uth is no surprise, since she was born and grew up in Serbia and was thus raised in the tradition of Orthodox Christianity and its visual concomitants. Gold and silver leaf abound in the *sacer* spaceless space of her paintings, with their symbol-laden imagery. In Simonida's diptych *Cup of Hermes Tris-megistus*—her visual response to the story in Genesis 22 of the binding of Isaac—the figures of Sarah and Hagar occupy the right-hand panel, and gold and copper leaf are the media of their shadowy representation. They are shadowy because they are no longer part of the main story as it is offered in Genesis, but portrayed in gold and copper to underscore their value to the narrative: they are *there*, even if not part of the bibli-cal narrative.

In the main panel, there is more restoration as well as crossover of tra-dition. Not only are Abraham and Isaac physically connected, but a third, pale figure, with the same facial features, swoops down between them. Rising from his back are blood-red protrusions that are simultane-ously the fire of the sacrificial altar, angelic wings, and a pomegranate-like crown. This last aspect of the protrusions suggests, by way of the pomegranate's symbolism of fertility and plenty due to its myriad seeds, a symbolic allusion to the profusion of descendants promised to Abra-ham and fated to pour out through the double lines of generations that lead to and through both Ishmael and Isaac. Indeed this third figure, who looks like Abraham and Isaac, is both the winged angel of redemp-tive intervention (preventing Isaac's death) and Ishmael, restored to possibility in this scene. Ishmael is also the dark blue shadow whose body contours follow behind the outline of Isaac's copper-leaf body. The pale, ghostly, angelic figure between Abraham and Isaac—between the father and the son—is the Holy Spirit: this is a trinity—three figures distinct yet all emanating from the same center and bearing the same likeness.[20] These and other details connect this work to Gresser's *Last Supper*, asserting the common sources among sibling faiths whose practitioners have, over the centuries, pulled them farther and farther away from each other.[21]

⚬⚬⚬

The visual vocabulary of faith in the late twentieth century includes tradition-laden work by contemporary Muslim artists like Mohammed Zakariya who, trained in the calligraphic art of the Islamic tradition, applies it in the contemporary American world in which he lives and works. His art is embellished by geometric and floral forms, continuing that aspect of Islamic visual art that prefers rich color and abstraction to figurative representation. Zakariya's *Three Quotations from the Qur'an: Abraham, Ishma'el, Isaac* (1997) frames in circular forms three passages that refer to these three figures. The three passages are placed within a field that is multiply framed: indeed the double-layered marbling in contrastive styles and colors is reminiscent of prayer rugs with their seven "frames within frames." The three Qur'anic passages recall a long theological discussion within Islam: whether it was Isaac or Ishmael whom Abraham bound and offered to God. Whereas in Judaism and Christianity Genesis 22 makes it clear that it was Isaac, the Qur'an is ambiguous on the matter, so Islam considered arguments for both of Abraham's sons for a thousand years.

In the last quarter of the twentieth century, as the contacts between the Islamic and the Jewish and Christian worlds have become more complicated and varied, it would be surprising if some contemporary Muslim artists were not to follow a visual course different from that of artists like Mohamed Zakariya. One might, moreover, expect an interweave of religious and political issues within the visual art of places such as Palestine and Iran. In the latter, before and after the revolution of 1979 that finally overthrew the shah and installed the regime of the Ayatollah Khomeini, visually syncretistic, modernist political commentary emerged with artists like Siah Armajani and Hossein Zenderoudi. Armajani's *Sealed Letter* (1964) subsumes the words that precede nearly every *sura* of the Qur'an—"In the Name of Allah the Merciful

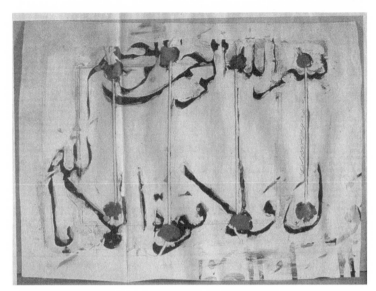

FIGURE 76
Siah Armajani:
Sealed Letter,
acrylic on
canvas. 1964

and Beneficent"—into an expressionist painting. Slabs of red and white color eradicate parts of the words—the red marks look almost like bullet holes shot through the words—and the crisp clarity with which the letters are traditionally shaped has been blurred. Indeed a second text is all but eradicated by the overlaid brushwork. Where does God hide within gun-toting dictatorships? (See Figure 76.)

Hossein Zenderoudi was busy for twenty years with conceptual syntheses before his painting titled *The Hand* (ca. 1980) was created. It builds from the protective *hamseh*—but in the popular national vocabulary it also represents the severed hand of the early Muslim martyr Hazrat Abbas. Hazrat Abbas died in 680 CE at the battle of Karbala and served as inspiration for the reborn militant Islam that shaped the 1979 revolution in Iran. Thus, the work has specific political implications, even as its primary conceptual underpinnings are broader. That breadth of intention is reinforced by the manner in which the artist has softened the image by inundating it with the sort of decorative patterning (referring, in its infinitizing quality, to God's infinity) and layered fields of calligraphic text (referring to God's word) that are typical of traditional Islamic art.

Myriad issues resonate into the twenty-first century. The preceding instances are token suggestions of the richer array of works that form that resonance. The sense of the *sacer* and the need to engage it, and the use of the visual image to help accomplish that engagement, are universal human phenomena. Such a sense and need have not diminished in our own time, nor are they likely to in the years to come. Whatever new directions visual self-expression may take in the Abrahamic (and other) traditions, those directions will continue to draw from a lush, varied, and interwoven heritage of symbols that cross millennia as well as national, ethnic, and religious borders. Such symbols are integral signs of the abiding human concern for the *sacer* and its relationship to humanity.

NOTES

Introduction

1. We recognize this word in the English adjective "sacerdotal." There are other Latin words for priest, the most familiar being *pontifex,* meaning "bridge-maker," which underscores the role of the priest as a provider of connections between the two realms.

2. From the verb *do, dare, dedi, datum.*

3. Again, the etymologies are instructive. Latin *templum* (Greek *temenos*) refers to a protected or secluded area; "sanctuary" is built on the Latin word *sanctus,* a derivative of *sacer;* "altar" comes directly from the Latin word for "high" or "high place" *(altus, alta, altum).*

4. The presumed order of etymological events is that first the two words combined (yielding *sacerfacere*) and then a series of sound changes set in, including metathesis (reversal of phonemes, as with the change of "-er" from *sacer* to "-re-"and vowel grade modifications (thus the "-re-" becomes "-ri-," for example). The last transformation would be the anglicization of the Latin word into the form we recognize (just as it would have been somewhat transformed as Latin evolved into the various Romance languages or lent some of its vocabulary to various other language families).

5. The surrogate is not necessarily an animal. In one of the more troubling of the Greek myths, Iphigenia, daughter of Agamemnon, is offered to the goddess Artemis to atone for the killing of an animal sacred *(sacer)* to the Goddess, so that Agamemnon's ships can sail to Troy. The fifth-century BCE Greek playwright Euripides found this disturbing enough to write a work that sends Iphigenia to the distant land of the Taurians, where she tends the shrine of the goddess. In other words, she is made *sacer* both in being sent out of the *profanus* of the Greek world and in serving the *sacer* realm of the goddess, rather than being killed. Note, however, that she is in effect dead. Because she is beyond the edge of the Greek world, she no longer participates in life; she will remain a virgin, tending the shrine, until her death.

6. Thus only a *sacerdos* such as Jacob could have a dream of that unique ladder; because he is a *sacerdos*, the spot that he thus marks contains a forever-after potency for his constituency. Similarly, the spot where Solomon builds the temple is chosen by his father, David, who is a king anointed by God through the hand of God's *sacerdos*, Samuel. That site, too, will be forever sacerdotal in the eyes of its constituents (who will eventually become Jews, Christians, and Muslims).

7. One can most succinctly grasp the paradox-laden concept of the *sacer* by examining the first instance in which the term itself seems to have been used in written form. In the heart of the old Roman forum is a stone, the *lapis niger* ("black stone"), on which an inscription—probably the oldest in Rome, dating from the late eighth or early seventh century BCE—appears in which a proto-Latin form of the term is used. The stone apparently marked a boundary between the general center of the early Roman community and a specific area, a grove marked off as reserved for a goddess. The inscription warns that anyone who upsets this boundary will, together with all his cattle (symbolizing one's material goods, property—one's wealth), be *sacer*. The warning provokes a threefold question: What does *sacer* really mean in this context? Why is the would-be boundary-disturber threatened with being made *sacer*? How can such a potential victim of his own error be brought back from a *sacer* condition to the *profanus*? In its context, *sacer* obviously means to be cursed, generally speaking. But what does it mean, in more precise terms, to be cursed? To be *sacer* is to be excluded from the *profanus*. If the *sacer* refers to everything that resides outside the realm of the familiar, and *profanus* refers to the realm of the familiar, then *profanus* also refers to the realm of the community. To be *sacer* is to be removed from the community. But what does it mean to be outside the community in the early Roman world? It means, among other things, not to be protected by the two fundamental ideas that bind a community together and protect its constituents. Religion is one—the root of which, *-lig-*, means a binding (see Note 8); *religio* is that which binds a community together with respect to its gods. *Lex* is the other—the root of which, *-leg-*, also means a binding; *lex* or law binds a community together with respect to its constituent human parts. So to be *sacer* is to be no longer protected by the laws of gods and men that enable the members of a community to survive. An individual labeled *sacer* must leave the community before somebody or someone harms him with impunity. But why? Because of the threat that the act of upsetting the boundary stone has potentially brought upon the community of which the offender is part. The realm of the *sacer* is a realm of analogues; its various aspects are subaspectual parallels of each other. And therefore *every* boundary—but particularly the one separating the community at large (the *profanus*) from an area devoted to a goddess (the *sacer*)—is the analogue of the ultimate boundary between *profanus* and *sacer*. The transgression of such a boundary can potentially wreak havoc on the community, as the transgression may have disturbed the *sacer*, which may thus become malignantly disposed toward the community of which the transgressor is part. The Roman tradition, by way of its Greek inheritance, is overrun with stories recounting the fate of those who have, even inadvertently, transgressed one boundary or another with respect to the *sacer*, and the consequences for their communities. Oedipus, for example, relieves Greek Thebes of the plague of the sphinx—a border creature (where three elements meet, one human, one leonine, and one avian) that he encounters at a crossroads—and is rewarded by being made king. But along the way, without realizing it, he has twice transgressed boundaries and thereby offended the gods: he kills his father (whom he had also encountered at a crossroads) and sleeps with his mother, bearing several children by her. Ironically, his double offense to the *sacer* brings plague onto the commu-

nity of which he has been made king for having relieved it of the plague of the sphinx. The only way the *profanus* of Thebes can be relieved of that new plague is by Oedipus' departure from it into the *sacer*. Because Rome emphasized the importance of the larger community (rather than emphasizing the individual, as the Greeks were inclined to do) the actions of one person could have wonderful or terrible consequences for the community of which that individual was part. But what could Oedipus do to return to the community—or the individual who inadvertently upset the *lapis niger* and was thus forced out of the *profanus* into the *sacer*? Clearly some act of expiation or appeasement was necessary. But *how* was this to be done? Where? When? By what means? Who was likely to know and be able to guide the offender back to the *profanus*? The one who knows such things—a priest, a prophet, or some other analogous kind of individual who has a connection with the *sacer* that the rest of us lack—is called a *sacerdos*, as we have seen. His instructions yield further paradoxes.

8. *Religio* derives from the Latin root "lig", meaning "to bind"; more precisely, "*re-lig-io*" means to "bind" something "back" or "again" to something else. In this case, its purpose is both to bind the constituent members of a given *profanus* (community) together with respect to the community's understanding of what the *sacer* is and to bind the *profanus* back to the *sacer* as that *profanus* understands the *sacer* that created the *profanus*.

9. "Monotheism" derives from the Greek prefix *mono-*, meaning "one" combined with *theos,* meaning "god"; "polytheism" derives from the Greek prefix *poly-*, meaning "many," plus *theos*. Some theologians would argue that Zoroastrianism is ultimately monotheistic, since Ohrmazd (Ahura Mazda) and Ahriman, although opposed elements, may ultimately be understood in a manner that makes Ohrmazd a singular deity, and Ahriman an opposer analogous in stature to that of Satan vis-à-vis God in the Christian tradition.

10. Two things become obvious when we consider, for example, Hesiod's *Theogony,* the poem that has as its subject the birth of the Gods and the transformation of reality from an original state of *chaos* ("yawning emptiness") to the *kosmos* ("order") of the current universe established by Zeus. The first is that he cannot have been witness to the events he describes in a *profanus* fashion; he must have received the information from the *sacer* itself—the gods, or their handmaidens, the muses, have inspirited him with the knowledge he shares with us. Thus he is indeed a *sacerdos,* intermediating between gods and humans. The second is that the story he tells cannot be false; surely the gods would strike him down were he to tell untruths about them. So his account, his *mythos,* must be a gods'-truth account. And that is the sense of the word *mythos* in Greek until the fifth century BCE, when for various reasons the term begins to acquire the legend-bound (as opposed to fact-bound) connotation it retains to this day in English.

11. The Babylonian words *Enuma Elish* mean "when on high" or "when in heaven." This is the opening phrase of that creation myth—Near Eastern literature uses the opening word or phrase of a work to "name" it; the idea of an encapsulating "title" is Greek. (This is why each of the five Books of Moses is called by its first significant word in Hebrew but by an actual content-summarizing title in Greek.)

12. Mesopotamia means "between the rivers" in Greek—an allusion to the most defining attribute of that piece of territory. Its political, linguistic, and cultural identity changed over the millennia, from domination by the Sumerians to domination by the Akkadians, various phases and configurations of Babylonian and Assyrian empires and the Achaemenid Persians—by which time the area was in constant contact with the Greek world. Through the various changes of hegemony (and I have drastically simplified that progression in the previous sentence), key literary works such as the *Enuma*

Elish continued to be passed down, even as the language of telling and occasional details of content changed over the course of several millennia of transmission.

13. See any edition of Liddell and Scott's *Greek-English Lexicon* or *Webster's New World Dictionary* for this breakdown. *Symballein* derives from *ballein,* meaning "to throw" and the prefixed intensifier/reflexive *syn-* (which, standing alone rather than as a prefix, means "with.")

Chapter One

1. Bison and aurochs are seen as well.

2. See in particular, David Lewis-Williams, *The Mind in the Cave: Consciousness and the Origins of Art* (London: Thames & Hudson, 2002). See also Jean Clottes and David Lewis-Williams, *The Shamans of Prehistory: Trance and Magic in the Painted Caves* (New York: Harry N. Abrams, 1998); and Jean-Marie Chauvet et al., *Dawn of Art: The Chauvet Cave, The Oldest Known Paintings in the World* (New York: Harry N. Abrams, 1996). The theories set forth in these and related works corroborate one or more of my assertions.

3. There are variant versions of some of the details within the mythic narrative, such as that the human tax was paid annually or every seven years.

4. The Greek *labyros* means "double ax." The pre-Greek suffix *-inthos* means "place of," of which a second example is Corinth[os].

5. The name combines two elements: *tauros,* meaning "bull," and *Minos.*

6. Plato's *Critias,* for example, which centers on a discussion of an Atlantis-like island civilization that is ultimately destroyed by the gods, has often been understood to have had Minoan Cretan civilization as its inspiration. The idea then intersects the archaeological supposition that the extinction of that civilization was in part due to the explosion of the island of Thera (Santorini) and its repercussions.

7. An entirely different argument for what Knossos was—not a city, but a necropolis—has been cogently argued by H. G. Wunderlich in *The Secret of Crete* (Athens: Efstathiades Group, 1998). For the purposes of this discussion, however, the importance of the bull as a symbol of fertility, and the notion of the bull games as a rite of passage, hardly changes. What is depicted would be the rite of passage to the *sacer* of the next world rather than the *profanus* of adulthood. Similar issues would apply to the prevalence of dolphins and other images in the art of Knossos: they reflect the widespread association of that beast with safe passage through the sea. Dolphins had a reputation throughout antiquity of helping or even rescuing sailors lost at sea.

8. That Oedipus, the hero-*sacerdos,* meets a border creature at a crossroads is not surprising, since such a site symbolizes the meeting of realms. At a second crossroads he meets and kills the man he does not recognize as his father.

9. I am using the familiar, Greek-derived version of Sargon's name, as with the Egyptian names that I mention. Sharu-kin would be a closer approximation of the Assyrian version of his name.

10. "Cherubim" is derived from Hebrew *kharubim,* which is in turn derived from Akkado-Assyrian *karubu,* referring to such fierce guardian creatures. The psychological reality of that ferocity—of the notion that the cherubs might be expected to pursue those seeking inappropriate entrance to the palace—is illustrated by an incident in the nineteenth century. The English archaeologist Austen Henry Layard was conducting an excavation and invited the sheikh who owned the land and had given him permission

to dig to witness the unearthing of the enormous creatures. The sheikh and his entourage arrived on horseback and, peering over the edge of the excavation pit to see the creatures, became immediately terrified of them and fled as fast as their steeds could carry them.

11. The term in Greek means either disorder or emptiness; *chaos,* from the verb *chaomai,* meaning "to yawn" or "to gape," is cognate with the English word "chasm." Whether a material-filled order of reality is preceded by emptiness or disorder doesn't matter for the purposes of our discussion.

12. The Sumerian word *ziggurat* is built around a root, *z-g,* that means something like "mountain," thus underscoring the significance of the ziggurat as a stylized, regularly ordered connector between earth and heaven.

13. The Parthenon is the Temple to Athena as Virgin, built on the rock outcropping that is Athena in her earlier, preclassical phase as Mother; therefore the Parthenon and Acropolis together offer the meeting of those two ideas, which in the ordinary *profanus* realm are opposites that, by definition, cannot meet. That the period in which the Parthenon was built culminated with Athenians' hubristic sense of themselves was apparent to Greeks who witnessed Athens' engagement and defeat in the Peloponnesian Wars that carried on from 431 to 404 BCE. See Note 22 below.

14. The word "aqueduct" means "water-leads" in Latin, from *aqua + ducere.*

15. The Latin *ambi* and the Greek *amphi* mean "both." The word "theater" comes from the Greek word *theao,* meaning "to look at, to see." So an amphitheater is a place where one looks at the action from both sides.

16. There are some slight exceptions to the rule of this distinction between Greek and Roman temple design. Greek temples in Sicily and southern Italy often have a front staircase—obviously influenced by the Italianate style—that cuts through the stereobate (which is nonetheless a continuous series of "stairs" around the entire base of the structure).

17. Pantheon means "all of the gods" in Greek. Just as educated Romans spoke Greek, and Roman culturati wrote in Greek, many terms referring to significant structures in the Roman world were Greek, rather than Latin.

18. By this point in the discussion, the reader is probably aware of the *sacer* paradox of seeing the sun both as one of the seven *planetes* and as a separate and clearly more important "eye of heaven." Similarly, it is associated with Apollo (and the moon is associated with his sister, Artemis), while it is also associated with Helios and his horse-pulled chariot.

19. In Hesiod's epic seventh-century *Theogony* ("The Coming to Be of the Gods") (lines 195–210), Aphrodite, goddess of love *(eros),* is the consequence of an extraordinary act of strife *(eris),* the castration of Ouranos by his son, Kronos, who tosses his father's genitals into the sea. It is out of the sea foam *(aphros)* that gathers around their remains that the goddess is born, carried onto the island of Cyprus.

20. The statement that "man is the measure of all things" is specifically ascribed to Protagoras in Plato's *Cratylus* 386a and *Theaetetus* 152a.

21. In the Phoenician/Canaanite context, the image of the "woman at the window" is associated with a temple devoted to a goddess of fertility, whose sacerdotal representative she is understood to be. She is a sacred prostitute, whose purpose is to assist in the maintenance of male sexual potency so as to assure the survival of the community through its never-failing fertility.

22. Indeed there were those in later antiquity who interpreted the defeat of the Athenians in the Peloponnesian Wars, just getting underway as the Parthenon was completed, as a consequence of the Athenian hubris manifest in such depictions. See Note 13, above.

Chapter 2

1. Or so the *mythos* of the Hebrew Bible tells us, and believing Jews, Christians, and Muslims accept without question his historicity. So shall we for the purposes of this narrative.

2. I am oversimplifying in order to get to the point of this discussion; a careful reading of the Hebrew Bible shows that Abraham's sense of God is far more limited than ours. Generations after him, the Second Commandment at Sinai (Exodus 20, and repeated in Deuteronomy 5) enjoined against having any "other gods *before me*," as though the notion of there being only one God, absolutely, was too difficult for the Israelites at Sinai to grasp, and therefore God eased his demand (assuming that ours is the correct understanding of God and that God has not changed). It would be nearly a millennium beyond Sinai before a full sense of God's universal uniqueness was grasped by the Judaean descendants of the Israelites.

3. The last chapter of 2 Samuel refers to David purchasing a "threshing floor" from Arauwna the Jebusite. For etymological reasons it seems clear that the term *arauwna* is derived not from a proper name but from a common noun, whose northern Semitic cognate is *eriwne*, meaning "leader." So it is from the head of the Jebusite community that the purchase would have been made—its *sacerdos*. It is also logical that the threshing floor would have been a sacred threshing floor—set aside for the grain god. The biblical narrative would naturally play this down to accentuate the unique condition under which David selects the spot for the Israelite temple. But if this hypothesis is correct, then here, as elsewhere in history, we see the transference of a *sacer* spot from one culture or tradition to another.

4. The Qur'an is ambiguous as to which son—Isaac or Ishmael—was offered by Abraham. The consequent array of discussion by Muslim scholars over the centuries has also debated the location of the offering: for some it is Mount Moriah; for others it is in the *hijaz*, the area where Muhammad would be born more than 2,500 years later. Muhammad is said to be the descendant of Ishmael and an Arab woman selected to be his wife by his father, Abraham. See Reuven Firestone, *Journeys in Holy Lands: The Evolution of the Abraham-Ishmael Legends in Islamic Exegesis* (Albany: State University of New York Press, 1990), for an excellent discussion of this issue.

5. Not only can the Phoenicians and the northern Canaanites be construed as the same people, but the terms are equivalent. The Semitic *kinahnu*, which we render as Canaanite (by way of transliterating the Hebrew *k'na'ani*), is derived from *kinahna*, which refers to the area between the east Mediterranean coast and the Jordan River and the area due north of it—now Israel, Palestine, and Lebanon. The term *kinahna* is the word for the tiny shellfish that, when crushed by the thousands and left to rot in varying amounts of water and urine for varying periods of time, yields a rich dye, *murex*, of red, purple, or blue. It was so expensive that only the rich—particularly royalty—could afford it (hence, "royal blue," "royal purple"). It also lent its name to the area that produced it, since it was essential to the local economy. The Greek *phoinikos*, which we transliterate as "Phoenician," is a precise translation of *kinahnu;* it means "purple." (This is more obvious by way of the Latin equivalent, *purpurus.*) The Phoenicians/Canaanites are the "purple people."

6. Solomon agreed to pay Hiram whatever price he deemed appropriate for the work. In this respect, he was hardly an exemplar of clever Near Eastern bargaining skill, nor is this incident consistent with his legendary wisdom. See 1 Kings 5:9ff.

7. See 2 Chronicles 3:17. Although there is considerable scholarly debate regarding the significance of these names, the architectural positioning of such a pair of columns

is clarified by the excavations at Hatzor, in northern Israel. Temple "G" offers an apparently typical northern Canaanite edifice—a "long house" structure with an internal division into three parts and two columns before the front entrance, and it seems that the builders of Solomon's temple followed this structural prescription.

8. This connection is only implied in the rendering of the Ten Commandments in Exodus 20, but it is explicit in the version offered in Deuteronomy 5. There is a good deal of symbolism related to "seven-ness," as we shall see in the following chapters.

9. The derivation of the word *shabbat* ("sabbath") and its underlying concept is, in a sense, double. The Hebrew verb *shavat,* used in Genesis 2:1, means "rested" ("and on the seventh day God *rested* from His work . . . ." But the word is also cognate with the Babylonian *s(h)apatu,* which referred to the day associated with the new moon—that is, no moon—approximately every four weeks when, since it was regarded as a bad luck day (no moon suggested a negative focus on the *profanus* by the *sacer*), Babylonians desisted from any enterprise that might suffer as a consequence. *Shabbat* transforms—reverses—the sense of the day from negative to positive, while retaining the essence of its functional quality: a day of rest. The biblical text offers a revolution within the Near Eastern religious context.

10. Centuries earlier, Moses and the "children of Israel" had also been commanded to build a sanctuary in the wilderness (the construction of which was supervised by the artisan Betzal-El, whose very name, meaning "in the shadow of God", indicated the source of his inspiration). That sanctuary was the forerunner, in a sense, of the temple in Jerusalem as far as its essential sacerdotal role and qualities are concerned. We can therefore look to it, perhaps half a millennium before the time of Solomon's temple, for the earliest example of visual self-expression in the Israelite tradition. One might say that the Hebrew Bible *leads* toward Solomon's temple: it *begins* in Exodus 35–38, with the movable tabernacle in the wilderness. In the innermost precinct of that tabernacle the Tablets of the Law were kept. Included among the appurtenances was, again by divine prescription, the first seven-branched candelabrum—or perhaps the very candelabrum that was later placed in Solomon's temple. This original *menorah* (the root of the word is *ner,* meaning "candle"—oil, wax, paraffin, or otherwise) may well have been modeled on the moriah plant, which, growing in and around the Holy Land, naturally sprouts seven shoots: a central one, with three shoots on either side. The predominance of botanical terminology in the discussion of the *menorah* in the wilderness tabernacle in Exodus 25:31–36 offers corroboration of such a hypothesis. (See the impressive discussion of this by Nogah Reuveni in his pamphlet, "Ecology in the Bible" (Kiryat Ono, Israel: Neot Kedumim, 1974).

11. This is another oversimplification for the sake of brevity. In Exodus 20, we read of the worship of the God of Israel by Moses' Midianite father-in-law, Jethro, after "he had seen all that the Lord God had done for Moses and the Children of Israel"—which suggests that Jethro and his constituency joined the covenantal relationship (Jethro would later advise Moses on how to organize his judicial infrastructure along more reasonable hierarchic lines). This passage militates against viewing the Israelites' evolving relationship with God in terms that are ethnocentrically narrow, even at that early point.

12. See Notes 14 and 15 below for more on Herod.

13. Matatthias and his five sons are more correctly called Hasmoneans—a term that identifies them as priests in the community of Modi'in (not far from Jerusalem) where they served. Maccabee seems to have been an epithet applied to Judah, the key leader among the five brothers, and may have been derived through a pun from a

physical attribute—it means "hammer" or "hammerhead" and perhaps referred to his stocky build, with a thick neck. See Solomon Zeitlin, *The Rise and Fall of the Judaean State*, vol. 1 (Philadelphia: Jewish Publication Society, 1978).

14. One of the more interesting moments in Judaean history, given subsequent Jewish and Christian history, is that in which John Hyrcanus, son of Simon (the last of the five Maccabee brothers), conducted a successful military campaign against the Idumaeans to the south of Judaea around 107–105 BCE. Having achieved victory, the Judaeans offered their long-term enemies the choice of death, exile, or conversion to the faith of Israel. Not surprisingly, the Idumaean leadership—Herod's grandfather—opted for the last of these choices, and thus Herod was a third-generation "Jew" on his father's side. However, in a world where ethnicity still counted heavily, the fact that he was *not* an ethnic Judaean would have been at least as significant to his Jewish Judaean constituents as the fact that he *was* half Jewish; to his pagan Judaean constituents (politically Judaean, since Judaea had grown to encompass inhabitants who did not worship the God of Israel, particularly in Herod's time and through his own political and military machinations) his Judaism would have been at least irrelevant or at most a negative attribute. Herod evidently worshipped the God of Israel, whose main cult center was in Jerusalem. But aside from his father being ethnically Idumaean, his mother was ethnically Nabataean and religiously pagan. As king of the polity Judaea, his nationality would be Judaean, and he would have been embraced by both pagan and Jewish Judaeans. This is further complicated by the fact that what we recognize as Judaism was not yet fully formed by Herod's time. Furthermore, the terminological distinction that we make in English between "Jewish" and "Judaean," where the first refers to religious conviction and the second to nationality, polity, or ethnicity, did not exist in any of the languages in use in Herod's time. *Yehoodi* in Hebrew, *Yehoodae* in Aramaic, *Yoodaios* in Greek, and *Yoodaius* in Latin all meant both "Jew(ish)" and "Judaean." Thus, the determination of anyone's identity in that realm, not just Herod's, is fraught with definitional conundra.

15. Herod did not rebuild the temple per se, as is often erroneously suggested.

16. For popular but effective overviews of the archaeology of the temple mount area, see Hershel Shanks, *The City of David: A Guide to Biblical Jerusalem* (Washington, D.C.: Biblical Archaeology Society, 1973); and Yigael Yadin, ed., *Jerusalem Revealed: Archaeology in the Holy City, 1968–1974* (Jerusalem: Israel Exploration Society, 1976). A great deal of research has been conducted since these two books were published, of course, but no new information contradicts the assumptions regarding Herod's putative taste, renovations, and expansions.

17. The Greek word *syn-agogê*, meaning "gathering together," roughly translates the Hebrew *knesset* and, in turn, is rendered in Latin as *con-gregatus*. However, the Greek word that was used at the time to refer to a place of gathering for prayer and fellowship with each other and with the *sacer* is *proseuchê*; *synagogê* referred to the congregation, not to the edifice. The full Hebrew rendering is *bet-knesset*, meaning "house of gathering."

18. Herod's needs for protection were real. Not only was he unloved by the majority—perhaps the totality—of his Judaean subjects (both Jewish and pagan, of whom he had a large constituency following the further expansion of the Judaean kingdom under his leadership), but he had good reason to fear that his first Roman ally, Marc Antony, might sell him out for love: Cleopatra coveted Judaea as a province for her Ptolemaic Egyptian kingdom. Therefore, comfortable but extremely defensible fortresses, such as Massada and Herodion, were important potential refuges—even if they were never used

as such. The Roman penchant for reshaping space, discussed in Chapter 1, included painting away the walls. The four sequential and overlapping styles of Roman wall painting all transform the walls of a room, either breaking its totality up into smaller parts, and sometimes offering the illusion that painted stucco is marble, or replacing the wall with landscapes or with the illusion of lower walls, over the tops of which one may discern distant vistas. The palace complex of Herod at Massada, cascading as three platforms hanging from the northern face of the shiplike rock, exhibits the first of these tendencies. The back walls of the lower level are punctuated by Corinthian-capped pilasters (suggesting that the synagogue columns may also have been Corinthian-capped), continuing the illusion of a circular peristyle, the first part of which is created by the actual columns that supported the roof extending from the rock face out to the edge of the platform facing north. In addition, the bases of the pilasters and the lower parts of the wall between them were stuccoed to present *trompe l'oeil* marble soffits. Above, within the full palace itself that occupied part of the top area, was a bath complex in the Roman style, with a frigidarium, a tepidarium, and a calidarium, decorated with handsome mosaics, reflecting that development in Hellenistic-Roman art as well.

19. The synagogue would also have functioned in part *as a boulê* because that is the obvious place where adult males would gather for any matter of communal significance, not only to address God—and any decision regarding a matter of significance would be undertaken with God's presumed "approval" taken into consideration.

20. Both Josephus' description and the archaeologists' spade give ample evidence of Herod's stylistic predilection with respect to the temple mount area, and evidence from other sites, such as his palace at Herodion, offers further corroboration.

21. It should be noted that his demand may have had as its focus patterns of belief and not ethnicity; that is, those who would be put out were those who refused to be part of the spiritual community of the Judaeans, regardless of their ethnicity.

22. The term derives from the combination of the Greek terms for "God" *(theos)* and "power" *(krasis)*.

23. Such literatures began as orally transmitted discussions. They would not begin to achieve a written form until some time—perhaps two hundred years—after the time of Jesus. The two primary types that emerged are *midrash* (from a root, *d-r-sh*, meaning "to dig [that is, beneath the surface of a text]"—which fills in lacunae in our understanding of divine writ (for example, heaven and earth, the death of Moses)—and *mishnah* (meaning "to turn over [that is, a subject, again and again]"), which offers commentary on how to live one's life within the shadow of the covenantal relationship. Within the third through sixth centuries CE, commentary on the *mishnah,* called *gemara* (meaning "completion") would complete the first layers of what is called *talmud* (meaning "learning"). The *talmud* responds to issues and questions by referencing divine writ, but it is not a commentary on it per se, as *midrash* is.

24. Josephus suggests that the destruction was accidental and not intentional, certainly not intended by the Roman leadership. Since that leadership was a patron of his historiography of these events, his words have been treated with skepticism until fairly recently.

25. See Note 23. *Midrash* and *talmud* are the basis for two primary forms of traditional Jewish literary expression: *agada*—meaning legend-bound material—and *halacha,* which literally means "[the way to] go" and refers to legalistic material. However, *midrash* has some *halachic* material, and *talmud* has some *agadic* material. Both forms of expression have continued to receive additional layers of commentary on commentary into the modern era.

26. The first quote is from Micah 4:1; the second is from Ezekial 39:7.

27. Here, too, one notes changes and exceptions to traditional tenets in the modern era. A substantial percentage of the followers of the Lubavitcher Rebbe Schneerson—one of a number of claimants, with constituents, to the legacy of the founder of Hassidism, Israel Baal Shem Tov (ca. 1700–1760), in turn representing one group among many within the Jewish people of the past several centuries—view him as the messiah. When Rabbi Schneerson had a stroke and went into a coma several years before his death, many of his followers believed that that development was merely the prelude to his rising from his bed to declare himself the messiah; since his death, some of his followers have maintained a vigil at his grave site, still hoping for and anticipating his resurrection and with it the arrival of the messianic era.

28. Note that there is an important nuance shift between the word *religio* as I have previously used it and the more specific Roman legal usage instanced here.

29. The traditional English spelling of "Mecca" and "Medina" ignores the fact that there is no vowel sound "e" in Arabic. "Macca" and "Madina" are closer to Arabic pronunciation.

30. The enormous volume of Islamic legalistic literature parallels the Jewish (more than either of them do the Christian) legalistic material. It is referred to overall as *shari'a*—meaning "path," which is very close in conception to the Hebrew/Jewish *halacha* (see Note 25).

31. See Note 4 regarding the question of whether Abraham offered Isaac or Ishmael.

32. The culmination of the *isra'* ("night journey") is referred to as the *mir'aj* ("ascent").

Chapter Three

1. The etymology of "catacomb" is probably from Latin *cata tumba* ("at/by the grave"; *tumba* becomes *cumba* by dissimilation). In turn, *cata* comes from Greek *kata* ("down").

2. See Nelson Glueck, "A Newly Discovered Temple of Atargatis and Hadad at Khirbet et-Tannur, Transjordania," *AJA* 41 (1937): 361–376; "The Nabataean Temple of Khirbet et-Tannur," *BASOR* 67 (1937): 19–26; and *Deities and Dolphins: The Story of the Nabataeans* (New York: Farrar-Strauss, 1965). Even more dominant among Nabataean symbols that offer symbolism leading to Christian imagery in the catacombs is that of the dolphin.

3. This story, found in *Midrash Rabbah Shemot* II.2 (that is, the *midrash* on passages from the book of Exodus), was part of an oral tradition that would have been known to both sides of the Judaean community that eventually became Jewish and Christian.

4. See Exodus 3:1–15.

5. Moreover, if we keep in mind the larger terminology that underlies all of this, Isaac *is* sacrificed in the sense of being made *sacer*—in that he becomes part of the covenantal relationship shared by his father with God—as Christ is sacrificed both in the sense of dying and in the sense of being made *sacer* by being gathered in by God the Father to dwell eternally in the *sacer*.

6. We recall too that one of the pagan predecessor gods to Christ is Dionysus, god of the vine and of wine, whose mother is human and whose father is divine, and who dies and is resurrected.

7. See Chapter 1. "Halo" derives from Greek *halios*, meaning "sun."

8. See Chapter 1 for a brief discussion of the Egyptian image of the *Ba* aspect of the soul imaged as a bird.

9. See Genesis 18:1–16.

10. See Quintillian, *The Training of Ovator,* Book I.11 and Book XI.3, ca. 93 CE.

11. *Orans* is derived from Latin *orare,* meaning "pray, beseech."

12. Christ is also beardless in the Good Shepherd motifs.

13. The phrase *bar mitzvah* means "son of the commandment" in Aramaic—the *lingua franca* of Judaea around the time of Jesus. A Judaean boy marked the transition from spiritual childhood to adulthood at the age of thirteen by demonstrating his command of the Torah through a public reading and discussion of the ethical principles set forth in the passage he read. This is continued in the Jewish tradition to this day.

14. See, most famously, the personified god who is the Danube River on the column of Trajan in Rome (ca. 113 CE), as the emperor and his soldiers depart their camp to battle the barbarians.

15. See, for example, the arches of Titus and Septimius Severus, with their relief-carved victory figures in their spandrels.

16. The term "synoptic" derives from the Greek words *syn,* meaning "with," and *ops,* meaning "eye," hence "shared view/one vision." The gospel according to John is different in overall vision from the other three (and was probably recorded considerably later than the others).

17. This is analogous to the use of five hemispheres in the Ahenny Cross.

18. The "Temple to all the Gods" (which is what *pantheon* means) was apparently first built by Augustus' best friend, key general, and eventual son-in-law, Agrippa, but was completely rebuilt during the reign of Hadrian. See Chapter 1.

19. Justinian built his version (the still-extant version) of the Haghia Sophia in the aftermath of an earthquake in 532–537 CE that destroyed the previous structure, which had replaced the original edifice built during the reign of Constantine.

20. The sixth-century theologian Pseudo-Dionysus, otherwise known as Dionysus the Areopagite, is credited with developing the idea of a nine-rung hierarchy of angelic hosts, some, but not all, of which are mentioned in different passages in the Hebrew Bible and New Testament. The order endorsed by the Catholic Church (from highest to lowest) is Seraphim, Cherubim, Thrones, Dominions, Virtues, Powers, Principalities, Archangels, and Angels/Guardians.

21. It is timeless not only because of the presence of thirteenth-century figures but also because of the image of John the Baptist, who would not be present if this were simply a Crucifixion scene, having been beheaded by the Romans some time earlier.

22. For example, in Psalm 42:1: "As the deer (stag, hart) panteth after the water brooks, so panteth my soul after thee, O God."

23. Whereas the word "Romanesque" derives from its visual relationship to its Roman antecedents—it means "Roman-like" and thus the Romanesque arch, for example, may be understood as a more vertically attenuated version of the Roman arch—the word "Gothic" (derived from the language of the same name) means "Godish," reflecting the nineteenth-century art historical interpretation of that style as God-focused along just the lines I am describing.

24. The exception to this is the Italian Gothic style with its strong horizontal emphasis. Cathedrals such as those at Siena and Orvieto most obviously exemplify this, with their alternating bands of dark and light stones, but even the most vertically charged of Italian Gothic churches—the Cathedral of Milan—offers a far more squat and earthbound mien than is true for Gothic churches and cathedrals in Spain, England, France,

Switzerland, Austria, or Germany. It is as if Italian earthiness (which is addressed in the discussion of Renaissance art), even in matters of spirituality, is expressed by this unique form of Gothic style.

25. It is no longer in Moissac, but in its entirety has been reconstructed within the Palais de Chaillot Museum in Paris.

26. In his *The Lives of the Most Excellent Painters, Sculptors, and Architects, written by Giorgio Vasari, Painter and Architect of Arezzo* [first published in 1550 but] *revised and extended by the same, with their portraits and with the addition of the Lives of living artists and those who died between the years 1550 up to 1567* (this, then, the full title of the 1568 second edition), Vasari speaks (at the end of his preface) of "the new way of drawing and painting," and in the end includes sculpture and architecture, which he relates to the Greeks. However, he does not use the term "renaissance."

27. The text of Genesis merely refers to "fruit." The analysis of the text by the scholastic philosophers of the eleventh through thirteenth centuries arrived at the conclusion that the fruit must have been an apple, based on a pun in Latin. The word *malum*, depending upon whether or not there is a pronunciational macron over the "a," means either "apple" or "evil."

28. This is based also on a specific biblical text: Song of Songs 2:3 (all of which is in any case treated as an allegory of the love relationship between Israel and God by Judaism and in Christianity is recast with regard to the principal figures in the salvational narrative, God the Father, the Virgin Mary, and God the Son): "As the apple tree among the trees of the wood, so is my beloved among the sons. I sat down under his shadow with great delight, and his fruit was sweet to my taste." The passage overall alludes, in Christian thought, to Christ; and as Christ is the new Adam, so the Virgin Mary is the new Eve, completing the circle of love.

29. For example, Frederick Hartt, in his *Italian Renaissance Art* (New York: Harry N. Abrams, 1973), 518. What underlies this interpretation is the idea that the man with the scroll might logically be construed as a prophet and that the prophet most likely to be depicted in the context of the Nativity of the Child born of a Virgin is Isaiah.

30. Erwin Panofsky dates it a bit earlier, 1433–1434. See his *Early Netherlandish Painting: Its Origins and Character* (The Charles Eliot Norton Lectures at Harvard University, 1947–1948) (New York: Harper & Row, Icon Editions, 1971): 193.

31. The church was named for Eloisa Martorana, founder of the convent to which the church was passed when Sicily came under Spanish control.

32. Hartt (178) refers to it as a portrait of Isaiah but the gesture is a familiar one of sending forth the dove, so that, although Isaiah is obviously connectable to this scene by way of allusion to the passage referring to a Maiden giving birth, previous Christian iconography and the specifics of the context would favor God the Father as sending forth the Holy Spirit toward the Virgin Mary.

33. The quote comes from St. Thomas Aquinas' *Summa Theologiae* I, qu I, art 9, c.

34. *The Revelations of St. Brigitte* of Sweden from the fourteenth century had become extremely popular in Germany, the Lowlands, and also Italy by this time.

35. See Meyer Schapiro, "*Muscipula Diaboli*: The Symbolism of the Merode Altarpiece," in *Art Bulletin* 27 (1945): 182–187.

36. By variations, I mean that the Magi may or may not be there simultaneously with the shepherds, just as some Nativity scenes are rendered with neither group, the

moment being represented coming before the arrival of those who were led to recognize and adore the Holy Child.

37. Judas takes the sop in wine to signify his betrayal (the sop is Christ's body, the wine is blood and thus his sacrifice; the sop in wine is, in John 13:26, handed to him by Jesus as a signifier of the fact that Judas will be the one to betray him—a sop not blessed by Christ the way the bread eaten by the other apostles is, since Judas reaches for it before Christ has recited the blessing over the bread).

38. Not to be confused with the number seven as the number of completion and perfection (among other things), which derives from the inclusion of the seventh day (a day of rest) in the Genesis creation cycle, and in turn, as we have seen, from much earlier Near Eastern sources that connect to what we observe in the motion of the heavenly elements.

39. This subject appears on the Vatican walls for reasons that are as political as they are allusive of divine intervention and thus spiritual. The expulsion of the Seleucid general—who at the behest of his king intended to steal the temple treasury but was instead miraculously put to flight by a heavenly rider in golden armor—was intended to evoke comparisons with the papal struggle to expel rebellious cardinals from the Vatican circle who were attacking the papacy at the behest of the king of France. Thus, we see the pontiff, by way of *symmetria,* balancing the action on the left side of the fresco, entering the picture carried by attendants on his *sella gestatoria.* This also reminds us that the symbolism of the subject leaps across time within the space before our eyes—in this case the two eras visually connected by the central scene in which Onias, the high priest at the temple, is shown praying for divine intervention at the altar—as we have seen in Christian religious art again and again in earlier periods. Nor is this the only instance of such a combination among the Raphael *stanze.* The *Stanza dell'Incendio* is so-named because of the fresco of *The Fire in the Borgo* that dominates it. In this case it is Julius II's successor, the Medici Pope Leo X who is depicted in the background, just off-center, praying that a fire in the vicinity of the Vatican be extinguished. While a heroic mountain of figures in the foreground right are engaged in bringing the water that will put the fire out—and the woman in the center foreground has upraised arms that parallel the diagonal surge of that mountain and counterposes its progression of counter-diagonals while her arms lead our eye along another diagonal toward the pontiff and his own arms echoing hers in reverse—in the foreground left we observe the Trojan hero Aeneas, carrying his father on his shoulders and leading his son by the hand. Behind them the water of the righthand side is balanced by fire; the burning city of Troy is subsumed in the middle ground. In summary, there is continuity from pagan Troy to the founding of pagan Rome to its transformation as Christian Rome; the difficult politics of those transitions and the politics of papal reality were subsumed under the arch of salvation mediated by the successor to St. Peter as God's designated *sacerdos.*

40. Vasari commented on the intellectual direction of Botticelli, referring to him as a *persona sofistica.* The artist avoids producing what might be stilted depictions of esoteric allegories by being such a consummate visual poet. Consider, for example, the physiological absurdities of his Aphrodite in "The Birth of Venus"—no shoulders, and a left arm that appears swollen by a score of bee-stings—which we don't even notice due to the exquisite face and hair to which our eyes are immediately drawn.

41. His upraised staff dispels the clouds that obscure the *sacer* and make it a mystery, reflecting his long association with both hidden *(hermetic)* knowledge and the interpretation and explanation of things intellectually and spiritually esoteric (thus the word "hermeneutics"). Midway through the previous century, Boccaccio had, in his

Genealogia deorum (Studies in the Birth of the [Pagan] Gods), referred to the ability of the staff of Hermes to dispel mental clouds: *Hac praeterea virga dicunt Mercurium . . . et tranare, id est turbationes auferre.*

42. This motif is also found on the mantle of the *Madonna Poldi-Pezzoli* and also fills the heavenly spheres in Botticelli's illustrations for an edition of Dante's *Paradiso.*

43. My choice of the term "contrapuntal," drawn from the vocabulary of music, is not casual since, as Edgar Wind so astutely points out, another key layer in all of this is the Neoplatonic connection to Plato's association of mathematics and music as the highest of human attainments, closest to the realm of the Forms (Ideas). See Edgar Wind, *Pagan Mysteries in the Renaissance* (New York: Norton Library, 1968): Chapters 7 and 8.

44. See *Hebrews* 4:13: "All things however are naked and open to his (God's) eyes," and Horace, *Carmina* I.24,7, referring to "naked Truth"—and even Petronius, *Satyricon* 88: "Naked Virtue used to please people in prior times [as opposed to the present]"— to name a few examples.

45. See Hesiod, *Theogony,* 154–195. The castration is engineered by Ouranos' wife, Gaia (Kronos' mother), who hides her son by the entrance to her womb, wherefrom he reaches out, and with a rusty sickle, *harvests* (that is Hesiod's verb) his father's genitals when the latter comes, at nightfall, to lie with his wife. Kronos will, in turn, swallow his children, lest they overthrow him, but his wife, Rhea, manages by a ruse to rescue Zeus, who, after having been raised by the muses on the island of Crete, in adulthood leads the other gods in the revolt that places him on the throne of supremacy and, from Olympus, places all the parts of the world as we know it into an intelligible order (Greek: *kosmos*).

46. Genesis 1:2. The verb traditionally translated as "hovered" would be more accurately rendered as the more active "swooped," since the Hebrew verb *merakhefet* is found elsewhere in the Pentateuch with reference to an eagle swooping around its aerie. Pico makes his assertion in his work *Heptaplus* III: 2.

47. This is specifically suggested by the Neoplatonic poet and philosopher Poliziano, who describes the same moment that is depicted by Botticelli in a line that culminates with the words *"e par che 'ciel ne goda"*: "and the sky rejoices in her," that is, the one who is Ouranos' new incarnation. See Poliziano, *Giostra* I:99. For a more detailed exposition, see Wind, *Pagan Mysteries,* 133–136.

48. Drawing from Empedocles, the fifth-century BCE Greek mystic and philosopher, Ficino writes of this admixture in *Conversationes* I:2,3, *Bibl.* 90, p. 1321. In our terms, love is the ultimate *sacerdos*. Not to beat a horse, but we are reminded of how important the contrast between the terms *sacer* and "sacred," and *profanus* and "profane" can be, since the latter terms, applied in the title that somehow accrued at some time to Titian's painting, misguide the viewer as to its symbolic intentions.

49. The lawsuit pertained to the virtuous Count Orgaz's legacy to the Parish of St. Thomas of an annual donation of 2 sheep, 16 chickens, 2 wineskins, 2 cords of firewood, and 800 maravedis. By 1564 the annual contribution had ceased. So Pastor Andres brought a suit at the Chancery of Valladolid against the community that was refusing to fulfill the commitment stipulated by their deceased lord, which he won in 1569. To celebrate that triumph and commemorate the goodness of the count, Pastor Andres commissioned an epitaph in Latin, which also referred to the miracle that had been officially recognized in 1583. Pastor Andres commissioned the star of Toledano painters, who arrived not long before from an abortive attempt to become the court painter to King Phillip II. The painting thus weaves the political position of the nobility

(in which the artist sees himself) with the economic conflict and resolution involving the church and the community with an intense religious sensibility toward mysticism and miracles.

50. Interestingly, Phillip II, the king of Spain who turned aside El Greco's bid for royal patronage (which rejection is what brought the artist from Madrid to Toledo) is shown among the figures in heaven witnessing the upper miracle. (He is the sixth figure from the left, beginning with John the Baptist, who gestures with his hand on his chest.) If Pastor Andres is out of time, Phillip is out of place; political and socioeconomic statement meet spiritual aspiration in the sacerdotal realms of El Greco's canvas.

Chapter 4

1. For the purposes of this discussion, Judaism is being treated simply as a religion, and the discussion is limited to symbols. However, it should be noted that a further complication attending the definition of "Jewish art" is the complex issue of defining Judaism. In the course of the nineteenth and twentieth centuries, the question of whether Judaism is best understood as a religion, or as a nationality, ethnicity, culture, body of customs and traditions, or as a civilization arises and with it the question of how to define Jewish art. Beyond that underlying issue is the question of whether the framework of definition should encompass symbols, style, subject, content, or intent and whether the art itself or the identity of the artist should be the basis of the definition.

2. This curved variant on the triangular Greek pediment is called a Syrian gable because it was apparently invented in Syria. The Romans in turn adopted it—one may see an excellent example of a Roman Syrian gable over the main doorway of the palace complex of the Emperor Diocletian (ca. 285–305) in Split, Yugoslavia. Whether the Jews picked up the idea of the Syrian gable directly from the Syrians or through the Romans is an open question—and for our purposes not important. Indeed that Syrian gable will prove most important for us not with regard to its own symbolic significance, but because, in subsequent eras, the use of such an architectural element will be understandable as a symbolic allusion to the early ancient synagogue.

3. See Chapter 6. For more on the Star of David, see Gershom Scholem, "The Star of David: The History of a Symbol," in his *The Messianic Idea in Judaism and Other Essays on Jewish Spirituality* (New York: Schocken Books, 1971); and Ori Z. Soltes, "Komar and Melamid, Jewish Questions and Art," in *Komar and Melamid: Symbols of the Big Bang,* Exhibition Catalogue, Yeshiva University Museum, New York, October 24, 2002—February 2, 2003.

4. Anaximander was the first of the pre-Socratic philosophers to suggest that there was a substratum—a *hypokeimenon*—underlying the four elements, as opposed to one of the four underlying the other three. This fifth element, in Roman-Latin terms is the *quint*(fifth)-essence.

5. The image of the *shofar* also connotes hope for the restoration of the temple, since Jewish tradition understands Mount Moriah, where Abraham offered Isaac to God, to be the subsequent site of the temple.

6. Moreover, each of these flora has its own symbolism. The *lulav* (originally only a palm branch) is made up of three fronds—the palm, the myrtle, and the willow. These represent Abraham, Isaac, and Jacob—or the backbone, the eye, and the mouth; the

etrog, a large lemon-like citrus fruit, symbolizes Joseph—or the heart—among a number of other interpretations.

7. Indeed a careful reading of the Second Commandment suggests that it is directed against the manufacture of images for *worship*, not the manufacture of images, per se.

8. Among the earliest of these is Santa Maria Antiqua in the old Forum Romanum and dating from the sixth century.

9. It is interesting to note how, by this era, a seasonal calendar similar to our own seems to have shifted into place, rather than the traditional Near Eastern form presenting two or three seasons. It would have been attractive for symbolic reasons: most obviously as connected to that fourness conveyed by the four-letter name of God—YHWH. It functions as an intermediary between created and creation, for which relationship the cycle of seasons is so essential. But it must also be noted that the names of the seasons are not actually the names of seasons, but rather of months. In other words "the period of Tishri," "the period of Tevet," "the period of Nisan," the period of Tammuz" are not designations that accord with the natural calendar but with a man-made series of divisions—in this case with connections to festivals that are ordained by God. So the intent is focus not on the natural clock but on the covenantal clock. It might also be noted that these month names derive, in large part, from Babylonian-Persian god-names. The adoption and adaptation of elements from the pagan world is as present within the vocabulary of the calendar as it is in other areas that lead us from that world into the worlds of Christianity and Judaism.

10. This is reminiscent of that earlier borrowing pattern that yielded the arrangement of benches in the early synagogues from Massada to Capernaum reflecting the internal structure of pagan Greek town halls.

11. *Aron HaKodesh* means "sacred/holy ark"; *bimah* means "raised place" and is a Yiddishization of Hebrew *bamah*, itself probably a borrowing in Hebrew of Greek *bemos*.

12. *Alt-Neu* means "old-new" in German, but the phrase probably puns on the Hebrew phrase *al tenai*, meaning "would that it were"—the "it" referring to the restoration of the temple. This synagogue understands itself as a substitute until "it would be."

13. As in the opening passage of *Pirkei Avot* ("Ethics of the Fathers"). The phrase, which interprets Leviticus 18:30 and Deuteronomy 22:8 toward regulations that assure against even unintentional violations of God's commandments, is well exemplified by the *kashrut* regulation not to mix dairy and meat products that derives from an interpretation of the commandment not to seethe a kid in its mother's milk (Exodus 23:19).

14. In part this may reflect the first substantive dispersions from the Holy Land during the Roman period, westward across the Mediterranean. But a synagogue in Krakow, for instance, will be north by northwest of Jerusalem; one in Moscow will be due north.

15. Even as God is the opposite of what we are, in having created us God is also and paradoxically assumed by us to be somehow like us (or rather, we must be like God, since we assume that a creation reflects its creator).

16. The term *ghetto* is a creation of the Venetians. The word is simply Venetian dialect for *gieto*, meaning "foundry." The area to which the Jews were confined in 1517 was in the vicinity of the Venetian iron foundry. The term gradually acquired the broader reference to the area in any European city to which Jews were confined for living quarters. Its equivalent in the Muslim world is *mellah*.

17. An interesting note regards the Grand German Synagogue, the earliest of the Venetian synagogues, originally devised in 1528 to accommodate the growing German

and central European—Ashkenazi—Jewish population in Venice. The floor remains entirely unchanged from the early sixteenth century, with its asymmetrical shape accommodating the available space upon which to construct it. At that time, the *bimah* was placed, in central European style, in the center of the room, but the renovations of the late seventeenth and early eighteenth centuries included moving the *bimah* to the wall opposite the *aron,* as the Ashkenazi community in Sephardic-Levantine Italian Venice became simply more Venetian. (The epitome of this is the *stylistic* renewal of the women's gallery in the early eighteenth century, inspired by Longhena's gallery devised for the Scuola Sefardita: the Spanish Synagogue). The *aron* is configured as a threefold *aedicula,* offering another variation on the theme of symbolizing the three-courtyard configuration of the temple in Jerusalem and of diasporatic Judaism itself.

18. Recall that the Hebrew word for "circumcision"—*brit* (transformed into the Ashkenazi, Yiddish-language form, *bris*)—actually means "covenant."

19. Deer symbolize the beloved in medieval Arabic poetry, and then by emulation, Hebrew poetry, but the image often becomes a triple metaphor, since the beloved is in turn either the faithful whom God, the Lover, pursues, or God, pursued by the man of faith.

20. Whereas Christianity would continue to expand the specifics of its vision of the afterlife toward the Dantean depictions of Heaven, Hell, and Purgatory, Judaism would not. In the long run, except where, on a folkloristic level and through the influence of Christianity one finds some such discussion and description, the mainstream form of rabbinic Judaism remains completely vague regarding what happens after death, beyond suggesting that there is a particularly good place for the righteous in some sort of hereafter and perhaps included in their portion is some form of rebirth into eternal life.

21. The association of Jews with magicians is the other side of the issue of ascribing to Jews horns and other negative, *sacer*-evoking attributes.

22. It is, to repeat, the symbolic concept of "east" rather than the physical geographic direction that is at issue. And again, in Hebrew, the word *mizrah* ("east") functions as an acronym for the words *MeeTzad Zeh Ruach haHayim*: "from this side (direction) [comes] the Spirit of Life." The Garden of Eden is referred to in *Genesis* 2 as having been planted "eastward."

23. That is, "May the Lord bless thee and keep thee; may the Lord cause his countenance to shine upon thee; may the Lord bless thee with peace."

24. The German Rabbi Ephraim of Regensburg, in the twelfth century, offers the earliest reference to such a special container for spices used in Jewish ritual. The use of spices for this purpose but without a special container began still earlier.

25. There is considerable irony here, when we realize that the Jews' neighbors associated the Jews with the demons they all feared.

26. As a note of interest, most Jewish silver and gold ceremonial objects (and not only spice boxes) were the handiwork of Christian artisans, since restrictions on the professions permitted to Jews often made it impossible for them to create their own objects in silver and gold. It is no surprise that most of the details of style and symbol are not specifically Jewish: Gothic windows, Renaissance shields, baroque figures, rococo swirls of foliage, and neoclassical swags of ribbon are drawn from the arsenal of Western Christian décor.

27. See *'Avodah Zarah* 8a; and *Brachot* 24.9, PRE 23 and 31, and *Targum Yerushalmi* Gen 8:20.

28. In between, of course, the most signal event to transpire at the same location was the offering of Isaac. So the same spot marks the sacrifice of the unicorn by Adam, the offering of Isaac by Abraham and Isaac, and the building of the Temple by Solomon.

29. The seven species referred to in Deuteronomy 8:7–8 are wheat, barley, grapes, figs, pomegranates, olives, and dates or date honey.

30. Scholarly consensus is that the Sarajevo *Haggadah* was created in the fourteenth century in or around Barcelona, Spain; was carried from there, perhaps at the time of the 1492 expulsion of Jews from Spain, to Italy; and ended up eventually in Yugoslavia. This is concisely discussed in the preface by Cecil Roth to the facsimile edition of the Sarajevo *Haggadah*.

31. In other words, the demonization process had led to the belief that Jews possess horns, as Satan and the Anti-Christ do, and decrees in some locales regarding horned headgear were designed to let a Christian know that the wearer of such a hat was a dangerous Jew.

32. This was, in fact, the last book to be accepted by the rabbis into the Hebrew biblical canon. It was accepted because of the powerful theme that it puts forth of a righteous people overcoming its apparently more powerful enemies. The reluctance to canonize it, on the other hand, stemmed largely from the fact that the name of God is never mentioned in it. That reluctance has left its residue in the fact that, at *Purim*, rather than simply opening a Bible to the Book of Esther, we read from a separate scroll—a *Megillah* as it is called in Hebrew. We read the *Megillat Esther* (in its entirety) almost as if, while part of the Bible, this story, where God's name nowhere appears, is apart from that sacred text.

33. See Ori Z. Soltes, "Images and the Book of Esther: From Manuscript Illumination to *Midrash*," in *The Book of Esther in Modern Research*, ed. Sidnie White Crawford and Leonard J. Greenspoon (London and New York: T&T Clark International; Continuum Press, 2003): 137–175.

34. First Maccabees 4:56 and Second Maccabees 10:6 both refer to the celebration as lasting eight days. Later a tradition developed that a miracle also took place: when the temple in Jerusalem had been recleansed after the Maccabean triumph, a small amount of sacred oil lasted in the temple's seven-branched menorah for the eight days necessary to prepare more sacred oil. Eight candles therefore recall this miracle; a ninth is added to kindle the others. From an original tradition of eight separate lamps, the *Hanukkiyah* developed as one eight-(nine)-branched lamp and offers, from at least the twelfth century onward, the ongoing evidence of vital visual response to that experience. There are two basic types: the tree style, with its branches rising like (and conceptually connecting to) the branches of the seven-branched menorah of the temple, and the bench style, with its wicks below, which can usually both hang on a wall or rest on a surface. The variety of forms within this distinction is extensive, reflecting the diversity in time and space of Jewish diasporatic experience.

35. For the issue of whether it was Isaac or Ishma'el and whether the site was the future Jerusalem or near Macca, see Chapter 2 and Chapter 6.

36. As always with such assertions, the interpretation is impossible to prove—it is an interpretation. My grounds for it are both the larger picture of the relationship among art, religion, and aspects of survival, including fertility, and the understanding of these issues in even a secular setting that Freud, Jung, and others have discussed.

37. The term "Al hambra" probably derives from the Arabic *al'Hamra,* meaning "the red"—a reference to the color of the outer walls of the complex, the more so when the late afternoon sun bathes them. But it also puns on the name of Ibn Ahmar, the first significant Nasrid leader.

38. This sense of venerating the *ka'aba* has its parallel in the Eastern Church in the veneration of icons *through* which to access the God one worships.

39. There is an obvious practical element to this: throughout the *dar al'Islam* it is almost always possible for "citizens" to ascertain the direction of Macca. For Jews scattered in Muslim, Christian, and other worlds, ascertaining the direction of Jerusalem might not be as easy.

40. Except for the rabbi who, once a year, on the Day of Atonement, goes down on his knees before the holy ark.

41. A *yatagan* is a short sword with a slightly curving blade.

42. This notion is certainly not unique to the context of the Ottoman sultanate, where it is merely implied; it is explicit in much of Pharaonic history and additionally in the history of the papacy.

43. It is still considered anathema by Orthodox Muslims to translate the Qur'an out of Arabic—the consequence of which is that a large percentage of the world's Muslims cannot read it, or at least not as they should. Jews are strongly encouraged to read the Torah in Hebrew—theoretically, at least, every child who studies for his/her Bar/Bat Mitzvah has achieved that capability—but there is no discomfort, per se, with reading in translation if Hebrew is not possible. Interestingly, Christianity even at the outset never laid claim to a particular language on God's behalf, perhaps because as it emerged in antithesis to Judaism, there were too many alternative linguistic possibilities to Hebrew, and Christianity was already reaching out to speakers of any and all languages. Where Christianity had an initial important linguistic stake was in the translation of the Hebrew Bible into Greek. That translation—the Septuagint (meaning "seventy" in Greek)—became Christianity's primary text, and the tradition emerged that the translation had been divinely inspired: seventy scholars, isolated from each other, arrived at precisely the same translation, which could only have come about through divine agency. But even that claim might be said to have been undercut by Saint Jerome's accomplishment of a new translation for the people—in Latin, the language of the people: *vulgus*—the Vulgate, in the fourth century.

44. To summarize, these forms are said to have been developed in the city of Kufa (in Iraq) in the second decade of Islam. The script form known as *kufic* itself bred several variants—but only one of these, a baseline-hugging, rounded horizontal Kufic, is used for writing a Qur'an. In the course of the following centuries, foliated and floriated Kufic found its way around the peripheries of mosques and across *mihrabs* and even onto more secular objects. Alongside it, other forms of *Mabsut wa-Musraqim* ("elongated and straight-lined") scripts, such as Mashq and Ma'il evolved. By contrast with Kufic and its siblings, a broad range of *Muqawar wa-Mudawwar* ("curved and round") scripts—flowing cursives—also developed, to be used in an endless array of contexts. The classical tradition identifies six cursives—Thuluth, Naskh, Muhaqqaq, Rahani, Riqa, and Tawqi—but individual calligraphers have invented variants across time and space. There are also those script styles that may be seen to have synthesized elements of both general categories.

45. David James, *Islamic Art: An Introduction* (London, New York, Sydney, Toronto: Hamlyn Publishing Group, 1974): 26.

46. The most fundamental Muslim statement refers to there being only one God: "There is no God but God."

47. The Jewish art of Hebrew-language micrography, in which the entire image is made up of the tiny letters of a text for which the image is a referent—for example, the image of Moses at the burning bush might be depicted using the words of that narrative in Exodus in lieu of ordinary lines—is somewhat parallel to *gulzar*.

Chapter 5

1. The seventeenth century, while marked by an exponential growth in secularizing thinking, was also rife with messianic speculation in both the Jewish and Christian communities. The "ingathering of the exiles" meant locating all the exiles of Israel; and there were Christian groups who thought they had found the Lost Ten Tribes in the Amazon and in China. Jews in the Ottoman Empire were drawn to the false messianic figure, Shabbetai Tzvi. And Cromwell's "Fifth Monarchy Men" supporters were certain that his rule would usher in the messianic era in the English Kingdom of God on Earth. With this in mind, Cromwell was easily convinced by the Amsterdam rabbi, Manasseh Ben Israel (Spinoza's first teacher and eventual ex-communicator) to officially invite the Jews back to England, from which they had been expelled four centuries earlier.

2. In the summer of 1666 Wren submitted plans for the remodeling of St. Paul's as a colonnaded domed structure—just before a disastrous fire destroyed the older building. By 1669 it became clear that an entirely new edifice would be necessary; the burnt remains of the earlier building would not sustain new work. Wren's so-called "First Model" was ready the following year, received royal approval, but then was regarded as inadequate, so that he produced the "Great Model" design in 1673—largely modeled directly on Michelangelo's unexecuted project for St. Peter's in Rome. This, too, was rejected as insufficiently liturgical, without a traditional nave or choir. So Wren devised a third plan in 1675, which offered the cruciform plan with its projecting transepts; this plan was approved, construction began in June of that year, and the entirety was completed by 1710.

3. At that time, the river that ran from the White House to the Capitoline (now Pennsylvania Avenue) was the Tiber River, furthering the allusion. When George Washington, instead of seeking a third presidential term or making himself king for life, chose instead to go back to his farm in Mt. Vernon, he was repeatedly likened to Cincinnatus, one of the founding fathers of the Roman Republic. Livy writes of Cincinnatus as the ideal farmer-soldier of the early Roman Republic who, having played a significant role in the liberation of the Romans from the last, most oppressive of the Etruscan kings, and helping both to found and to stabilize a new republic (*res publica*: "people's thing"), instead of seeking some kingship-for-life, chose to go back to his farm.

4. The first proposed Seal of the United States, suggested by Benjamin Franklin, depicted the Israelites arriving to safety as the Red Sea began to swallow up the Pharaoh and the Egyptians.

5. The final touch, Lincoln's decision to crown the capitol dome with the figure of Freedom (set on December 2, 1863, at a time when the republic was rent by Civil War), symbolized ongoing hopes and aspirations: that the republic, restored, would be one nation under the God of freedom who serves all races.

6. There is irony here, since the revocation of the Edict of Nantes by Louis XIV a few years earlier, in 1685, which sent perhaps 200,000 Protestant Huguenots as highly skilled refugees from France to England, Holland, and elsewhere, may be seen as a precipitator of the alliance and the war that followed. So religion had been a *prelude* to the events that, when they moved forward, left religious issues behind.

7. Reform Judaism, born in 1811 in Hamburg, Germany, sought to reshape Judaism and strip it of what were perceived to be anachronistic medievalisms. Among its features was a firm statement that Jews in the Diaspora are not in exile: post-Emancipation communities are as validly and permanently placed as ancestral communities in Israel-Judaea had been. Jews are not awaiting a messiah and the ingathering of the exiles back

to the Holy Land and the rebuilding of the temple in Jerusalem. Thus, the term "temple" rather than "synagogue" is ideological and not merely incidental.

8. All of these structures are marked by an exterior pattern of alternating horizontal bands of dark and light stone.

9. It was designed by the (non-Jewish) architect Charles Greco.

10. Limits of space confine this discussion to Europe and the United States. Symbolic language in synagogue shape and décor can be followed across these centuries from Fez, Morocco, to Kai Feng Fu, China.

11. The "historical" painting is based on a detail from a novel written by Chariton, the earliest known Greek novelist (second century CE), whose hero is properly called Chaireas, not Coroesus.

12. The principle of religious toleration, nonetheless, was not born in America, although perhaps it reached its fullest and most clear-cut articulation here at the inception of American nationhood. But the effect of a range of revolutions in which traditional socioeconomic, scientific, and philosophical principles were assaulted and in the context of which the nature, presence, and very existence of God were also being summarily reexamined could not fail to yield certain concrete results. In various states in parts of central and western Europe, acts of "Emancipation," as they were termed, made it possible for Jews to become part of the socioeconomic and cultural mainstream rather than remaining on the fringes of the various nation-states of which they were part.

13. Practically speaking, the fact that most of these scenes were done in engraving format meant that they could be disseminated for widespread viewing.

14. See, for example, Edward Lucie-Smith, *A Concise History of French Painting* (New York and Toronto: Oxford University Press, 1978): 221–222.

15. For more on Pissarro's interest in the science of seeing and on the social import of art (and incidentally the relationship between that and the artist's Jewishness), see Ori Z. Soltes, *Tradition and Transformation: A History of Jewish Art and Architecture* (Cleveland, Ohio: Electric Shadows, 1984–1990), segment 5B of a twenty-six-part video course; and also Soltes, Introduction to *Fixing the World: American Jewish Painters in the Twentieth Century* (Hanover, N.H.: University Press of New England, 2002).

16. Both quotes are from *Memoirs from the Baths of Diocletian,* ed. Joseph Guttman and Stanley Chyet (Detroit: Wayne State University Press, 1975).

17. See Albert Aurier, "Symbolisme en Peinture—Paul Gauguin," *Mercure de France* (Paris, 1891).

18. As far back as 1859 the French poet, Charles Baudelaire had enunciated the notion of correspondences among the senses and between the senses and a world beyond them. (In the 1859 issue of *Salon Review* he wrote: "It is imagination which has taught man the moral implication of color, line, sounds and scents. At the beginning of the world it created analogy and metaphor.") This notion was wedded to a fin-de-siècle malaise that Max Nordau called "the impotent despair of a sick man who feels himself dying by inches in the midst of an eternally living nature blooming forever." Nordau was writing in *Degeneration* (London, 1895) about the entire sense of despair and emotional attenuation—the neurotic atmosphere—that he perceived in various visual and other manifestations dominating Vienna, Paris, and especially London. Baudelaire's notions also connected to Mallarmé's idea of poetry as "the expression through human language, reduced to its essentials, of the mysterious meaning of aspects of existence" (*La Vogue,* no. 2 [1893]: 70). Thus, various artistic groups were connected to a widespread series of literary events. The end of the century saw the appearance of Edouard Schure's book *Les*

Grands Inities (1889) and the bible of secular mysticism, Madame Blavatsky's *Secret Doctrine* (1893). The Rosicrucian Order was revived, between 1892 and 1897, in salons that interwove mystical sensibility with the dandyism of the decadents. Joseph Peladin, leader of the *Ordre de la Rose+Croix Catholique*, noted in his *Rules of the Salon of the Rose+Croix* (Paris, 1891): "The Order favors first the Catholic ideal and mysticism. After Legend, Myth, Allegory, the Dream, the Paraphrase of great poetry, and finally, all Lyricism." Androgynous figures, who symbolize the fusion of opposites, the end of all seeking and human completion (for the ultimate search is for the missing half of the self, and the unified androgyne has been reunited with his or her missing half—as in Plato's *Symposium,* where Aristophanes speaks about love as the process of regaining one's lost half since the human being was split by the gods early on into male and female halves) were part of Peladin's ideology, expressed visually by artists associated with his salon. Overt religious symbolism derived from the visual vocabulary of the Christian past was championed, for "the heavens will have their Louvre and the hearts of masterpieces will adore throughout eternity their creator as we worship God" (Josephin Peladin, *La Quest du Graal* [Paris, 1892], quoted in Jacques Letheve, "Les Salons de la Rose+Croix," *Gazette des Beaux-Arts,* December 1960: 370).

19. Freud reported that in the aftermath of his father's death (in 1895) he began to have dreams in which he expressed great anger toward the paternal progenitor against whom such an emotion had never been apparent to Freud—and certainly had not been expressed when he was awake or when his father was alive. He began to realize that the state of sleep and dreaming opened doors kept shut when, awake, we are in control and controlled by conscious thought. In turn, then, if one could access the material of dreams, one could gain insights into aspects of our inner life otherwise repressed. Moreover, since even in the *sacer* reality of dreams we struggle to repress, sometimes the material accessed is articulated by the dream in indirect—symbolic—terms. So the analyzer of the dreams—the psychoanalyst—must both elicit an untrammeled flow of remembered content from his patient and interpret the symbolic language of that overt content for its covert meanings. All of this found its way onto the symbolist canvasses of the same era.

20. Dante named his heroine Beatrice after Beatrice Portinari, whom Dante loved—probably from a distance (each of them was married to someone else)—but who died when he was twenty-five years old. Her death inspired him to make the gradual change from extroverted politics to introverted study and poetry.

21. Quoted from the 1959 translation of *A Rebours,* by Robert Baldick (London, 1959).

22. So-called because physicians before Freud had insistently viewed it as a women's malady; the term derives from Greek *hystera,* meaning "womb."

23. Albert Edward Elsen, *Rodin's Gates of Hell* (Minneapolis: University of Minnesota Press, 1960): 3. See also Elsen, *Auguste Rodin: Readings on His Life and Work* (Englewood Cliffs, N.J.: Prentice-Hall, 1965).

Chapter 6

1. An obvious change in this area is the exponential increase in the production of Judaica by Jewish artists, since until the twentieth century Jewish communities generally relied on Christian craftsmen for such work.

2. Given the scholarly argument that the image of the Tower of Babel in Genesis is based on that of the Great Ziggurat in Ur, religion-bound metaphor works on both

sides of the fence: for those to whom such a structure is a Tower of Babel it is as illegitimate as a temple as are any pagan structures, including ziggurats, disavowed as such by the Abrahamic faiths.

3. Consider this image in relationship to Dutch still lifes of the sixteenth and seventeenth centuries: the flotsam and jetsam of existence and flickering candles have been transformed from symbols of the brevity of life into symbols of the hellishness of life in the *profanus*.

4. The night of November 8–9, 1938, was marked by both carefully orchestrated and haphazard violence against Jews, their homes, places of business, and synagogues across Germany. Ironically, thereafter such street violence was rare; a cleaner, more clinical solution to the Jewish problem—the Final Solution—was being worked out in meticulous detail by Hitler's brass.

5. In the context of defending himself against what his father construed as blasphemous acts and words regarding his (Dali's) deceased mother's memory, Dali rationalized that such acts and words grew out of dreams, and "in a dream, one can commit a blasphemous act against people one adores in real life and dream of spitting on one's mother . . . In some religions the act of spitting often takes on a sacred character." In his diary is a quote from Freud to the effect that "the hero is the man who resists his father's authority and overcomes it." The symbolism of drawers in and out of a figure, with respect to that which is revealed and concealed, both twists the issue of visual concealment/revelation so important to Greek and subsequent Western art in a new direction and relates to Freud's categories referring to the revealing unconscious and concealing conscious mind: the id and ego. Specifically, in Freud's psychoanalytic theory, the drawers represent the unconscious (which expresses itself, among other ways, in dreams) but can also symbolize, more specifically, according to Dali's *The Secret Life*, "a kind of allegory destined to illustrate a certain forbearance, to scent out the countless narcissistic smells that waft out of our drawers."

6. Michael Tapié, "Salvador Dali: An Appreciation," in *Dali: A Study of His Life and Work* (Greenwich, Conn.: New York Graphic Society, 1958): 83.

7. See Carol Mann, *Modigliani* (New York & Toronto: Oxford University Press, 1980): 38–39, 182–192 (especially 192) and words written about him in the summer of 1919 by Lunia Czechowska: "He spoke about Italy which he would never see again, about his daughter who he would never watch growing up."

8. The very name of the school is symbolic, since it is named for the craftsman cited as the creator of the tabernacle in the wilderness at the end of the book of Exodus, who is viewed as the first "Jewish" artist (Exodus 35:30–39:43). Strictly speaking, of course, Bezalel Ben Uri was the first *Israelite* craftsperson mentioned by name, but even more than is generally the case for Jews, Bezalel ideology charted a direct line from Abraham to contemporary Jewish life, as though the terms "Jewish," "Jew," and "Judaism" could apply simply throughout those 4,000 years.

9. For a fuller discussion of Schatz and Bezalel than is possible here, see Ori Z. Soltes, "The Birth of Israeli Art," exhibition essay for the "The Legacy of Bezalel: The Israeli Arts and Crafts Movement," Mizel Museum of Judaica, Denver, Colo., 1988; or Soltes, "Bezalel: The Evolution of a Heritage," exhibition essay for the exhibit of that name at the B'nai B'rith Klutznick National Jewish Museum, Washington, D.C., 1998; or Soltes, "Political, Jewish, and Otherwise: Fifty (Ninety-Two) Years of Israeli Art," in *Israel at Fifty*, Vol. 11 of *Studies in Jewish Civilization*, ed. Leonard Greenspoon and Bryan F. Le Beau (Omaha, Neb.: Creighton University Press, 2001). For more extensive information, see Nurit Shilo-Cohen, ed., *Bezalel, 1906–1929*, catalogue of an exhibition at the Israel Museum,

Jerusalem, 1983—especially Chapter 3 (by Gideon Ofrat-Friedlander) and Chapter 4 (by Yigal Zalmona).

10. Born in Budapest in 1860 to a family that moved to Vienna when he was eighteen, Herzl was a highly assimilated Jew and the successful writer of light, fashionable plays. In 1892 he was appointed to the staff of the *Neue Freie Presse,* the most significant Viennese newspaper, and was sent to Paris as its correspondent. He had encountered anti-Semitism while at the university but arrived in Paris precisely when that sentiment was rising precipitously through the efforts of Edouard Drumont, author of *La France Juive,* the ultimate work of nineteenth-century French anti-Semitism. Two years later Herzl's play *The New Ghetto* made it clear how significant this subject had become for him; it offers the observation that even assimilated Jews live in an invisible ghetto in a non-Jewish world. That same year the trial of Alfred Dreyfus began with all of its anti-Semitic overtones. Herzl's coverage of events for his newspaper led to the conclusive shaping of his thinking toward Zionism. That thinking culminated, in turn, with his authorship of a small book prescribing the creation of a Jewish state and his convening of the first Zionist Congress, held in Basel in August 1897, which was attended by more than 200 delegates from throughout the world. The book grew out of notations in his diary and a discussion with and long letter (dated 3 June 1895) to Baron de Hirsch. Inspired, Herzl then wrote, within his diary, an "Address to the Rothschilds," which amounted to a 65-page pamphlet offering an outline of how a Jewish state could be fashioned. Eventually, after considerable reworking, the piece was published as *The Jewish State* in February 1896.

11. Quoted in Frances K. Pohl, *Ben Shahn* (San Francisco: Pomegranate Artbooks, 1993): 12.

12. See, for example, Barbara Rose, *American Art Since 1900: A Critical History,* 4th ed. (New York: Praeger, 1973): 173–210. The closest Ms. Rose comes to acknowledging something beyond aesthetics is her passing phrase, with regard to Pollock, that his triumphs "lay in wrestling a transcendent order from primordial chaos" (174), and that, with regard to Rothko, the "centralized image is still in a sense a symbol—of oneness or wholeness or transcendental unity—but of a much more abstract and conceptual nature than the more literal Surrealist symbols" (196). Her comments are perfectly accurate, but go no further than this and find no substantial connection between the canvas image and the world outside it. Only in the past several years has the notion of sociopolitical content within abstract expressionism begun to follow from the assertion offered in Segment 9b ("From the Holocaust to Abstract Expressionism") of my 1984–1990 video series, *Tradition and Transformation.* See Note 15 in Chapter 5.

13. The notion of a secular messiah was not absent from twentieth-century Jewish thought. After all, Theodore Herzl both saw himself in such terms and was perceived as such by others. The notion that he could and would rescue hundreds of thousands of Jews at risk in a world rampant with anti-Semitism—that he could find a cure for that theretofore incurable disease—fueled his crafting of the Jewish nationalist movement, which, in his hands, was shaped without regard for traditional Jewish religious thought.

14. See Ori Z. Soltes, *Reach for the Moon: The Paintings of Ruth Dunkell* (New York, 2002; published privately by Sam Dunkell): 4–6. The quote is drawn from a conversation between the artist and the author.

15. From a passage written by the artist and quoted in Ori Z. Soltes, *Everyman a Hero: The Saving of Bulgarian Jewry* and *The Art of Susan Schwalb,* catalogue for a pair of exhibits by those names, B'nai B'rith Klutznick National Jewish Museum, Washington, D.C., 1993.

16. Nesterova's painting is filled with ironic subtexts. On a New York City park bench in her 1993 *New York, Park,* the man who apparently concentrates on a book about birds might be taken for a bird-watcher in Central Park (almost a contradiction in terms, but then, there *are* birds, and not only pigeons, in that park in the middle of the city)—perfectly appropriate to the endless supply of traditional double-speak contradictions-in-terms that characterized the Soviet world. A woman on the other side of the bench turns slightly toward him—and us—as if eavesdropping: she seems to watch the watcher out of the corner of her eye. That is, it seems that spies are exchanging observations—or spying on each other—behind the innocent guise of a book. It is a bilingual book (a book that speaks two languages, official and unofficial, or double-speak), in English and Hebrew (because this is heavily Jewish New York, not Moscow), which is absurd in the context. The former era of spying between Moscow and New York (the USSR and the US); the former condition of spying within spying that marked Soviet life, particularly for those living unofficial or protest lives; the former condition of apartness from straightforward acceptance for Jews (Hebrew-speakers) in Moscow; the sense of New York as "dominated" by Jews—the "cosmopolites" whom Soviet authorities so frequently expressed fear of and contempt for—all of this is parodied here. For more on Nesterova's work, see Alexandre Gertsman, ed., *Natalya Nesterova: Russian Wanderings* (New York: IntArt Press, 2000).

17. The word "pomegranate" means "seed/grain *apple,*" and in some threads of the tradition the pomegranate is the fruit associated with the Fall.

18. For clarity's sake, a rapid review: St. Petersburg was founded by Peter the Great and named for the saint of the same name in 1703. The city was intended to be Russia's new "Window on the West." After the revolution, the city was renamed Petrograd, thereby imposing upon its name a Slavic rather than Germanic form. In 1924, with the death of the founding father of the Soviet Union, the city was renamed in his honor: Leningrad. This remained its name until the time of Perestroika and, in its aftermath, the collapse of the Soviet Union, after which the name reverted—almost, not completely—to Petersburg, thereby erasing its Soviet history, as it were, but avoiding the religious inclinations of its Romanov history.

19. Soviet socialist realism is marked both by a hyper-realist style and by subjects that are idealized: happy, healthy youths (and occasional older people, but who are also emphatically happy and healthy) in dynamic urban and rural settings that trumpet Soviet success.

20. Indeed we may recognize that all of these elements are inspired not only in a general way by the icon tradition but specifically by the famous "Holy Trinity" icon of Andrei Rublev (1360–1430), in which the three angels that Abraham receives are presented as if equal components of the triune God with which Abraham is speaking.

21. In Hellenistic and Roman pagan antiquity, Hermes Trismegistus referred to Hermes' role as a protector of those who pass a three-way crossroads, but also to Hermes synthesized to the Egyptian god Thoth, who in that capacity is the author of the *Hermetica,* writings that teach a doctrine of salvation achieved not through a savior but through esoteric knowledge. Simonida reconnects the pagan past to the crossroads where the Abrahamic faiths converge. Abraham, Isaac, Ishmael, Sarah, and Hagar (even Osiris-Horus and Hermes-Thoth)—are all present and interwoven in this painting, the message of which (and Hermes is, above all, the messenger god in his classical Greek identity) pertains to the intersection of three (or more) conceptual and spiritual paths.

INDEX